Jonathan Swift, Stanley Lane-Poole

Selections From the Prose Writing of Jonathan Swift

Jonathan Swift, Stanley Lane-Poole
Selections From the Prose Writing of Jonathan Swift
ISBN/EAN: 9783744685399

Printed in Europe, USA, Canada, Australia, Japan

Cover: Foto ©Thomas Meinert / pixelio.de

More available books at **www.hansebooks.com**

SELECTIONS

FROM THE

PROSE WRITINGS

OF

JONATHAN SWIFT

WITH A PREFACE AND NOTES
BY
STANLEY LANE-POOLE

NEW YORK
D. APPLETON AND COMPANY
1, 3, AND 5 BOND STREET
MDCCCLXXXV

CONTENTS

	PAGE
PREFACE	vii
A TALE OF A TUB	1
Epistle dedicatory to Prince Posterity	3
The Introduction	10
What is Man but a Micro-coat? (Section II.)	20
A Digression in Praise of Digressions	26
A Digression concerning Madness	31
From a Farther Digression	44
THE BATTLE OF THE BOOKS	47
The Spider and the Bee	49
The Battle	55
The Episode of Bentley and Wotton	60
THE ABOLISHING OF CHRISTIANITY IN ENGLAND	67
A MEDITATION UPON A BROOMSTICK	87
GULLIVER'S TRAVELS	91
Gulliver's Reception in Lilliput	93
The Inventory of the Man-Mountain	100
Factions in the State of Lilliput	108
The Capture of the Fleet of Blefuscu	112
Arrival in Brobdingnag	115
The King of Brobdingnag's Inquiry	123
The Humours of the Laputians	132
The Academy of Lagado	136
A particular Account of the Struldbrugs	144
The Gray Houyhnhnm	149
The Virtues of the Houyhnhnms	156
ENGLISH POLITICAL TRACTS	161
The Examiner. No. 15	163
The Examiner. No. 16	170
The Conduct of the Allies	178

CONTENTS

	PAGE
A Proposal for correcting, improving, and ascertaining the English Tongue	187
Tracts Relating to Ireland	203
The Swearers' Bank	205
The Drapier's Fourth Letter	210
A Modest Proposal for preventing the Children of poor people in Ireland from being a burden to their parents and country, and for making them beneficial to the public	229
Polite Conversation	241
Notes	261

PREFACE

IT is the melancholy privilege of a classical author to be more often talked about than read; and Swift has enjoyed this distinction to the full. It would be an interesting experiment to take a census of the number of ordinary readers who have any acquaintance with his writings beyond a boyish recollection of *Gulliver's Travels* and perhaps an impression that the too familiar pass-words "sweetness and light" are to be found in the *Battle of the Books*. Professional students of English literature must of course know their Swift; but the multitude of critical and biographical essays, that inevitably follow in the train of every classic, furnish the general reader with only too easy a mode of acquiring a surface knowledge at second or third hand, and the majority of the polite commonplaces that are always in stock about Swift may be traced to Thackeray's slight lecture, or to the brilliant but superficial chapter in Taine. We are all proud of our greatest satirist; but as to making a detailed study of his works, nobody thinks of such an adventure. A distant acquaintance with *Gulliver*, and an inquisitive interest in Stella and Vanessa, will carry one comfortably through the world, and it were unreasonable to require more of the harassed reader in an age when every one is a Deucalion and every stone a book.

One disadvantage that Swift shares with his contemporary Defoe is his bulk. There is certainly something deterring to many tastes in a classic, let him be never so famous, who cannot be comfortably lodged in less than nineteen sizeable volumes. Scott's second edition, 1824, is still, in spite of its want of method and accuracy, the standard text of Swift, and it has recently been luxuriously and only too faithfully reprinted without any diminution of its size. Nineteen volumes, with never a novel among them, or at best an allegorical tale or two, and for subject first and last one gigantic pillory of the human species, may fairly be allowed to make a severe demand upon the jaded appetite of the modern reader. The true book lover knows how to appreciate long editions; I am not, however, thinking at present of book lovers, but of book readers, who need as careful preparation as ever Foulis or Bodoni bestowed upon their folios, though the preparation must be of a different or even opposite nature. Nineteen honest brown backs are dear to a lover of books, but they scare a mere reader, whose weaker faith must be fortified by small doses, and whose unaccustomed organs can only digest food when it has been well minced.

Thus it happens that Swift is not read except by a few avowed students. My own introduction to him in his entirety was under far more unfavourable auspices than Scott's. I claim to belong to the book lovers, and an edition that spreads along a whole shelf has no terrors for me. But I was condemned to learn my Swift in the most atrocious form that ever printer and binder conspired to produce for the torment of their victims. The accident that compelled me to read Swift was an illness. There is nothing like a good long illness for the cultivation of pure literature. It should not be too severe or needlessly painful, for then you may overshoot the mark and be too weary to read or be read to. It is possible to have too much of even the best things. But a proper, comfortable illness, that keeps you in bed, yet leaves you free to read; that banishes all the interruptions of life, the constitutional walks, the stupid visits, the annoying correspondence, the dressing and the undressing, and all the other amenities of modern civilization, and allows you to lie at peace and read your fill, is among the best gifts of the gods. You soon forget to be sleepy and lazy; your mind displays an unwonted activity, and you become conscious of an insatiable craving for books.

At first the attentions of well-meaning friends will provide you with all the most recent additions to the circulating library, and you will daily consume your thirty-one-and-sixpenny-worth of guileless incapacity. But this will not last long; you will get rid of your friends, by natural brutality or by simulating an infectious disorder; you will refuse to pay the carriage of library parcels; and you will then abandon yourself to the luxury of reposeful reading of some great author who has stood neglected on your upper shelf for years, and has sadly listened to your glib criticisms of his works, when he knows you have never even taken him into your hands. You will read and re-read the neglected one as you have seldom read anything of late :— slowly, with enjoyment of each well-turned sentence, each pregnant thought; the mere act of reading will be a delight, instead of the scramble it too often is, and you will remember that author as long as you live, and continue to read and re-read him when you know his every page by heart. If the gods could condescend to mortal literature, in such a way would they read. They may talk of an Academy for England; but what we most want is a statutory illness, which everyone shall be compelled to take at reasonable intervals, and during which he shall be locked up in the company of a real book, till he and it are grown firm friends. A Bill to banish the productions of circulating libraries from all sick rooms, and for the provision by the state of a sufficient diet of good authors, would almost serve the turn; but the compulsory illness is the true remedy for literary ignorance.

In such an illness I chanced to forgather with Swift. I had passed through the thirty-one-and-sixpenny phase, and was experiencing the inevitable reaction, when I remembered two solid volumes on the traditional top-shelf, which I had not explored. They contained Swift's works. I had no recollection when or why I bought them: and when I opened them for the first time, I marvelled greatly what perversity had led to such a purchase.

There are two ways of getting a literary gallon into a pint pot. One is the evaporative process, by which the thinner and airier portions of the fluid are suffered to depart in vapour, and a residue of sound liquor, mellowed by time and full of the distinctive bouquet of the vintage, preserves all of it that was worth keeping. This might be applied to Swift with success, for there is much that is unequal in his work, and it is quite possible and desirable to distil the true essence out of the mixed brew that we find in the complete editions. The other method is one of mechanical compression, unknown to distillers, but familiar to buyers of books, whereby each particle of the liquor is squeezed and shaken into half its natural size, with the loss too often of taste and colour, and is then crammed into a mean vessel, of the thinnest and basest metal, which cannot be lifted without spilling the contents, and in which the pot-boy knocks a hole at every drawing.

My Swift had been subjected to the latter process. Two tall columns,—not "tall" in the celestial sense beloved of collectors, but only long of "form" and short of margin,—filled each page with closely serried ranks of undersized letters; and each volume held near a thousand such pages between its shattered boards. Here, indeed, was the whole of Swift,— or more than the whole, for there was a good deal that he never wrote,—but so hustled and pressed and "cropped," that a moral effort was needed to keep the outraged sight upon the pages. Accident, however, ruled the event. There was nothing else to read; something printed was essential; and so the two huge volumes came down from their dusty obscurity, and Swift became my intimate companion, then and thenceforward. I have never ceased to be grateful to those two ungainly volumes, and the illness that forced me to study them: and though I now rejoice in the possession of Scott's luxurious edition, the mangled remains of the clumsy but painstaking edition of 1841 are still religiously preserved as objects of tender solicitude.

You may get much pleasure by reading chosen portions of an author, as I hope some will gain from these Selections; but to enjoy a great writer fully you must read him through and then read him again. It is a happy accident that forces one to read such a one in earnest; and however one may agree with Sir John in the general principle, there can be no doubt that such reading "upon compulsion" is the best fate that can befall a man. Selections have their justification. They serve a double object,—to introduce and to remind. They provide the unadventurous reader with the easiest way to learn a little of an author he feels he ought to know; and they recall the fruits of fuller study to the memories of those who have passed on to other fields. "The unlearned will thank me for informing, and the learned will forgive me for reminding them," was the exordium of the old scholar: and this is the best motto that can be prefixed to a book of selections from a great classic.

In Swift's case there are other reasons for such selection. Much of his work was concerned with the politics of his day, and this part has lost something of its flavour to all but historical students. Too often his best writings are defaced by a coarseness of illustration, which though it may find its parallel in the literature of the age can hardly be excused, and can certainly not be tolerated in a book for general reading. Swift's coarseness, however, is not of the worst kind, as anyone will allow who has made any extensive research among the pamphlets and skits of his time, nor is it so pervasive as is commonly imagined. It is quite possible to purge his text of every trace of indelicacy without injuring either his sense or his style. The number of such omissions in the present selection is quite trifling; yet there remains not a line in this volume which might not be recited in a drawing-room.

Another reason for excision is that his satire sometimes stings a foe who has been so long forgotten that it takes an antiquary to discover the bite. Swift's remarks on the fleeting existence of a pun apply scarcely less closely to satire. Nothing, he says, is so very tender as a modern piece of wit, or is so apt to suffer in the carriage. "Some things are extremely witty to-day, or fasting, or in this place, or at eight o'clock, or over a bottle, or spoke by Mr. What d' y' call 'm, or in a summer's morning: any of which by the smallest transposal or misapplication is utterly annihilate. Thus wit has its walks and purlieus, out of which it may not stray the breadth of a hair, upon peril of being lost. The moderns have artfully fixed this mercury, and reduced it to the circumstances of time, place, and person. Such a jest there is that will not pass out of Covent Garden; and such a one that is nowhere intelligible but at Hyde-park corner. Now though it sometimes tenderly affects me to consider, that all the towardly passages I shall deliver in the following treatise will quite grow out of date and relish with the first shifting of the present scene, yet I must needs subscribe to the justice of the proceeding: because I cannot imagine why we should be at the expense to furnish wit for succeeding ages, when the former have made no sort of provision for ours." What Swift said ironically, for the benefit of the small wits of his time, applies in earnest to not a few of his own taunts, which have lost their savour merely because the exciting cause has been long buried. What can be less interesting than a parody of an unknown poem or play? But this is the fate of many of Swift's jibes at the abuses of his age; and ignorance of the objects has brought neglect and inappreciation upon the jest. Swift's comments on Prior's journey, and Wharton's vices, and the theology of Mr. Collins, need a second commentator to make them intelligible to a latter-day reader.

But if satire has its perishable elements, it possesses also qualities that will commend it to the shrewder minds so long as the world lasts. "As wit is the noblest and most useful gift of human nature, so humour is the most agreeable; and where these two enter far into the composition of any work, they will render it always acceptable to the world." And of all forms of humour satire has perhaps the most durability. "Satire is a sort of glass," begins the preface to the *Battle of the Books*, "wherein beholders do generally discover everybody's face but their own; which is the chief reason for that kind reception it meets with in the world." It will not win the widest popularity among the general, for it demands a sense of humour and perhaps a slight vein of cynicism which are not present in every mind, and it postulates a mind, which is not contained in every skull. But among those who are able to understand it, satire has a power of fascination that no other written thing possesses.

Swift exercises this peculiar fascination upon all who fairly come within reach of his pen. Some of his irony has lost its point by age and our forgetfulness of the past; but the great mass of his work is on that large field which embraces human nature without regard to time or place,—with the *ludibrium rerum humanarum*, the "ridiculous tragedy" of life,—and is as applicable to the follies and hypocrisies of the present day, as it was to the days of Wharton and Walpole. Man seen at Lilliput through the wrong end of a telescope is as fruitful of instructive humour as he was when *Gulliver* was first published; the contrasts between the Houyhnhnms and the Yahoos have as terrible a meaning now as then; the mocking laughter of the *Tub* and the *Books* rings as scornfully now as ever it did in the opening of the eighteenth century. Swift's satire is as enduring as our language, and will in turn delight and chill and terrify mankind so long as books have power.

There is something in this satire that is alone and without exact parallel in literature. It is always in terrible earnest. We smile with Thackeray, for we feel that the humourist is ridiculing himself as much as anybody, and is laughing with us while he pretends to anathematize. With Swift it is no laughing matter. He hates and loathes the meannesses and unrealities of life with the fervour of a prophet of old; he denounces them with the Burden of Moab. Weakness and deception do not amuse but enrage him; he does not pity the feeble race that descends to shams and subterfuge, he despises it heartily. His whole heart is filled with unspeakable contempt for "the animal called man," and all his writings give utterance to his disgust.

But he did not sneer for the sake of sneering; he showed the right while he scarified the wrong; he did not paint that loathsome picture of the Yahoos without a fellow portrait of the "Great Virtues of the Houyhnhnms," or satirize the vices of his country without contrasting the excellence of the government of Brobdingnag. Swift was the Carlyle of his time, but with twice Carlyle's breadth and a thousand times his intellectual keenness. The "Philosophy of Clothes" is Swift's, as *Sartor* allows, and the general tenor of the two men's jeremiads is singularly parallel. Carlyle has a certain Teutonic idealism and romance which Swift hardly shows; nevertheless Swift had his standards as well as his Scottish successor. Each despises "the animal called man," and each loves his Peter or Jack,— his Sterling or Arbuthnot. "If there were but a dozen Arbuthnots in the world," wrote Swift, "I would burn my *Travels.*" Each had the same belief in great men, and the same distrust of the multitude— "mostly fools." Each lacked that broad sympathy which belongs to the very greatest natures, and each accordingly fell into that slough of gloomy despairing misanthropy, from which only wide sympathies can save those whose eyes are "quick to see offences." But the defects are integral parts of the character. You cannot pour the vials of wrath upon the world if you are able to see its better side; sympathy destroys the power of denunciation, and the lash will be laid on with a tremulous hand if the whipper is full of compassion for the whipped. The character that strikes cannot be joined to the heart that pities, or the blows will fall feebly and miss their aim. The highest natures may combine the sword that smites with the balm that heals,—as Shakspere did,—but it will be at the sacrifice of the sword's edge. Swift did not possess this highest nature; he could love and pity on occasion, but his mission was to scourge, and like most executioners he grew hardened to his work. It is the too common fate of the schoolmaster.

The terrible earnestness of Swift's wrath, the *saeva indignatio* of his own epitaph, gives him a peculiar power. Lighter satire amuses us; we enjoy the wit and discernment of the writer, and join in his pleasant half-malicious laugh. But Swift's satire goes home to us; we feel that he sees into the realities of things, and that the shams and canting impostures he exposes are real and hateful things which still destroy the honesty and truth of life. With Swift as with Carlyle the detestation of falsehood and hypocrisy was the one ruling idea, and the vehemence with which they denounced the pettinesses and shams of life carries us away. It is difficult to turn from either of these earnest haters of wrong and falsehood to the half-hearted criticisms of the generality, without a feeling of contempt. I remember, when I had read *Sartor Resartus* for the first time, taking up a volume of essays by a very distinguished critic of these days, whom I had frequently read with keen pleasure; and flinging it incontinently away. The bathos was too precipitate. It is the same with Swift. He towers above other men by the scathing force and passion of his indignation, by the terrible, perhaps exaggerated, earnestness which underlies his lightest travesties.

His earnestness is reflected in his style. No English is so pointed and so direct as Swift's. Every sentence is a keen knife that cuts straight to the core; there is no hesitation or swerving; there is never a word wasted. His sentences follow one another logically and equably, in the order dictated by the subject, without any apparent regard for the graces of expression, nor even, sometimes, for the ordinary rules of grammar. He wrote rapidly, as the thoughts seized him, nor "ever leaned his head upon his left hand to study what he should write next." Yet Swift's prose is never ungainly; it is simple and clear and direct, absolutely free from affectation or "curious care," never seeking mere rhetorical effects; but it is not the less polished to a smooth and brilliant surface;—not the polish of elaboration, but the fine chiselled surface that marks a mind that thought clearly and exactly. If, as Mr. Matthew Arnold says, "uniformity, regularity, precision, balance," be the best names for the essentials of good prose, these qualities are conspicuous in Swift's English. But precision is the quality that strikes one as more salient in his style than perhaps in any other English prose. His words always say precisely what he means, neither more nor less; and that after all is the end of language with one who has something to say. If he can say exactly what he means, without rhetorical exaggeration or bald insufficiency, he writes well; if he can do all this, and also make his sentences glitter like burnished daggers, he is a master of prose style. In all this Swift stands supreme: there is more graceful language, more glowing, more imaginative, but none more masculine, straightforward, and expressive of the precise idea of the writer. A safer model of style cannot be found in the whole range of English literature.

But there is another quality in Swift as characteristic as his incisive style or his cynical satire, and this is his extraordinary power of detailed realization of purely fictitious images. It is this that gives, not only his narrative, but his illustrations, his "proposals," and "schemes," their lifelike probability. As Mr. Leslie Stephen has put it, "Swift's peculiarity is in the curious sobriety of fancy which leads him to keep in his most daring flights upon the confines of the possible. In the imaginary travels of Lucian and Rabelais, with which *Gulliver* is generally compared, we frankly take leave of the real world altogether. We are treated with arbitrary and monstrous combinations, which may be amusing, but which do not challenge even a semblance of belief. In *Gulliver* this is so little the case that it can hardly be said in strictness that the fundamental assumptions are even impossible. Why should there not be creatures in human form with whom, as in Lilliput, one of our inches represents a foot, or, as in Brobdingnag, one of our feet represents an inch? the assumption is so modest that we are presented, it may be said, with a definite and soluble problem. We have not, as in other fictitious worlds, to deal with a state of things in which the imagination is bewildered, but with one in which it is agreeably stimulated. We have certainly to consider an extremely exceptional case, but one to which all the ordinary laws of human nature are still strictly applicable. Imagine giants and dwarfs as tall as a house or as low as a footstool, and let us see what comes of it. That is a plain, almost mathematical problem; and we can therefore judge his success and receive pleasure from the ingenuity and verisimilitude of his creations.

"'When we have once thought of big men and little men,' said Johnson, perversely enough, 'it is easy to do the rest.' The first step might, perhaps, seem in this case to be the easiest, yet nobody ever thought of it before Swift, and nobody has ever had similar good fortune since. There is no other fictitious world the denizens of which have become so real for us and which has supplied so many images familiar to every educated mind. But the apparent ease is due to the extreme consistency and sound judgment of Swift's realization. The conclusions follow so inevitably from the primary data, that when they are once drawn we agree that they could not be otherwise, and infer, rashly, that anybody else could have drawn them. It is as easy as lying; but everybody who has seriously tried the experiment knows that even lying is by no means so easy as it appears at first sight. In fact, Swift's success is something unique. The charming plausibility of every incident throughout the two first parts, commends itself to children, who enjoy definite concrete images, and are fascinated by a world which is at once full of marvels surpassing Jack the Giant Killer and the wonders seen by Sindbad, and yet as obviously and undeniably true as the adventures of Robinson Crusoe himself." This is, of course, more even than the edge of the satire, the true cause of *Gulliver's* popularity, and not among children only.

In arranging the present selection, I have sought to give especial prominence to this peculiar power of realization, which lends a unique charm to Swift's narrative. Of the extracts from *Gulliver*, which fill a third of this volume, half were chosen on account of the microscopic realism of the pictures they present of purely imaginary states of existence. Such extracts are the "Reception in Lilliput," perhaps the most successful example of the logical expansion of a fanciful hypothesis in English literature; the "Inventory," where the same idea is consistently developed; the "Capture of the Fleet"; and the meeting with the

Gray Houyhnhnm, which to my mind possesses a grace and charm which cannot be matched in all the rest of the wonderful book. The other extracts from *Gulliver* show Swift's vein of cynical satire in its most sober and restrained dignity. We feel, as Hazlitt said, that we are reading the measured judgments of some inhabitant of a higher sphere, who looks down with sovereign contempt upon the hollow pretences, the puny rivalries, the gratuitous falsehoods, which go to help out the " ridiculous tragedy " called life. The King of Brobdingnag's " Inquiry " reads as coldly and judicially as a state paper. The passion and scorn that underlie the calmest irony in Swift is here so subdued that it might almost pass unsuspected. There is little of the exuberant slashing ridicule of the *Tub* or the *Books;* it is rather the expression of the contemptuous despair of one who has seen through life, and pronounces it altogether vanity. The quiet hopelessness of the satire reaches its most gloomy stage in the picture of the Struldbrugs, where Swift turns the Tithonus myth into a horrible reality, and shows us old age in its most revolting and dismal aspect.

I have drawn less freely than some will perhaps approve from the voyage to Laputa ; but when it was necessary to exclude even some of the most celebrated passages in Lilliput and Brobdingnag, it was inevitable that the inferior work of the third voyage should be represented very briefly. The hitherto unpublished addition to Laputa, however, printed in the Notes, will make some amends for the omissions in the text.

The studiously restrained contempt of the satire and the extraordinary lifelike quality of the narrative make *Gulliver* Swift's greatest work ; but there are many who would give a nearly equal rank to the *Tale of a Tub*. Swift himself, in the dreary decline of his powers, was observed to turn over the pages of his earliest work, and exclaim, "Good God, what a genius I had when I wrote that book!"—and genius is written on every page of it. The vigorous young intellect rejoices in its strength, and wantons and riots in its work of destruction. He has already found out that all is vanity and hypocrisy, and he tears the mask from the solemn shams and decorums of the world with shouts of derisive laughter. He is divesting himself of "prejudices," he says, and is confident that he, and he alone, is free from the conventional impostures and plausible formulas of the world. He exposes the cant of religion and the pretensions of letters and the unrealities of every established form of putative virtue, or genius with a keen enjoyment of the ruin he lays bare. He anticipates the philosophy of clothes when he shows that it is the robe makes the difference between the mayor and the bishop; and he works out the dominant idea of the relativity and accidental character of all so-called greatness, when he draws his famous parallel between madness and genius, and explains the common attributes of Curtius and Empedocles.

In style, and as an artistic whole, the *Tale of a Tub* is Swift's masterpiece. The satire is more pointed and concise than in *Gulliver*, the thought more full and vigorous, the ideas and language more sustained and nervous. But to our modern taste there is much in the story of the three brothers that is painful and repellent. Without intending to do more than expose religious shams, Swift deals with what, to many people, are very sacred things, with a rude and coarse brutality that make the *Tale* hateful to sensitive readers. Fortunately the introduction into it of "Digressions" (a satire upon the "padding" of Grub Street) affords an opportunity for selection. While the religious part of the satire must necessarily be omitted from a volume which everyone should be able to read without offence, the digressions, which deal chiefly with the literary forms of imposture, are capable of being reproduced here with hardly any omissions, and though they do not adequately represent the almost boisterous humour of the work, they show Swift's style in its utmost perfection. As English, the "Epistle Dedicatory to Prince Posterity," complaining of the unfairness of his governor, Time, towards the literary productions of the age, is unsurpassed in all Swift's works.

The *Battle of the Books* is represented by the "Apologue of the Spider and the Bee," which gives the moral of the whole dispute, and by the Homeric combats which end it. The work cannot rank with the *Tub*, but it is a remarkable example of Swift's early mood, when he loved to run a-tilt against anything, for the mere enjoyment of sound knocks, and did not trouble himself about the merits of the case. The *Argument against abolishing Christianity* is introduced, partly because it is a singularly fine specimen of Swift's lighter satire, and is capable of being given in its entirety; and partly because it gives some hints of his opinions as a Churchman, which form the key to many difficulties in his political career. Swift was before all things a churchman, but his thorough contempt for abstract thought, as for abstract politics, made him rather a believer in a practically efficient church, the guardian of order and morals, than in any very spiritual institution. He was a staunch upholder of church and state, because his general contempt for mankind at large convinced him that they were about as good for flying as for thinking, and therefore needed authorized and qualified divines to do their theology for them. He detested sectarianism, not so much for its doctrinal differences as for its political dangers. A good deal of this may be read between the lines of the *Abolishing of Christianity*, but it is impossible in a limited space to give an adequate representation of the ecclesiastical views which formed so important a part of the convictions of the Dean of St. Patrick's; and although such tracts as the *Sentiments of a Church of England Man* are interesting from the biographer's point of view, as literature they must take a quite subordinate position in the works of Swift.

The same criticism applies to his political papers, which are chiefly occupied with questions that have long passed out of our horizon, and which need some historical preparation for their due understanding. Swift's pamphlets cannot indeed be ignored in the record of his work, for they formed the main support of a weak administration, and for ever established the press in the powerful position it has since held. Following Defoe's *Review*, Swift may be said to have created the "leading article" by his weekly *Examiners*, which supplied the Tory ministry with the arguments they would have used if they had had wit to think of them; and the long series of these articles, with the culminating triumph of the *Conduct of the Allies*, had no unimportant share in bringing about the disgrace of Marlborough, and the short-lived supremacy of the Harley ministry. There is no disguising the fact that these political tracts read very ill in the present day, when we are accustomed to have our political pabulum very neatly dished up for fastidious palates. Two *Examiners* are given in these selections out of thirty-three that Swift wrote, and they are, I think, the most interesting, and as literature the best, of the series; but they are certainly flat. No modern leader-writer, however commonplace, would write such heavy stuff now. The explanation probably is, as Mr. Leslie Stephen remarks, that Swift's pamphlets were rather blows than words; he had serious political effects to produce, and what he had to prove must be said in plain words, for the honest Tory squire of the country party to understand,—and obey. However this may be, very few of Swift's political writings have a literary value, and too many have a vindictive tone of personal hatred, that destroys their balance and ruins their literary effect. The extract from the *Conduct of the Allies*, the best and most potent of all his English tracts, will serve to show Swift's manner in this species of composition, and contains as clear an epitome of his views on statesmanship as could be found in a few vigorous paragraphs. Here we see that peace policy, that denunciation of the war as the doing of a ring of Whig stock-jobbers and monied men, and that belief in the landed interest and in the Establishment, which formed the keynote to Swift's politics, and the ground of his secession to the Tories.

Of the rest of the selection little need be said. It

was decided that it must be limited to prose, since the introduction of Swift's verse would have resulted in an inadequate representation of both; and the same restrictions of space compelled the rejection of the Journals and Correspondence, which were not written for publication, and have a biographical rather than a literary value. The *Essay on improving the English Tongue* is inserted as the only piece that Swift ever put his name to, and also as one of the few writings of his that are not satirical, except so far as a proposal for an Academy for England must always involve some unconscious irony. The somewhat antiquated views upon the origin and the history of our language may be forgiven in consideration of the fine appeal at the end for more substantial recognition of learning at the hands of the state:—an appeal which still retains its force in our time, when the revenue of England is devoted more readily to any object than the encouragement of science and learning; in spite of the fact that "the smallest favour given by a great prince as a mark of esteem to reward the endowments of the mind never fails to be returned with praises and gratitude, and loudly celebrated to the world." .

The last twenty-five years of Swift's sane life may be called his Irish period. During this time he was generally resident in Ireland, and his pen—apart from *Gulliver*—was almost wholly devoted to Irish concerns. He wrote about Irish trade, or no-trade; on banks, currency, agriculture, fisheries, grazing, road-making, planting, reclaiming bogs, labelling beggars, abolishing the Irish language, and utilizing infants as articles of food. In all these we find the essential virtues of Swift's style: all are treated in the inflexibly logical fashion; objections are reduced to absurdity or laughed out of existence; arguments driven home with a sledge-hammer, accompanied by a dispersing of sharp splinters into the soft places of bystanders. Some are naturally of merely temporary interest: others contain far-reaching views on the melancholy condition of Ireland under English rule. Many notable extracts might be made in illustration of the state of the country and the corruption of the government; but for literary purposes the famous *Fourth Drapier's Letter*, which caused a reward to be offered for the author's detection, and the even more celebrated *Modest Proposal*, with the little-known but ingenious caricature of the bubbles of the period, entitled *The Swearer's Bank*, are probably sufficient. They show that Swift's hand had not lost its cunning; and they also show, what many would regard as contradictory in his character, that he was an earnest Irish patriot. His "perfect hatred of tyranny and oppression," which by his own account was the cause of his championship of Ireland, was entirely of a piece with the wrath against wrong that inspired the *Tub* and *Gulliver*. He defended Ireland from a sense of justice rather than love or pity; for he positively hated the land of his exile, and regarded Dublin only as a "good enough place to die in." Nor can we claim for him a wide sympathy with the Irish proper, of whom he scarcely thought, or with the Ulster Presbyterians, whom he abhorred: his voice was for the narrow Ireland of the Englishry. Nevertheless, he worked a marvellous change in the country at large. Right or wrong about Wood's halfpence and other matters, he created public opinion in a "nation of slaves," and used it as a political force against a bad law and a vicious system of government.

Part of the *Polite Conversation* concludes the selection: this, with the *Directions to Servants*, formed Swift's last prose works. The *Directions* are so radically disgusting from first to last, that I cannot bring myself to stain these pages by a single extract: but the *Polite Conversation* shows us the now venerable Dean of St. Patrick's in a light and genial vein that leaves a pleasant taste, despite the knowledge that the sparkling string of inconsequent repartee was written by a man who had long abandoned hope.

"No English is more robust than Swift's," is the verdict of a sound critic, "no wit more scathing, no life in private and public more sad and proud, no death more pitiable." In this pithy summary a true note is touched which no student of Swift can forget. That life full of proud sadness is among the chief titles of Swift to the interest and admiration of all ages. The troubled spirit may rest,—*ubi saeva indignatio ulterius cor lacerare nequit*,—but the sad proud story will not be forgotten while there are ears to hear and hearts to understand. The personality of the desolate Dean stands out among his contemporaries like a riven oak amidst a forest of saplings. As we wander through the forest, we stop and admire the supple grace of the young trees, but all the while the old oak, seared with the thunder-bolt, towers above us in lonely majesty: him we dare not praise, but stand in sudden awe. So when we ramble through the wonderful correspondence that has descended to us from the library of St. Patrick's Deanery, we revel in the sparkling wit and light grace of the Popes and Gays, the Arbuthnots and Priors, the Lady Betty Germains and Duchesses of Queensberry of the brilliant epoch; we do homage to the daring mind of Bolingbroke; and catch glimpses of Addison and Steele and Congreve in the distance: but all the while we are conscious of a greater presence, of a master intellect before whom all these lesser luminaries pale and fade; a personality compared to which those others are "as moonlight unto sunlight, and as water unto wine."

We see him, in his busy years in London, writing his *Examiners* all evening, and then in bed scribbling his "little language" to Stella, till his fingers ache with cold, or hurrying away unshorn in the early morning, after a brief postscript to his loved journal, to prepare, at the urgent entreaty of Harley, some fresh broadside in defence of the ministry. He is dining with St. John and the favoured few at the Saturday councils, or dropping in at Will's or the St. James's Coffee House, to chat with Addison, or ask for a letter from Ireland, where he left his heart. Or again he is spending long silent days with Pope at Twickenham, or enjoying stolen visits to the Vanhomrighs, or dispensing what little gaiety and sprightliness he possessed with the charming Lady Betties of the period. We follow him to the quiet and hated retreat of St. Patrick's, and see him defending, as it never before had been defended, the country of his forced adoption, passing his only hours of sympathy with that mysterious partner of his life who was ever near but never close: or watch him reverently as he sets a seal on a life's strange love, in the despairing memorable words, "only a woman's hair.' We tremble at his forced gaiety with the jovial pathetic Sheridan in his bear-garden at Cavan; and pity his decorous dinners with Delaney; and note the sign of a disappointed life in his one solace, to write to his English friends and bemoan his fate.

So comes the last sad scene, when the disease that had tormented him through life overcame the till then indomitable will, and the mind that for half a century had known no rest,—that had guided an empire and guarded a stricken land, that had delighted and terrified men with its power and humour and vengeful scorn,—at last found sleep; the torch that had shone with scathing brilliancy upon the dark corners of the earth flickered and died out. In every phase and each relation, Swift stands alone and companionless in his unique personality. We feel the tragedy of his lonely life in the midst of its busiest engagements. We feel that, loved as he was by some, and feared and respected by most, he was without an equal to understand him and enter into his heart, that he knew it and had steeled himself to live a life of solitude in the midst of a crowd. "No public and private life was more sad and proud;" none was ever more affecting. To realize Swift's life is to know human nature in its sternest, gloomiest, most rebellious, most mysterious moods. But to realize it fully is beyond the power of any but a Swift.

A TALE OF A TUB

WRITTEN FOR THE UNIVERSAL
IMPROVEMENT OF MANKIND

The *Author's Apology*, prefixed to the 5th edition, states that "the greatest part" of the *Tale* "was finished about thirteen years since, 1696, which is eight years before it was published. The author was then young, his invention at the height, and his reading fresh in his head. By the assistance of some thinking, and much conversation, he had endeavoured to strip himself of as many real prejudices as he could. . . . Thus prepared, he thought the numerous and gross corruptions in religion and learning might furnish matter for a satire that would be useful and diverting. He resolved to proceed in a manner that should be altogether new, the world having been already too long nauseated with endless repetitions upon every subject. The abuses of religion he proposed to set forth in the allegory of the coats and the three brothers, which was to make up the body of the discourse: those in learning he chose to introduce by way of digressions." The title was derived, according to the *Author's Preface*, from a custom seamen use "when they meet a whale, to throw him out an empty tub by way of amusement, to divert him from laying violent hands upon the ship." Such a whale is Hobbes's *Leviathan*, "which tosses and plays with all schemes of religion and government," and to divert Hobbes's kindred from "tossing and sporting with the commonwealth" Swift flings them his treatise until such time as a more complete engine of defence shall be set up. The *Tale* is outwardly a narrative of the career of three brothers, Peter, Martin, and Jack, who represent respectively the Roman Church, the Reformed or Anglican Church, and Protestant Dissent; but the history of their adventures and the diverse modes in which they contrive to interpret their father's will, the New Testament, in accordance with their own desires, and to accommodate the miraculous coats, Christianity, which he had bequeathed to them to the varying fashions of each season, fills but a third of the treatise, and even here the satire reaches much further than ecclesiastical divisions and scholastic hairsplittings. In the several digressions the story is wholly set aside, and the author allows his humour to play unfettered upon cant and hypocrisy of all kinds. Of the eleven sections which, together with sundry prefaces and dedications, and a conclusion, make up the work, the Second, Fourth, Sixth, and Eleventh, alone are occupied with the allegory of the three brothers: the remaining seven are digressions, though not all so styled, "on critics," "in the modern kind," "in praise of digressions," on the Æolists, or pretenders to immediate inspiration, who derive all things from wind, "on madness," etc. The epistle to Prince Posterity, and Sections I., VII., and IX., together with passages from II. and X., are here selected to represent the work: but there is hardly a line that can well be spared from Swift's masterpiece.

THE EPISTLE DEDICATORY
TO
HIS ROYAL HIGHNESS PRINCE POSTERITY

SIR,

I HERE present your highness with the fruits of a very few leisure hours, stolen from the short intervals of a world of business, and of an employment quite alien from such amusements as this : the poor production of that refuse of time which has lain heavy upon my hands during a long prorogation of parliament, a great dearth of foreign news, and a tedious fit of rainy weather; for which and other reasons, it cannot choose extremely to deserve such a patronage as that of your highness, whose numberless virtues, in so few years, make the world look upon you as the future example to all princes : for although your highness is hardly got clear of infancy, yet has the universal learned world already resolved upon appealing to your future dictates with the lowest and most resigned submission ; fate having decreed you sole arbiter of the productions of human wit in this polite and most accomplished age. Methinks, the number of appellants were enough to shock and startle any judge of a genius less unlimited than yours: but, in order to prevent such glorious trials, the person, it seems, to whose care the education of your highness is committed, has resolved, as I am told, to keep you in almost a universal ignorance of our studies, which it is your inherent birthright to inspect.

It is amazing to me that this person should have the assurance, in the face of the sun, to go about persuading your highness that our age is almost wholly illiterate, and has hardly produced one writer upon any subject. I know very well, that when your highness shall come to riper years, and have gone through the learning of antiquity, you will be too curious to neglect inquiring into the authors of the very age before you: and to think that this insolent, in the account he is preparing for your view, designs to reduce them to a number so insignificant as I am ashamed to mention; it moves my zeal and my spleen for the honour and interest of our vast flourishing body, as well as of myself, for whom, I know by long experience, he has professed, and still continues, a peculiar malice.

It is not unlikely that, when your highness will one day peruse what I am now writing, you may be ready to expostulate with your governor upon the credit of what I here affirm, and command him to show you some of our productions. To which he will answer, (for I am well informed of his designs,) by asking your highness, where they are? and what has become of them? and pretend it a demonstration that there never were any, because they are not then to be found. Not to be found! who has mislaid them? are they sunk in the abyss of things? It is certain that in their own nature they were light enough to swim upon the surface for all eternity. Therefore the fault is in him who tied weights so heavy to their heels as to depress them to the centre. Is their very essence destroyed? who has annihilated them? But, that it may no longer be a doubt with your highness, who is to be the author of this universal ruin, I beseech you to observe that large and terrible scythe which your governor affects to bear continually about him. Be pleased to remark the length and strength, the sharpness and hardness, of his nails and teeth; consider his baneful, abominable breath, enemy to life and matter, infectious and corrupting: and then reflect, whether it be possible for any mortal ink and paper of this generation to make a suitable resistance. O! that your highness would one day resolve to disarm this usurping *maître du palais* of his furious engines, and bring your empire *hors de page*.

It were needless to recount the several methods of tyranny and destruction which your governor is pleased to practise upon this occasion. His inveterate malice is such to the writings of our age, that of several thousands produced yearly from this renowned city, before the next revolution of the sun, there is not one to be heard of: unhappy infants! many of them barbarously destroyed before they have so much as learnt their mother tongue to beg for pity. Some he stifles in their cradles; others he frights into convulsions, whereof they suddenly die; some he flays alive; others he tears limb from limb. Great numbers are offered to Moloch; and the rest, tainted by his breath, die of a languishing consumption.

But the concern I have most at heart is for our corporation of poets; from whom I am preparing a petition to your highness, to be subscribed with the names of one hundred and thirty-six of the first rate; but whose immortal productions are never likely to reach your eyes, though each of them is now a humble and earnest appellant for the laurel, and has large comely volumes ready to show for a support to his pretensions. The never-dying works of these illustrious persons, your governor, sir, has devoted to unavoidable death; and your highness is to be made believe that our age has never arrived at the honour to produce one single poet.

We confess Immortality to be a great and powerful goddess; but in vain we offer up to her our devotions and our sacrifices, if your highness's governor, who has usurped the priesthood, must, by an unparalleled ambition and avarice, wholly intercept and devour them.

To affirm that our age is altogether unlearned, and devoid of writers in any kind, seems to be an assertion so bold and so false, that I have been some time thinking the contrary may almost be proved by uncontrollable demonstration. It is true, indeed, that although their numbers be vast, and their productions numerous in proportion, yet are they hurried so hastily off the scene, that they escape our memory and elude our sight. When I first thought of this address, I had prepared a copious list of titles to present your highness, as an undisputed argument for what I affirm. The originals were posted fresh upon all gates and corners of streets; but, returning in a very few hours to take a review, they were all torn down, and fresh ones in their places. I inquired after them among readers and booksellers; but I inquired in vain: the memorial of them was lost among men, their place was no more to be found; and I was laughed to scorn for a clown and a pedant, without all taste and refinement, little versed in the course of present affairs, and that knew nothing of what had passed in the best companies of court and town. So that I can only avow in general to your highness, that we do abound in learning and wit; but to fix upon particulars is a task too slippery for my slender abilities. If I should venture in a windy day to affirm to your highness, that there is a large cloud near the horizon in the form of a bear, another in the zenith with the head of an ass, a third to the westward with claws like a dragon; and your highness should in a few minutes think fit to examine the truth; it is certain they would all be changed in figure and position: new ones would arise, and all we could agree upon would be, that clouds there were, but that I was grossly mistaken in the zoography and topography of them.

But your governor perhaps may still insist, and put the question,—What is then become of those immense bales of paper which must needs have been employed in such numbers of books? can these also be wholly annihilate, and so of a sudden, as I pretend? What shall I say in return of so invidious an objection? It ill befits the distance between your highness and me, to send you for ocular conviction to an oven or a sordid lantern. Books, like men their authors, have no more than one way of coming into the world; but there are ten thousand to go out of it and return no more.

I profess to your highness, in the integrity of my heart, that what I am going to say is literally true this minute I am writing: what revolutions may happen before it shall be ready for your perusal, I can by no means warrant; however, I beg you to accept it as a specimen of our learning, our politeness, and our wit. I do therefore affirm, upon the word of a sincere man, that there is now actually in being a certain poet, called John Dryden, whose translation of Virgil was lately printed in a large folio, well bound, and if diligent search were made, for aught I know, is yet to be seen. There is another, called Nahum Tate, who is ready to make oath that he has caused many reams of verse to be published, whereof both himself and his bookseller, if lawfully required, can still produce authentic copies, and therefore wonders why the world is pleased to make such a secret of it. There is a third, known by the name of Tom Durfey, a poet of a vast comprehension, a universal genius, and most profound learning. There are also one Mr. Rymer, and one Mr. Dennis, most profound critics. There is a person styled Dr. Bentley, who has written near a thousand pages of immense erudition, giving a full and true account of a certain squabble of wonderful importance between himself and a bookseller: he is a writer of infinite wit and humour; no man rallies with a better grace and in more sprightly turns. Farther, I avow to your highness that with these eyes I have beheld the person of William Wotton, B. D., who has written a good sizeable volume against a friend of your governor, (from whom, alas! he must therefore look for little favour,) in a most gentlemanly style, adorned with the utmost politeness and civility; replete with discoveries equally valuable for their novelty and use; and embellished with traits of wit, so poignant and so apposite, that he is a worthy yoke-mate to his forementioned friend.

Why should I go upon farther particulars, which might fill a volume with the just eulogies of my contemporary brethren? I shall bequeath this piece of justice to a larger work, wherein I intend to write a character of the present set of wits in our nation: their persons I shall describe particularly and at length, their genius and understandings in miniature.

In the meantime, I do here make bold to present your highness with a faithful abstract, drawn from the universal body of all arts and sciences, intended wholly for your service and instruction: nor do I doubt in the least, but your highness will peruse it as carefully, and make as considerable improvements, as other young princes have already done, by the many volumes of late years written for a help to their studies.

That your highness may advance in wisdom and virtue, as well as years, and at last outshine all your royal ancestors, shall be the daily prayer of,

   Sir,
     your highness's
       most devoted, &c.

Decemb.
1697.

THE INTRODUCTION

WHOEVER has an ambition to be heard in a crowd, must press, and squeeze, and thrust, and climb, with indefatigable pains, till he has exalted himself to a certain degree of altitude above them. Now, in all assemblies, though you wedge them ever so close, we may observe this peculiar property, that over their heads there is room enough, but how to reach it is the difficult point; it being as hard to get quit of number, as of hell:

Evadere ad auras,
Hoc opus, hic labor est.

To this end the philosopher's way, in all ages, has been by erecting certain edifices in the air: but, whatever practice and reputation these kind of structures have formerly possessed, or may still continue in, not excepting even that of Socrates, when he was suspended in a basket to help contemplation, I think, with due submission, they seem to labour under two inconveniences. First, That, the foundations being laid too high, they have been often out of sight and ever out of hearing. Secondly, That the materials, being very transitory, have suffered much from inclemencies of air, especially in these north-west regions.

Therefore, towards the just performance of this

great work, there remain but three methods that I can think of; whereof the wisdom of our ancestors being highly sensible has, to encourage all aspiring adventurers, thought fit to erect three wooden machines for the use of those orators who desire to talk much without interruption. These are the pulpit, the ladder, and the stage itinerant. For as to the bar, though it be compounded of the same matter, and designed for the same use, it cannot, however, be well allowed the honour of a fourth, by reason of its level or inferior situation exposing it to perpetual interruption from collaterals. Neither can the bench itself, though raised to a proper eminency, put in a better claim, whatever its advocates insist on. For, if they please to look into the original design of its erection, and the circumstances or adjuncts subservient to that design, they will soon acknowledge the present practice exactly correspondent to the primitive institution, and both to answer the etymology of the name, which in the Phœnician tongue is a word of great signification, importing, if literally interpreted, the place of sleep; but, in common acceptation, a seat well bolstered and cushioned for the repose of old and gouty limbs: *senes ut in otia tuta recedant.* Fortune being indebted to them this part of retaliation, that, as formerly they have long talked while others slept, so now they may sleep as long while others talk.

But if no other argument could occur to exclude the bench and the bar from the list of oratorial machines, it were sufficent that the admission of them would overthrow a number which I was resolved to establish, whatever argument it might cost me; in imitation of that prudent method observed by many other philosophers and great clerks, whose chief art in division has been to grow fond of some proper mystical number, which their imaginations have rendered sacred, to a degree that they force common reason to find room for it in every part of nature; reducing, including, and adjusting, every genus and species within that compass, by coupling some against their wills, and banishing others at any rate. Now, among all the rest, the profound number THREE is that which has most employed my sublimest speculations, nor ever without wonderful delight. There is now in the press, and will be published next term, a panegyrical essay of mine upon this number; wherein I have, by most convincing proofs, not only reduced the senses and the elements under its banner, but brought over several deserters from its two great rivals, SEVEN and NINE.

Now, the first of these oratorial machines, in place as well as dignity, is the pulpit. Of pulpits there are in this island several sorts; but I esteem only that made of timber from the *sylva Caledonia*, which agrees very well with our climate. If it be upon its decay, it is the better both for conveyance of sound, and for other reasons to be mentioned by and by. The degree of perfection in shape and size, I take to consist in being extremely narrow, with little ornament, and, best of all, without a cover, (for, by ancient rule, it ought to be the only uncovered vessel in every assembly, where it is rightfully used,) by which means, from its near resemblance to a pillory, it will ever have a mighty influence on human ears.

Of ladders I need say nothing: it is observed by foreigners themselves, to the honour of our country, that we excel all nations in our practice and understanding of this machine. The ascending orators do not only oblige their audience in the agreeable delivery, but the whole world in the early publication, of their speeches; which I look upon as the choicest treasury of our British eloquence, and whereof, I am informed, that worthy citizen and bookseller, Mr. John Dunton, has made a faithful and painful collection, which he shortly designs to publish, in twelve volumes in folio, illustrated with copper-plates. A work highly useful and curious, and altogether worthy of such a hand.

The last engine of orators is the stage itinerant, erected with much sagacity, *sub Jove pluvio, in triviis et quadriviis*. It is the great seminary of the two former, and its orators are sometimes preferred to the one, and sometimes to the other, in proportion to their deservings; there being a strict and perpetual intercourse between all three.

From this accurate deduction it is manifest that for obtaining attention in public there is of necessity required a superior position of place. But, although this point be generally granted, yet the cause is little agreed in; and it seems to me that very few philosophers have fallen into a true, natural solution of this phenomenon. The deepest account, and the most fairly digested of any I have yet met with, is this: that air being a heavy body, and therefore, according to the system of Epicurus, continually descending, must needs be more so, when loaded and pressed down by words; which are also bodies of much weight and gravity, as it is manifest from those deep impressions they make and leave upon us; and therefore must be delivered from a due altitude, or else they will neither carry a good aim, nor fall down with a sufficient force.

*Corpoream quoque enim vocem constare fatendum est,
Et sonitum, quoniam possunt impellere sensus.*
—LUCR. Lib. iv.

And I am the readier to favour this conjecture, from a common observation, that, in the several assemblies of these orators, nature itself has instructed the hearers to stand with their mouths open and erected parallel to the horizon, so as they may be intersected by a perpendicular line from the zenith to the centre of the earth. In which position, if the audience be well compact, every one carries home a share, and little or nothing is lost.

I confess, there is something yet more refined in the contrivance and structure of our modern theatres. For, first, the pit is sunk below the stage, with due regard to the institution above deduced; that, whatever weighty matter shall be delivered thence, whether it be lead or gold, may fall plumb into the jaws of certain critics, as I think they are called, which stand ready opened to devour them. Then, the boxes are built round, and raised to a level with the scene, in deference to the ladies: because that large portion of wit, laid out in raising protuberances, is observed to run much upon a line, and ever in a circle. The whining passions and little starved conceits are gently wafted up, by their own extreme levity, to the middle region, and there fix and are frozen by the frigid understandings of the inhabitants. Bombastry and buffoonery, by nature lofty and light, soar highest of all, and would be lost in the roof, if the prudent architect had not, with much foresight, contrived for them a fourth place, called the twelve-penny gallery, and there planted a suitable colony, who greedily intercept them in their passage.

Now this physico-logical scheme of oratorial receptacles or machines contains a great mystery; being a type, a sign, an emblem, a shadow, a symbol, bearing analogy to the spacious commonwealth of writers, and to those methods by which they must exalt themselves to a certain eminency above the inferior world. By the pulpit are adumbrated the writings of our modern saints in great Britain, as they have spiritualised and refined them from the dross and grossness of sense and human reason. The matter, as we have said, is of rotten wood; and that upon two considerations; because it is the quality of rotten wood to give light in the dark : and secondly, because its cavities are full of worms; which is a type with a pair of handles, having a respect to the two principal qualifications of the orator, and the two different fates attending upon his works.

The ladder is an adequate symbol of faction, and of poetry, to both of which so noble a number of authors are indebted for their fame. Of faction because * * * * *Hiatus in MS.* * * * * * * Of poetry, because its orators do *perorare* with a song; and because, climbing up by slow degrees, fate is sure to turn them off, before they can reach within many steps of the top; and because it is a preferment attained by transferring of property, and a confounding of *meum* and *tuum*.

Under the stage itinerant are couched those productions designed for the pleasure and delight of mortal man; such as, Six-penny-worth of Wit, Westminster Drolleries, Delightful Tales, Complete Jesters,

and the like; by which the writers of and for GRUB
STREET have in these latter ages so nobly triumphed
over Time; have clipped his wings, pared his nails,
filed his teeth, turned back his hour-glass, blunted his
scythe, and drawn the hob-nails out of his shoes. It
is under this class I have presumed to list my present
treatise, being just come from having the honour con-
ferred upon me to be adopted a member of that illustrious fraternity.

Now, I am not unaware how the productions of the
Grub Street brotherhood have of late years fallen under
many prejudices, nor how it has been the perpetual
employment of two junior start-up societies to ridicule
them and their authors, as unworthy their established
post in the commonwealth of wit and learning. Their
own consciences will easily inform them whom I
mean; nor has the world been so negligent a looker-
on, as not to observe the continual efforts made by the
societies of Gresham and of Will's to edify a name and
reputation upon the ruin of OURS. And this is yet a
more feeling grief to us, upon the regards of tenderness
as well as of justice, when we reflect on their proceedings not only as unjust, but as ungrateful, undutiful,
and unnatural. For how can it be forgot by the world
or themselves, to say nothing of our own records, which
are full and clear in the point, that they both are
seminaries, not only of our planting, but our watering
too? I am informed, our two rivals have lately made
an offer to enter into the lists with united forces, and
challenge us to a comparison of books, both as to
weight and number. In return to which, with licence
from our president, I humbly offer two answers: first,
we say, the proposal is like that which Archimedes

made upon a smaller affair, including an impossibility
in the practice; for where can they find scales of
capacity enough for the first, or an arithmetician of
capacity enough for the second? Secondly, we are
ready to accept the challenge ; but with this condition,
that a third indifferent person be assigned, to whose
impartial judgment it should be left to decide which
society each book, treatise, or pamphlet, do most
properly belong to. This point, God knows, is very
far from being fixed at present ; for we are ready to
produce a catalogue of some thousands, which in all
common justice ought to be entitled to our fraternity,
but by the revolted and new-fangled writers [are] most
perfidiously ascribed to the others. Upon all which,
we think it very unbecoming our prudence that the
determination should be remitted to the authors themselves ; when our adversaries, by briguing and cabal-
ling, have caused so universal a defection from us, that
the greatest part of our society has already deserted to
them, and our nearest friends begin to stand aloof, as
if they were half ashamed to own us.

This is the utmost I am authorised to say upon so
ungrateful and melancholy a subject ; because we are
extreme unwilling to inflame a controversy whose continuance may be so fatal to the interests of us all, desir-
ing much rather that things be amicably composed ;
and we shall so far advance on our side, as to be ready
to receive the two prodigals with open arms whenever
they shall think fit to return from their husks ; and, like
an indulgent parent, continue to them our affection and
our blessing.

But the greatest maim given to that general reception which the writings of our society have formerly

received, next to the transitory state of all sublunary things, has been a superficial vein among many readers of the present age, who will by no means be persuaded to inspect beyond the surface and the rind of things; whereas, wisdom is a fox, who, after long hunting, will at last cost you the pains to dig out; it is a cheese, which, by how much the richer, has the thicker, the homelier, and the coarser coat, and whereof to a judicious palate the maggots are the best; it is a sackposset, wherein the deeper you go, you will find it the sweeter. Wisdom is a hen, whose cackling we must value and consider, because it is attended with an egg; but then, lastly, it is a nut, which, unless you choose with judgment, may cost you a tooth, and pay you with nothing but a worm. In consequence of these momentous truths, the grubæan sages have always chosen to convey their precepts and their arts shut up within the vehicles of types and fables; which having been perhaps more careful and curious in adorning than was altogether necessary, it has fared with these vehicles, after the usual fate of coaches over-finely painted and gilt, that the transitory gazers have so dazzled their eyes and filled their imaginations with the outward lustre, as neither to regard nor consider the person or the parts of the owner within. A misfortune we undergo with somewhat less reluctancy, because it has been common to us with Pythagoras, Æsop, Socrates, and other of our predecessors.

However, that neither the world nor ourselves may any longer suffer by such misunderstandings, I have been prevailed on, after much importunity from my friends, to travel in a complete and laborious dissertation upon the prime productions of our society; which, besides their beautiful externals for the gratification of superficial readers, have darkly and deeply couched under them the most finished and refined systems of all sciences and arts ; as I do not doubt to lay open by untwisting or unwinding, and either to draw up by exantlation, or display by incision.

WHAT IS MAN BUT A MICRO-COAT?

[FROM SECTION THE SECOND.]

ABOUT this time it happened a sect arose, whose tenets obtained and spread very far, especially in the *grand monde*, and among every body of good fashion. They worshipped a sort of idol, who, as their doctrine delivered, did daily create men by a kind of manufactory operation. This idol they placed in the highest part of the house, on an altar erected about three foot : he was shown in the posture of a Persian emperor, sitting on a superficies, with his legs interwoven under him. This god had a goose for his ensign : whence it is that some learned men pretend to deduce his original from Jupiter Capitolinus. At his left hand, beneath the altar, hell seemed to open, and catch at the animals the idol was creating ; to prevent which, certain of his priests hourly flung in pieces of the uninformed mass, or substance, and sometimes whole limbs already enlivened, which that horrid gulf insatiably swallowed, terrible to behold. The goose was also held a subaltern divinity, or *deus minorum gentium*, before whose shrine was sacrificed that creature whose hourly food is human gore, and who is in so great renown abroad, for being the delight and favourite of the Ægyptian Cercopithecus. Millions of these animals were cruelly slaughtered every day, to appease the hunger of that consuming deity. The chief idol was also worshipped as the inventor of the yard and needle ; whether as the god of seamen, or on account of certain other mystical attributes, has not been sufficiently cleared.

The worshippers of this deity had also a system of their belief, which seemed to turn upon the following fundamentals. They held the universe to be a large suit of clothes, which invests everything: that the earth is invested by the air ; the air is invested by the stars ; and the stars are invested by the *primum mobile*. Look on this globe of earth, you will find it to be a very complete and fashionable dress. What is that which some call land, but a fine coat faced with green ? or the sea, but a waistcoat of water-tabby ? Proceed to the particular works of the creation, you will find how curious journeyman Nature has been to trim up the vegetable beaux ; observe how sparkish a periwig adorns the head of a beech, and what a fine doublet of white satin is worn by the birch. To conclude from all, what is man himself but a micro-coat, or rather a complete suit of clothes with all its trimmings? as to his body there can be no dispute ; but examine even the acquirements of his mind, you will find them all contribute in their order towards furnishing out an exact dress : to instance no more, is not religion a cloak, honesty a pair of shoes worn out in the dirt, self-love a surtout, vanity a shirt, and conscience a pair of breeches?

These postulata being admitted, it will follow in due course of reasoning that those beings, which the world calls improperly suits of clothes, are in reality the most refined species of animals; or, to proceed higher, that they are rational creatures, or men. For is it not manifest that they live, and move, and talk, and perform all other offices of human life? are not beauty, and wit, and mien, and breeding, their inseparable proprieties? in short, we see nothing but them, hear nothing but them. Is it not they who walk the streets, fill up parliament-, coffee-, play-houses? It is true, indeed, that these animals, which are vulgarly called suits of clothes, or dresses, do, according to certain compositions, receive different appellations. If one of them be trimmed up with a gold chain, and a red gown, and a white rod, and a great horse, it is called a lord mayor; if certain ermines and furs be placed in a certain position, we style them a judge; and so an apt conjunction of lawn and black satin we entitle a bishop.

Others of these professors, though agreeing in the main system, were yet more refined upon certain branches of it; and held that man was an animal compounded of two dresses, the natural and celestial suit, which were the body and the soul: that the soul was the outward, and the body the inward clothing; that the latter was *ex traduce*, but the former of daily creation and circumfusion; this last they proved by scripture, because in them we live, and move, and have our being; as likewise by philosophy, because they are all in all, and all in every part. Besides, said they, separate these two and you will find the body to be only a senseless unsavoury carcase. By all which it is manifest that the outward dress must needs be the soul.

To this system of religion were tagged several

subaltern doctrines, which were entertained with great vogue; as particularly, the faculties of the mind were deduced by the learned among them in this manner: embroidery was sheer wit, gold fringe was agreeable conversation, gold lace was repartee, a huge long periwig was humour, and a coat full of powder was very good raillery: all which required abundance of *finesse* and *delicatesse* to manage with advantage, as well as a strict observance after times and fashions.

I have, with much pains and reading, collected out of ancient authors this short summary of a body of philosophy and divinity, which seems to have been composed by a vein and race of thinking, very different from any other systems either ancient or modern. And it was not merely to entertain or satisfy the reader's curiosity, but rather to give him light into several circumstances of the following story; that, knowing the state of dispositions and opinions in an age so remote, he may better comprehend those great events which were the issue of them. I advise, therefore, the courteous reader to peruse with a world of application, again and again, whatever I have written upon this matter. And leaving these broken ends, I carefully gather up the chief thread of my story, and proceed.

These opinions, therefore, were so universal, as well as the practices of them, among the refined part of court and town, that our three brother-adventurers, as their circumstances then stood, were strangely at a loss. For, on the one side, the three ladies they addressed themselves to were ever at the very top of the fashion, and abhorred all that were below it but the breadth of a hair. On the other side, their father's will was very precise; and it was the main precept in it, with the greatest penalties annexed, not to add to or diminish from their coats one thread, without a positive command in the will. Now, the coats their father had left them were, it is true, of very good cloth, and, besides, so neatly sewn, you would swear they were all of a piece; but at the same time very plain, and with little or no ornament: and it happened that before they were a month in town great shoulder-knots came up: straight all the world was shoulder-knots; no approaching the ladies' *ruelles* without the *quota* of shoulder-knots. That fellow, cries one, has no soul; where is his shoulder-knot? Our three brethren soon discovered their want by sad experience, meeting in their walks with forty mortifications and indignities. If they went to the playhouse, the door-keeper showed them into the twelvepenny gallery. If they called a boat, says a waterman, I am first sculler. If they stepped to the Rose to take a bottle, the drawer would cry, Friend, we sell no ale. If they went to visit a lady, a footman met them at the door with, Pray send up your message. In this unhappy case, they went immediately to consult their father's will, read it over and over, but not a word of the shoulder-knot. What should they do? what temper should they find? obedience was absolutely necessary, and yet shoulder-knots appeared extremely requisite. After much thought, one of the brothers, who happened to be more book-learned than the other two, said, he had found an expedient. It is true, said he, there is nothing here in this will, *totidem verbis*, making mention of shoulder-knots: but I dare conjecture, we may find them *inclusivè*, or *totidem syllabis.* This distinction was immediately approved by all; and so they fell again to examine; but their evil star had so directed the matter, that the first syllable was not to be found in the whole writings. Upon which disappointment, he who found the former evasion took heart, and said: Brothers, there are yet hopes; for though we cannot find them *totidem verbis*, nor *totidem syllabis*, I dare engage we shall make them out *tertio modo*, or *totidem literis*. This discovery was also highly commended, upon which they fell once more to the scrutiny, and picked out S, H, O, U, L, D, E, R; when the same planet, enemy to their repose, had wonderfully contrived that a K was not to be found. Here was a weighty difficulty! but the distinguishing brother, for whom we shall hereafter find a name, now his hand was in, proved by a very good argument that K was a modern illegitimate letter, unknown to the learned ages, nor anywhere to be found in ancient manuscripts. Calendæ hath in Q. V. C. been sometimes written with a K, but erroneously; for in the best copies it is ever spelt with a C. And by consequence it was a gross mistake in our language to spell knot with a K; but that from henceforward he would take care it should be written with a C. Upon this all farther difficulty vanished; shoulder-knots were made clearly out to be *jure paterno:* and our three gentlemen swaggered with as large and as flaunting ones as the best.

A DIGRESSION IN PRAISE OF DIGRESSIONS

I HAVE sometimes heard of an Iliad in a nut-shell; but it has been my fortune to have much oftener seen a nut-shell in an Iliad. There is no doubt that human life has received most wonderful advantages from both; but to which of the two the world is chiefly indebted, I shall leave among the curious, as a problem worthy of their utmost inquiry. For the invention of the latter, I think the commonwealth of learning is chiefly obliged to the great modern improvement of digressions: the late refinements in knowledge running parallel to those of diet in our nation, which, among men of a judicious taste, are dressed up in various compounds, consisting in soups and olios, fricassees and ragouts.

It is true, there is a sort of morose, detracting, ill-bred people, who pretend utterly to disrelish these polite innovations; and as to the similitude from diet, they allow the parallel, but are so bold to pronounce the example itself a corruption and degeneracy of taste. They tell us that the fashion of jumbling fifty things together in a dish was at first introduced, in compliance to a depraved and debauched appetite, as well as to a crazy constitution: and to see a man hunting through an olio after the head and brains of a goose, a widgeon, or a woodcock, is a sign he wants a stomach and digestion for more substantial victuals. Farther, they affirm that digressions in a book are like foreign troops in a state, which argue the nation to want a heart and hands of its own, and often either subdue the natives, or drive them into the most unfruitful corners.

But, after all that can be objected by these supercilious censors, it is manifest the society of writers would quickly be reduced to a very inconsiderable number, if men were put upon making books with the fatal confinement of delivering nothing beyond what is to the purpose. It is acknowledged, that were the case the same among us, as with the Greeks and Romans, when learning was in its cradle, to be reared, and fed, and clothed, by invention, it would be an easy task to fill up volumes upon particular occasions, without farther expatiating from the subjects than by moderate excursions, helping to advance or clear the main design. But with knowledge it has fared as with a numerous army, encamped in a fruitful country; which, for a few days, maintains itself by the product of the soil it is on; till, provisions being spent, they are sent to forage many a mile, among friends or enemies, it matters not. Meanwhile, the neighbouring fields, trampled and beaten down, become barren and dry, affording no sustenance but clouds of dust.

The whole course of things being thus entirely changed between us and the ancients, and the moderns wisely sensible of it, we of this age have discovered a shorter and more prudent method to become scholars and wits, without the fatigue of reading or of thinking.

The most accomplished way of using books at present is two-fold: either, first, to serve them as some men do lords, learn their titles exactly, and then brag of their acquaintance; or, secondly, which is indeed the choicer, the profounder, and politer method, to get a thorough insight into the index, by which the whole book is governed and turned, like fishes by the tail. For, to enter the palace of learning at the great gate requires an expense of time and forms; therefore men of much haste and little ceremony are content to get in by the back door. For the arts are all in flying march, and therefore more easily subdued by attacking them in the rear. Thus men catch knowledge by throwing their wit on the posteriors of a book, as boys do sparrows with flinging salt upon their tails. Thus human life is best understood by the wise man's rule of regarding the end. Thus are the sciences found, like Hercules's oxen, by tracing them backwards. Thus are old sciences unravelled, like old stockings, by beginning at the foot. Besides all this, the army of the sciences has been of late, with a world of martial discipline, drawn into its close order, so that a view or a muster may be taken of it with abundance of expedition. For this great blessing we are wholly indebted to systems and abstracts, in which the modern fathers of learning, like prudent usurers, spent their sweat for the ease of us their children. For labour is the seed of idleness, and it is the peculiar happiness of our noble age to gather the fruit.

Now, the method of growing wise, learned, and sublime, having become so regular an affair, and so established in all its forms, the number of writers must needs have increased accordingly, and to a pitch that has made it of absolute necessity for them to interfere continually with each other. Besides, it is reckoned that there is not at this present a sufficient quantity of new matter left in nature to furnish and adorn any one particular subject to the extent of a volume. This I am told by a very skilful computer, who has given a full demonstration of it from rules of arithmetic. What remains, therefore, but that our last recourse must be had to large indexes and little compendiums? quotations must be plentifully gathered, and booked in alphabet; to this end, though authors need be little consulted, yet critics, and commentators, and lexicons, carefully must. But, above all, those judicious collectors of bright parts, and flowers, and *observandas*, are to be nicely dwelt on; by some called the sieves and bolters of learning, though it is left undetermined whether they dealt in pearls or meal, and consequently, whether we are more to value that which passed through, or what staid behind.

By these methods, in a few weeks, there starts up many a writer capable of managing the profoundest and most universal subjects. For, what though his head be empty, provided his commonplace-book be full; and if you will bate him but the circumstances of method, and style, and grammar, and invention; allow him but the common privileges of transcribing from others, and digressing from himself, as often as he shall see occasion; he will desire no more ingredients towards fitting up a treatise that shall make a very comely figure on a bookseller's shelf; there to be preserved neat and clean for a long eternity, adorned with the heraldry of its title fairly inscribed on a label; never to be thumbed or greased by students, nor bound to everlasting chains of darkness in a library: but, when the fulness of time is come, shall happily undergo the trial of purgatory, in order to ascend the sky.

Without these allowances, how is it possible we modern wits should ever have an opportunity to introduce our collections, listed under so many thousand heads of a different nature; for want of which, the learned world would be deprived of infinite delight, as well as instruction, and we ourselves buried beyond redress in an inglorious and undistinguished oblivion?

From such elements as these, I am alive to behold the day wherein the corporation of authors can outvie all its brethren in the guild. A happiness derived to us, with a great many others, from our Scythian ancestors; among whom the number of pens was so infinite, that the Grecian eloquence had no other way of expressing it than by saying that in the regions far to the north it was hardly possible for a man to travel, the very air was so replete with feathers.

The necessity of this digression will easily excuse the length; and I have chosen for it as proper a place as I could readily find. If the judicious reader can assign a fitter, I do here impower him to remove it into any other corner he pleases.

A DIGRESSION CONCERNING THE ORIGINAL, THE USE, AND IMPROVEMENT OF MADNESS IN A COMMONWEALTH

NOR shall it any ways detract from the just reputation of this famous sect [of the Aeolists], that its rise and institution are owing to such an author as I have described Jack to be; a person whose intellectuals were overturned, and his brain shaken out of its natural position; which we commonly suppose to be a distemper, and call by the name of madness or phrensy. For, if we take a survey of the greatest actions that have been performed in the world under the influence of single men; which are, the establishment of new empires by conquest; the advance and progress of new schemes in philosophy; and the contriving, as well as the propagating, of new religions; we shall find the authors of them all to have been persons whose natural reason had admitted great revolutions, from their diet, their education, the prevalency of some certain temper, together with the particular influence of air and climate. Besides, there is something individual in human minds, that easily kindles at the accidental approach and collision of certain circumstances, which, though of paltry and mean appearance, do often flame out into the greatest emergencies of life. For great turns are not always given by strong hands, but by lucky adaption, and at proper seasons; and it is of no import where the fire was kindled, if the vapour has once got up into the brain. For the upper region of man is furnished like the middle region of the air: the materials are formed from causes of the widest difference, yet produce at last the same substance and effect. Mists arise from the earth, steams from dunghills, exhalations from the sea, and smoke from fire; yet all clouds are the same in composition as well as consequences. Thus far, I suppose, will easily be granted me: and then it will follow that, as the face of nature never produces rain but when it is overcast and disturbed, so human understanding, seated in the brain, must be troubled and overspread by vapours ascending from the lower faculties to water the invention and render it fruitful.

Let us next examine the great introducers of new schemes in philosophy, and search till we can find from what faculty of the soul the disposition arises in mortal man of taking it into his head to advance new systems, with such an eager zeal, in things agreed on all hands impossible to be known: from what seeds this disposition springs, and to what quality of human nature these grand innovators have been indebted for their number of disciples. Because it is plain that several of the chief among them, both ancient and modern, were usually mistaken by their adversaries, and indeed by all except their own followers, to have been persons crazed, or out of their wits; having generally proceeded, in the common course of their words and actions, by a method very different from the vulgar dictates of unrefined reason; agreeing for the most part in their several models with their present undoubted successors in the academy of modern Bedlam; whose merits and principles I shall farther examine in due place. Of this kind were Epicurus, Diogenes, Apollonius, Lucretius, Paracelsus, Descartes, and others; who, if they were now in the world, tied fast, and separate from their followers, would, in this our undistinguishing age, incur manifest danger of phlebotomy, and whips, and chains, and dark chambers, and straw. For what man, in the natural state or course of thinking, did ever conceive it in his power to reduce the notions of all mankind exactly to the same length, and breadth, and height of his own? yet this is the first humble and civil design of all innovators in the empire of reason. Epicurus modestly hoped that, one time or other, a certain fortuitous concourse of all men's opinions, after perpetual justlings, the sharp with the smooth, the light and the heavy, the round and the square, would by certain *clinamina* unite in the notions of atoms and void, as these did in the originals of all things. Cartesius reckoned to see, before he died, the sentiments of all philosophers, like so many lesser stars in his romantic system, wrapped and drawn within his own vortex. Now, I would gladly be informed how it is possible to account for such imaginations as these in particular men, without recourse to my phenomenon of vapours ascending from the lower faculties to overshadow the brain, and there distilling into conceptions for which the narrowness of our mother-tongue has not yet assigned any other name besides that of madness or phrensy. Let us therefore now conjecture how it comes to pass that none of these great prescribers do ever fail providing themselves and their notions with a number of implicit disciples. And, I think, the reason is easy to be assigned : for there is a peculiar string in the harmony of human understanding, which, in several individuals, is exactly of the same tuning. This if you can dexterously screw up to its right key, and then strike gently upon it, whenever you have the good fortune to light among those of the same pitch, they will, by a secret necessary sympathy, strike exactly at the same time. And in this one circumstance lies all the skill or luck of the matter ; for, if you chance to jar the string among those who are either above or below your own height, instead of subscribing to your doctrine, they will tie you fast, call you mad, and feed you with bread and water. It is therefore a point of the nicest conduct to distinguish and adapt this noble talent with respect to the differences of persons and of times. Cicero understood this very well, [who,] when writing to a friend in England, with a caution, among other matters, to beware of being cheated by our hackney-coachmen, (who, it seems, in those days were as arrant rascals as they are now,) has these remarkable words : *Est quod gaudeas te in ista loca venisse, ubi aliquid sapere viderere.* For, to speak a bold truth, it is a fatal miscarriage so ill to order affairs, as to pass for a fool in one company, when in another you might be treated as a philosopher. Which I desire some certain gentlemen of my acquaintance to lay up in their hearts, as a very seasonable *innuendo.*

This, indeed, was the fatal mistake of that worthy gentleman, my most ingenious friend, Mr. Wotton ; a person, in appearance, ordained for great designs as well as performances : whether you will consider his

OF MADNESS IN A COMMONWEALTH 35

notions or his looks, surely no man ever advanced into the public with fitter qualifications of body and mind for the propagation of a new religion. O, had those happy talents, misapplied to vain philosophy, been turned into their proper channels of dreams and visions, where distortion of mind and countenance are of such sovereign use, the base detracting world would not then have dared to report that something is amiss, that his brain has undergone an unlucky shake; which even his brother modernists themselves, like ungrates, do whisper so loud, that it reaches up to the very garret I am now writing in!

Lastly, whosoever pleases to look into the fountains of enthusiasm, from whence, in all ages, have eternally proceeded such fattening streams, will find the springhead to have been as troubled and muddy as the current: of such great emolument is a tincture of this vapour, which the world calls madness, that without its help the world would not only be deprived of those two great blessings, conquests and systems, but even all mankind would unhappily be reduced to the same belief in things invisible. Now, the former *postulatum* being held, that it is of no import from what originals this vapour proceeds, but either in what angles it strikes and spreads over the understanding, or upon what species of brain it ascends; it will be a very delicate point to cut the feather, and divide the several reasons to a nice and curious reader, how this numerical difference in the brain can produce effects of so vast a difference from the same vapour, as to be the sole point of individuation between Alexander the Great, Jack of Leyden, and Monsieur Descartes. The present argument is the most abstracted that ever

I engaged in; it strains my faculties to their highest stretch: and I desire the reader to attend with the utmost perpensity; for I now proceed to unravel this knotty point.

There is in mankind a certain * *
* * * * * * *
Hic multa desiderantur. * * *
* * * And this I take to be a clear solution of the matter.

Having therefore so narrowly passed through this intricate difficulty, the reader will, I am sure, agree with me in the conclusion, that if the moderns mean by madness only a disturbance or transposition of the brain, by force of certain vapours issuing up from the lower faculties, then has this madness been the parent of all those mighty revolutions that have happened in empire, in philosophy, and in religion. For the brain, in its natural position and state of serenity, disposes its owner to pass his life in the common forms, without any thoughts of subduing multitudes to his own power, his reasons, or his visions; and the more he shapes his understanding by the pattern of human learning, the less he is inclined to form parties after his particular notions; because that instructs him in his private infirmities, as well as in the stubborn ignorance of the people. But when a man's fancy gets astride on his reason; when imagination is at cuffs with the senses, and common understanding, as well as common sense, is kicked out of doors; the first proselyte he makes is himself; and when that is once compassed, the difficulty is not so great in bringing over others; a strong delusion always operating from without as vigorously as from within. For cant and vision are, to the ear and the eye, the same that tickling is to the touch. Those entertainments and pleasures we most value in life are such as dupe and play the wag with the senses. For, if we take an examination of what is generally understood by happiness, as it has respect either to the understanding or the senses, we shall find all its properties and adjuncts will herd under this short definition, that it is a perpetual possession of being well deceived. And, first, with relation to the mind or understanding, it is manifest what mighty advantages fiction has over truth; and the reason is just at our elbow, because imagination can build nobler scenes, and produce more wonderful revolutions, than fortune or nature will be at expense to furnish. Nor is mankind so much to blame in his choice thus determining him, if we consider that the debate merely lies between things past and things conceived : and so the question is only this, whether things that have place in the imagination may not as properly be said to exist, as those that are seated in the memory; which may be justly held in the affirmative, and very much to the advantage of the former, since this is acknowledged to be the womb of things, and the other allowed to be no more than the grave. Again, if we take this definition of happiness, and examine it with reference to the senses, it will be acknowledged wonderfully adapt. How fading and insipid do all objects accost us that are not conveyed in the vehicle of delusion! how shrunk is everything as it appears in the glass of nature! so that, if it were not for the assistance of artificial mediums, false lights, refracted angles, varnish and tinsel, there would be a mighty level in the felicity and enjoyments of mortal men.

If this were seriously considered by the world, as I have a certain reason to suspect it hardly will, men would no longer reckon among their high points of wisdom the art of exposing weak sides and publishing infirmities; an employment, in my opinion, neither better nor worse than that of unmasking, which, I think, has never been allowed fair usage, either in the world or the playhouse.

In the proportion that credulity is a more peaceful possession of the mind than curiosity; so far preferable is that wisdom which converses about the surface, to that pretended philosophy which enters into the depth of things, and then comes gravely back with informations and discoveries that in the inside they are good for nothing. The two senses, to which all objects first address themselves, are the sight and the touch; these never examine farther than the colour, the shape, the size, and whatever other qualities dwell or are drawn by art upon the outward of bodies; and then comes reason officiously with tools for cutting, and opening, and mangling, and piercing, offering to demonstrate that they are not of the same consistence quite through. Now I take all this to be the last degree of perverting nature; one of whose eternal laws it is, to put her best furniture forward. And therefore, in order to save the charges of all such expensive anatomy for the time to come, I do here think fit to inform the reader that, in such conclusions as these, reason is certainly in the right; and that, in most corporeal beings which have fallen under my cognizance, the outside has been infinitely preferable to the in: whereof I have been farther convinced from some late experiments. Last week I saw a woman flayed, and you will hardly believe how much it altered her person for the worse. Yesterday I ordered the carcase of a beau to be stripped in my presence ; when we were all amazed to find so many unsuspected faults under one suit of clothes. Then I laid open his brain, his heart, and his spleen : but I plainly perceived at every operation, that the farther we proceeded we found the defects increase upon us in number and bulk : from all which, I justly formed this conclusion to myself, that whatever philosopher or projector can find out an art to solder and patch up the flaws and imperfections of nature, will deserve much better of mankind, and teach us a more useful science, than that so much in present esteem of widening and exposing them, like him who held anatomy to be the ultimate end of physic. And he whose fortunes and dispositions have placed him in a convenient station to enjoy the fruits of this noble art ; he that can, with Epicurus, content his ideas with the films and images that fly off upon his senses from the superficies of things ; such a man, truly wise, creams off nature, leaving the sour and the dregs for philosophy and reason to lap up. This is the sublime and refined point of felicity, called the possession of being well deceived; the serene peaceful state of being a fool among knaves.

But to return to madness. It is certain that, according to the system I have above deduced, every species thereof proceeds from a redundancy of vapours; therefore, as some kinds of phrensy give double strength to the sinews, so there are of other species which add vigour, and life, and spirit to the brain : now, it usually happens that these active spirits, getting possession of the brain, resemble those that haunt other waste and empty dwellings, which, for want of business, either vanish and carry away a piece of the house, or else stay at home and fling it all out of the windows. By which are mystically displayed the two principal branches of madness, and which some philosophers, not considering so well as I, have mistaken to be different in their causes, over hastily assigning the first to deficiency, and the other to redundance.

I think it therefore manifest, from what I have here advanced, that the main point of skill and address is to furnish employment for this redundancy of vapour, and prudently to adjust the season of it; by which means it may certainly become of cardinal and catholic emolument in a commonwealth. Thus one man, choosing a proper juncture, leaps into a gulf, thence proceeds a hero, and is called the saviour of his country; another achieves the same enterprise, but, unluckily timing it, has left the brand of madness fixed as a reproach upon his memory: upon so nice a distinction are we taught to repeat the name of Curtius with reverence and love; that of Empedocles with hatred and contempt. Thus also it is usually conceived that the elder Brutus only personated the fool and madman for the good of the public; but this was nothing else than a redundancy of the same vapour long misapplied, called by the Latins *ingenium par negotiis;* or, to translate it as nearly as I can, a sort of phrensy, never in its right element till you take it up in the business of the state.

Upon all which, and many other reasons of equal weight, though not equally curious, I do here gladly embrace an opportunity I have long sought for of recommending it as a very noble undertaking to sir

Edward Seymour, sir Christopher Musgrave, sir John Bowles, John Howe, esq., and other patriots concerned, that they would move for leave to bring in a bill for appointing commissioners to inspect into Bedlam and the parts adjacent; who shall be empowered to send for persons, papers, and records; to examine into the merits and qualifications of every student and professor; to observe with utmost exactness their several dispositions and behaviour; by which means, duly distinguishing and adapting their talents, they might produce admirable instruments for the several offices in a state, [ecclesiastical], civil, and military; proceeding in such methods as I shall here humbly propose. And I hope the gentle reader will give some allowance to my great solicitudes in this important affair, upon account of the high esteem I have borne that honourable society, whereof I had some time the happiness to be an unworthy member.

Is any student tearing his straw in piecemeal, swearing and blaspheming, biting his grate, foaming at the mouth? let the right worshipful the commissioners of inspection give him a regiment of dragoons, and send him into Flanders among the rest. Is another eternally talking, sputtering, gaping, bawling in a sound without period or article? what wonderful talents are here mislaid! let him be furnished immediately with a green bag and papers, and threepence in his pocket, and away with him to Westminster-Hall. You will find a third gravely taking the dimensions of his kennel; a person of foresight and insight, though kept quite in the dark; for why, like Moses, *ecce cornuta erat ejus facies*. He walks duly in one pace, entreats your penny with due gravity and ceremony;

talks much of hard times and taxes; bars up the wooden window of his cell constantly at eight o'clock; dreams of fire, and shop-lifters, and court-customers, and privileged places. Now, what a figure would all these acquirements amount to, if the owner were sent into the city among his brethren! Behold a fourth, in much and deep conversation with himself, biting his thumbs at proper junctures; his countenance checkered with business and design; sometimes walking very fast, with his eyes nailed to a paper that he holds in his hands: a great saver of time, somewhat thick of hearing, very short of sight, but more of memory; a man ever in haste, a great hatcher and breeder of business, and excellent at the famous art of whispering nothing; a huge idolater of monosyllables and procrastination; so ready to give his word to everybody, that he never keeps it; one that has forgot the common meaning of words, but an admirable retainer of the sound. If you approach his grate in his familiar intervals, Sir, says he, give me a penny, and I'll sing you a song: but give me the penny first. (Hence comes the common saying, and commoner practice, of parting with money for a song.) What a complete system of court skill is here described in every branch of it, and all utterly lost with wrong application! Another student struts up fiercely to your teeth, puffing with his lips, half squeezing out his eyes, and very graciously holds you out his hand to kiss. The keeper desires you not to be afraid of this professor, for he will do you no hurt: to him alone is allowed the liberty of the antechamber, and the orator of the place gives you to understand that this solemn person is a tailor run mad with pride. This considerable student is adorned with many other qualities,

upon which at present I shall not farther enlarge.——
Hark in your ear—I am strangely mistaken if all his address, his motions, and his airs, would not then be very natural, and in their proper element.

I shall not descend so minutely as to insist upon the vast number of beaux, fiddlers, poets, and politicians, that the world might recover by such a reformation; but what is more material, beside the clear gain redounding to the commonwealth by so large an acquisition of persons to employ, whose talents and acquirements, if I may be so bold as to affirm it, are now buried or at least misapplied; it would be a mighty advantage accruing to the public from this inquiry, that all these would very much excel, and arrive at great perfection, in their several kinds; which, I think, is manifest from what I have already shown, and shall enforce by this one plain instance: that even I myself, the author of these momentous truths, am a person whose imaginations are hard-mouthed and exceedingly disposed to run away with his reason, which I have observed, from long experience, to be a very light rider and easily shaken off; upon which account my friends will never trust me alone, without a solemn promise to vent my speculations in this or the like manner, for the universal benefit of human kind; which perhaps the gentle, courteous, and candid reader, brimful of that modern charity and tenderness usually annexed to his office, will be very hardly persuaded to believe.

FROM
A FARTHER DIGRESSION

IF the reader fairly considers the strength of what I have advanced in the foregoing section, I am convinced it will produce a wonderful revolution in his notions and opinions; and he will be abundantly better prepared to receive and to relish the concluding part of this miraculous treatise. Readers may be divided into three classes—the superficial, the ignorant, and the learned: and I have with much felicity fitted my pen to the genius and advantage of each. The superficial reader will be strangely provoked to laughter; which clears the breast and the lungs, is sovereign against the spleen, and the most innocent of all diuretics. The ignorant reader, between whom and the former the distinction is extremely nice, will find himself disposed to stare; which is an admirable remedy for ill eyes, serves to raise and enliven the spirits, and wonderfully helps perspiration. But the reader truly learned, chiefly for whose benefit I wake when others sleep, and sleep when others wake, will here find sufficient matter to employ his speculations for the rest of his life. It were much to be wished, and I do here humbly propose for an experiment, that every prince in Christendom will take seven of the deepest scholars in his dominions, and shut them up close for seven years in seven chambers, with a command to write seven ample commentaries on this comprehensive discourse. I shall venture to affirm that, whatever difference may be found in their several conjectures, they will be all, without the least distortion, manifestly deducible from the text. Meantime, it is my earnest request that so useful an undertaking may be entered upon, if their majesties please, with all convenient speed; because I have a strong inclination, before I leave the world, to taste a blessing which we mysterious writers can seldom reach till we have gotten into our graves: whether it is that fame, being a fruit grafted on the body, can hardly grow, and much less ripen, till the stock is in the earth; or whether she be a bird of prey, and is lured, among the rest, to pursue after the scent of a carcase; or whether she conceives her trumpet sounds best and farthest when she stands on a tomb, by the advantage of a rising ground and the echo of a hollow vault.

A
FULL AND TRUE ACCOUNT
OF THE
BATTLE
FOUGHT LAST FRIDAY
BETWEEN
THE ANCIENT AND THE MODERN BOOKS
IN SAINT JAMES'S LIBRARY

Swift's patron, Sir William Temple, had been drawn into a dispute "by a silly question raised in France on the respective merits of ancient and modern writers, wherein somebody having declared Corneille to be as much superior to Æschylus as Pascal was to Plato, Temple took up the cudgels for the ancients, on whose behalf he made assertions quite as preposterous, and incidentally declared the Epistles of Phalaris to be one of the triumphs of antiquity. Then came Wotton, a so-styled youthful prodigy of learning in those days, defending the moderns against Temple; then a new edition of Phalaris produced on behalf of Temple by Charles Boyle, afterwards Lord Orrery, his tutor Atterbury, and other Oxford scholars; and then from the other university the scornful challenge of Richard Bentley, first of scholars, who in a second edition of Wotton's book, declared the Phalaris epistles to be the egregious forgery which they too truly were. At this stage of the conflict, while Boyle, Atterbury and Smallridge were preparing the reply that elicited Bentley's crushing rejoinder, Swift came to the protection of Temple with the *Battle of the Books* [1697], and of all that constituted once the so famous controversy, its prodigious learning and its furious abuse, this triumphant piece of humour alone survives. It was circulated widely before Temple died, and not until four years later [1704] appeared in print."—*Forster*.

A history of the rivalry long subsisting between ancient and modern books, and an account of the manner in which it was revived among the volumes in the St. James's Library, of which Bentley was "regent" or curator, leads up to the allegory of the Spider and the Bee; after which the interposition of the Goddess Criticism, mother of Wotton, is described, and then the fray begins in earnest in a series of Homeric contests between the classics and their translators and commentators.

THE SPIDER AND THE BEE

THINGS were at this crisis when a material accident fell out. For upon the highest corner of a large window there dwelt a certain spider, swollen up to the first magnitude by the destruction of infinite numbers of flies, whose spoils lay scattered before the gates of his palace, like human bones before the cave of some giant. The avenues to his castle were guarded with turnpikes and palisadoes, all after the modern way of fortification. After you had passed several courts you came to the centre, wherein you might behold the constable himself in his own lodgings, which had windows fronting to each avenue, and ports to sally out upon all occasions of prey or defence. In this mansion he had for some time dwelt in peace and plenty, without danger to his person by swallows from above, or to his palace by brooms from below: when it was the pleasure of fortune to conduct thither a wandering bee, to whose curiosity a broken pane in the glass had discovered itself, and in he went; where, expatiating a while, he at last happened to alight upon one of the outward walls of the spider's citadel; which, yielding to the unequal weight, sunk down to the very foundation. Thrice he endeavoured to force his passage, and thrice the centre shook. The spider within, feeling the terrible convulsion, supposed at first that nature was approaching to her final dissolution; or else that Beelzebub, with all his legions, was come to revenge the death of many thousands of his subjects whom his enemy had slain and devoured. However, he at length valiantly resolved to issue forth and meet his fate. Meanwhile the bee had acquitted himself of his toils, and, posted securely at some distance, was employed in cleansing his wings, and disengaging them from the ragged remnants of the cobweb. By this time the spider was adventured out, when, beholding the chasms, the ruins, and dilapidations of his fortress, he was very near at his wit's end ; he stormed and swore like a madman, and swelled till he was ready to burst. At length, casting his eye upon the bee, and wisely gathering causes from events, (for they knew each other by sight,) A plague split you, said he ; is it you, with a vengeance, that have made this litter here? could not you look before you, and be d—d? do you think I have nothing else to do, in the devil's name, but to mend and repair after you?—Good words, friend, said the bee, having now pruned himself, and being disposed to droll : I'll give you my hand and word to come near your kennel no more ; I was never in such a confounded pickle since I was born.—Sirrah, replied the spider, if it were not for breaking an old custom in our family, never to stir abroad against an enemy, I should come and teach you better manners.—I pray have patience, said the bee, or you'll spend your substance, and, for aught I see, you may stand in need of it all toward the repair of your house.—Rogue, rogue, replied the spider, yet methinks you should have more respect to a person whom all the world allows to be so much your betters.

—By my troth, said the bee, the comparison will amount to a very good jest; and you will do me a favour to let me know the reasons that all the world is pleased to use in so hopeful a dispute. At this the spider, having swelled himself into the size and posture of a disputant, began his argument in the true spirit of controversy, with resolution to be heartily scurrilous and angry, to urge on his own reasons, without the least regard to the answers or objections of his opposite; and fully predetermined in his mind against all conviction.

Not to disparage myself, said he, by the comparison with such a rascal, what art thou but a vagabond without house or home, without stock or inheritance? born to no possession of your own, but a pair of wings and a drone-pipe. Your livelihood is a universal plunder upon nature; a freebooter over fields and gardens; and, for the sake of stealing, will rob a nettle as easily as a violet. Whereas I am a domestic animal, furnished with a native stock within myself. This large castle (to show my improvements in the mathematics) is all built with my own hands, and the materials extracted altogether out of my own person.

I am glad, answered the bee, to hear you grant at least that I am come honestly by my wings and my voice; for then, it seems, I am obliged to Heaven alone for my flights and my music; and Providence would never have bestowed on me two such gifts, without designing them for the noblest ends. I visit indeed all the flowers and blossoms of the field and garden; but whatever I collect thence enriches myself, without the least injury to their beauty, their smell, or their taste. Now, for you and your skill in architecture and other mathematics, I have little to say: in that building of yours there might, for aught I know, have been labour and method enough; but, by woful experience for us both, it is plain the materials are naught; and I hope you will henceforth take warning, and consider duration and matter, as well as method and art. You boast indeed of being obliged to no other creature, but of drawing and spinning out all from yourself; that is to say, if we may judge of the liquor in the vessel by what issues out, you possess a good plentiful store of dirt and poison in your breast; and, though I would by no means lessen or disparage your genuine stock of either, yet I doubt you are somewhat obliged, for an increase of both, to a little foreign assistance. Your inherent portion of dirt does not fail of acquisitions, by sweepings exhaled from below; and one insect furnishes you with a share of poison to destroy another. So that, in short, the question comes all to this: whether is the nobler being of the two, that which, by a lazy contemplation of four inches round, by an overweening pride, feeding and engendering on itself, turns all into venom, producing nothing at all but flybane and a cobweb; or that which, by a universal range, with long search, much study, true judgment, and distinction of things, brings home honey and wax.

This dispute was managed with such eagerness, clamour, and warmth, that the two parties of books, in arms below, stood silent a while, waiting in suspense what would be the issue; which was not long undetermined: for the bee, grown impatient at so much loss of time, fled straight away to a bed of roses, without looking for a reply, and left the spider, like an orator, collected in himself, and just prepared to burst out.

It happened upon this emergency that Æsop broke silence first. He had been of late most barbarously treated by a strange effect of the regent's humanity, who had torn off his title-page, sorely defaced one half of his leaves, and chained him fast among a shelf of moderns. Where, soon discovering how high the quarrel was likely to proceed, he tried all his arts, and turned himself to a thousand forms. At length, in the borrowed shape of an ass, the regent mistook him for a modern; by which means he had time and opportunity to escape to the ancients, just when the spider and the bee were entering into their contest; to which he gave his attention with a world of pleasure, and, when it was ended, swore in the loudest key that in all his life he had never known two cases so parallel and adapt to each other as that in the window and this upon the shelves. The disputants, said he, have admirably managed the dispute between them, have taken in the full strength of all that is to be said on both sides, and exhausted the substance of every argument *pro* and *con*. It is but to adjust the reasonings of both to the present quarrel, then to compare and apply the labours and fruits of each, as the bee has learnedly deduced them, and we shall find the conclusion fall plain and close upon the moderns and us. For pray, gentlemen, was ever anything so modern as the spider in his air, his turns, and his paradoxes? he argues in the behalf of you his brethren and himself with many boastings of his native stock and great genius; that he spins and spits wholly from himself, and scorns to own any obligation or assistance from without. Then he displays to you his great skill in architecture and improvement in the mathematics. To all this the bee, as an advocate retained by us the ancients, thinks fit to answer, that, if one may judge of the great genius or inventions of the moderns by what they have produced, you will hardly have countenance to bear you out in boasting of either. Erect your schemes with as much method and skill as you please; yet, if the materials be nothing but dirt, spun out of your own entrails, the edifice will conclude at last in a cobweb; the duration of which, like that of other spiders' webs, may be imputed to their being forgotten, or neglected, or hid in a corner. For anything else of genuine that the moderns may pretend to, I cannot recollect; unless it be a large vein of wrangling and satire, much of a nature and substance with the spider's poison, which, however they pretend to spit wholly out of themselves, is improved by the same arts, by feeding upon the insects and vermin of the age. As for us the ancients, we are content, with the bee, to pretend to nothing of our own beyond our wings and our voice: that is to say, our flights and our language. For the rest, whatever we have got has been by infinite labour and search, and ranging through every corner of nature; the difference is, that, instead of dirt and poison, we have rather chosen to fill our hives with honey and wax, thus furnishing mankind with the two noblest of things, which are sweetness and light.

THE BATTLE

THE destined hour of fate being now arrived, the fight began; whereof, before I dare adventure to make a particular description, I must, after the example of other authors, petition for a hundred tongues, and mouths, and hands, and pens, which would all be too little to perform so immense a work. Say, goddess, that presidest over history, who it was that first advanced in the field of battle! Paracelsus, at the head of his dragoons, observing Galen in the adverse wing, darted his javelin with a mighty force, which the brave ancient received upon his shield, the point breaking in the second fold.

* * * *

* * * * *Hic pauca desunt.*

They bore the wounded aga on their shields to his chariot * * * *
Desunt * * * *
nonnulla. * * * *

Then Aristotle, observing Bacon advance with a furious mien, drew his bow to the head, and let fly his arrow, which missed the valiant modern and went whizzing over his head; but Des Cartes it hit; the steel point quickly found a defect in his headpiece; it

pierced the leather and the pasteboard, and went in at his right eye. The torture of the pain whirled the valiant bowman round, till death, like a star of superior influence, drew him into his own vortex.
Ingens hiatus   *   *   *   *
hic in MS.   *   *   *   *
    *   *   when Homer appeared at the head of the cavalry, mounted on a furious horse, with difficulty managed by the rider himself, but which no other mortal durst approach; he rode among the enemy's ranks, and bore down all before him. Say, goddess, whom he slew first and whom he slew last! First, Gondibert advanced against him, clad in heavy armour and mounted on a staid sober gelding, not so famed for his speed as his docility in kneeling whenever his rider would mount or alight. He had made a vow to Pallas that he would never leave the field till he had spoiled Homer of his armour: madman, who had never once seen the wearer, nor understood his strength! Him Homer overthrew, horse and man, to the ground, there to be trampled and choked in the dirt. Then with a long spear he slew Denham, a stout modern, who from his father's side derived his lineage from Apollo, but his mother was of mortal race. He fell, and bit the earth. The celestial part Apollo took, and made it a star; but the terrestrial lay wallowing upon the ground. Then Homer slew Sam Wesley with a kick of his horse's heel; he took Perrault by mighty force out of his saddle, then hurled him at Fontenelle, with the same blow dashing out both their brains.

On the left wing of the horse Virgil appeared, in shining armour, completely fitted to his body: he was mounted on a dapple-gray steed, the slowness of whose pace was an effect of the highest mettle and vigour. He cast his eye on the adverse wing, with a desire to find an object worthy of his valour, when behold upon a sorrel gelding of a monstrous size appeared a foe, issuing from among the thickest of the enemy's squadrons; but his speed was less than his noise; for his horse, old and lean, spent the dregs of his strength in a high trot, which, though it made slow advances, yet caused a loud clashing of his armour, terrible to hear. The two cavaliers had now approached within the throw of a lance, when the stranger desired a parley, and, lifting up the vizor of his helmet, a face hardly appeared from within, which, after a pause, was known for that of the renowned Dryden. The brave ancient suddenly started, as one possessed with surprise and disappointment together; for the helmet was nine times too large for the head, which appeared situate far in the hinder part, even like the lady in a lobster, or like a mouse under a canopy of state, or like a shrivelled beau from within the penthouse of a modern periwig; and the voice was suited to the visage, sounding weak and remote. Dryden, in a long harangue, soothed up the good ancient; called him father, and, by a large deduction of genealogies, made it plainly appear that they were nearly related. Then he humbly proposed an exchange of armour, as a lasting mark of hospitality between them. Virgil consented (for the goddess Diffidence came unseen, and cast a mist before his eyes), though his was of gold and cost a hundred beeves, the other's but of rusty iron. However, this glittering armour became the modern yet worse than his own. Then they agreed to exchange horses; but, when it came to the trial, Dryden was afraid and utterly unable to mount.

* * *   *Alter hiatus*
* * *   *in MS.*

Lucan appeared upon a fiery horse of admirable shape, but headstrong, bearing the rider where he list over the field; he made a mighty slaughter among the enemy's horse; which destruction to stop, Blackmore, a famous modern (but one of the mercenaries), strenuously opposed himself, and darted his javelin with a strong hand, which, falling short of its mark, struck deep in the earth. Then Lucan threw a lance; but Æsculapius came unseen and turned off the point. Brave modern, said Lucan, I perceive some god protects you, for never did my arm so deceive me before; but what mortal can contend with a god? Therefore, let us fight no longer, but present gifts to each other. Lucan then bestowed the modern a pair of spurs, and Blackmore gave Lucan a bridle. * * * *
Pauca desunt. * * * * * *
* * * * * * * * *

Creech: but the goddess Dulness took a cloud, formed into the shape of Horace, armed and mounted, and placed in a flying posture before him. Glad was the cavalier to begin a combat with a flying foe, and pursued the image, threatening aloud; till at last it led him to the peaceful bower of his father, Ogleby, by whom he was disarmed and assigned to his repose.

Then Pindar slew ——, and ——, Oldham, and ——, and Afra the Amazon, light of foot; never advancing in a direct line, but wheeling with incredible agility and force, he made a terrible slaughter among the enemy's light horse. Him when Cowley observed, his generous heart burnt within him, and he advanced against the fierce ancient, imitating his address, his pace, and career as well as the vigour of his horse and his own skill would allow. When the two cavaliers had approached within the length of three javelins, first Cowley threw a lance, which missed Pindar, and, passing into the enemy's ranks, fell ineffectual to the ground. Then Pindar darted a javelin so large and weighty, that scarce a dozen cavaliers, as cavaliers are in our degenerate days, could raise it from the ground; yet he threw it with ease, and it went, by an unerring hand, singing through the air; nor could the modern have avoided present death if he had not luckily opposed the shield that had been given him by Venus. And now both heroes drew their swords; but the modern was so aghast and disordered that he knew not where he was: his shield dropped from his hands; thrice he fled, and thrice he could not escape; at last he turned, and lifting up his hand in the posture of a suppliant, Godlike Pindar, said he, spare my life, and possess my horse, with these arms, beside the ransom which my friends will give when they hear I am alive and your prisoner. Dog! said Pindar, let your ransom stay with your friends; but your carcase shall be left for the fowls of the air and the beasts of the field. With that he raised his sword, and, with a mighty stroke, cleft the wretched modern in twain, the sword pursuing the blow; and one half lay panting on the ground, to be trod in pieces by the horses' feet; the other half was borne by the frighted steed through the field. This Venus took, washed it seven times in ambrosia, then struck it thrice with a sprig of amaranth; upon which the leather grew round and soft,

and the leaves turned into feathers, and, being gilded before, continued gilded still; so it became a dove, and she harnessed it to her chariot. * * *
* * * * * * *Hiatus valde defendus in MS.*

THE EPISODE OF BENTLEY AND WOTTON.

Day being far spent, and the numerous forces of the moderns half inclining to a retreat, there issued forth from a squadron of their heavy-armed foot a captain whose name was Bentley, the most deformed of all the moderns; tall, but without shape or comeliness; large, but without strength or proportion. His armour was patched up of a thousand incoherent pieces; and the sound of it, as he marched, was loud and dry, like that made by the fall of a sheet of lead, which an Etesian wind blows suddenly down from the roof of some steeple. His helmet was of old rusty iron, but the vizor was brass, which, tainted by his breath, corrupted into copperas, nor wanted gall from the same fountain; so that, whenever provoked by anger or labour, an atramentous quality, of most malignant nature, was seen to distil from his lips. In his right hand he grasped a flail, and thus completely armed, he advanced with a slow and heavy pace where the modern chiefs were holding a consult upon the sum of things; who, as he came onwards, laughed to behold his crooked leg and humped shoulder, which his boot and armour, vainly endeavouring to hide, were forced to comply with and expose. The generals made use of him for his talent of railing; which, kept within government, proved frequently of great service to their cause, but, at other times, did more mischief than good; for, at the least touch of offence, and often without any at all, he would, like a wounded elephant, convert it against his leaders. Such, at this juncture, was the disposition of Bentley; grieved to see the enemy prevail, and dissatisfied with everybody's conduct but his own. He humbly gave the modern generals to understand that he conceived, with great submission, they were all a pack of rogues, and fools, and d—d cowards, and confounded loggerheads, and illiterate whelps, and nonsensical scoundrels; that, if himself had been constituted general, those presumptuous dogs, the ancients, would long before this have been beaten out of the field. You, said he, sit here idle; but when I, or any other valiant modern, kill an enemy, you are sure to seize the spoil. But I will not march one foot against the foe till you all swear to me that whomsoever I take or kill, his arms I shall quietly possess. Bentley having spoken thus, Scaliger, bestowing him a sour look, Miscreant prater! said he, eloquent only in thine own eyes, thou railest without wit, or truth, or discretion. The malignity of thy temper perverteth nature; thy learning makes thee more barbarous; thy study of humanity more inhuman; thy converse among poets, more grovelling, miry, and dull. All arts of civilizing others render thee rude and untractable; courts have taught thee ill manners, and polite conversation has finished thee a pedant. Besides, a greater coward burdeneth not the army. But never despond; I pass my word, whatever spoil thou takest shall certainly be thy own; though I hope that vile carcase will first become a prey to kites and worms.

Bentley durst not reply; but, half choked with spleen and rage, withdrew, in full resolution of performing some great achievement. With him, for his aid and companion, he took his beloved Wotton; resolving by policy or surprise to attempt some neglected quarter of the ancients' army. They began their march over carcases of their slaughtered friends; then to the right of their own forces; then wheeled northward, till they came to Aldrovandus's tomb, which they passed on the side of the declining sun. And now they arrived, with fear, toward the enemy's out-guards; looking about, if haply they might spy the quarters of the wounded, or some straggling sleepers, unarmed and remote from the rest. As when two mongrel curs, whom native greediness and domestic want provoke and join in partnership, though fearful, nightly to invade the folds of some rich grazier, they, with tails depressed and lolling tongues, creep soft and slow; meanwhile the conscious moon, now in her zenith, on their guilty heads darts perpendicular rays; nor dare they bark, though much provoked at her refulgent visage, whether seen in puddle by reflection or in sphere direct; but one surveys the region round, while the other scouts the plain, if haply to discover, at distance from the flock, some carcase half devoured, the refuse of gorged wolves or ominous ravens. So marched this lovely, loving pair of friends, nor with less fear and circumspection, when at a distance they might perceive two shining suits of armour hanging upon an oak, and the owners not far off in a profound sleep. The two friends drew lots, and the pursuing of this adventure fell to Bentley; on he went, and in his van Confusion and Amaze, while

Horror and Affright brought up the rear. As he came near, behold two heroes of the ancients' army, Phalaris and Æsop, lay fast asleep; Bentley would fain have despatched them both, and, stealing close, aimed his flail at Phalaris's breast. But then the goddess Affright, interposing, caught the modern in her icy arms, and dragged him from the danger she foresaw; both the dormant heroes happened to turn at the same instant, though soundly sleeping and busy in a dream. For Phalaris was just that minute dreaming how a most vile poetaster had lampooned him, and how he had got him roaring in his bull. And Æsop dreamed that, as he and the ancient chiefs were lying on the ground, a wild ass broke loose, ran about, trampling and kicking in their faces. Bentley, leaving the two heroes asleep, seized on both their armours, and withdrew in quest of his darling Wotton.

He, in the meantime, had wandered long in search of some enterprise, till at length he arrived at a small rivulet that issued from a fountain hard by, called, in the language of mortal men, Helicon. Here he stopped, and, parched with thirst, resolved to allay it in this limpid stream. Thrice with profane hands he essayed to raise the water to his lips, and thrice it slipped all through his fingers. Then he stooped prone on his breast, but, ere his mouth had kissed the liquid crystal, Apollo came, and in the channel held his shield betwixt the modern and the fountain, so that he drew up nothing but mud. For, although no fountain on earth can compare with the clearness of Helicon, yet there lies at bottom a thick sediment of slime and mud; for so Apollo begged of Jupiter, as a punishment to those who durst attempt to taste it with unhallowed lips, and for a lesson to all not to draw too deep or far from the spring.

At the fountain-head Wotton discerned two heroes; the one he could not distinguish, but the other was soon known for Temple, general of the allies to the ancients. His back was turned, and he was employed in drinking large draughts in his helmet from the fountain, where he had withdrawn himself to rest from the toils of the war. Wotton, observing him, with quaking knees and trembling hands, spoke thus to himself: O that I could kill this destroyer of our army, what renown should I purchase among the chiefs! but to issue out against him, man against man, shield against shield, and lance against lance, what modern of us dare? for he fights like a god, and Pallas or Apollo are ever at his elbow. But, O mother! if what Fame reports be true, that I am the son of so great a goddess, grant me to hit Temple with this lance, that the stroke may send him to hell, and that I may return in safety and triumph, laden with his spoils. The first part of this prayer the gods granted at the intercession of his mother and of Momus; but the rest, by a perverse wind sent from Fate, was scattered in the air. Then Wotton grasped his lance, and, brandishing it thrice over his head, darted it with all his might; the goddess, his mother, at the same time adding strength to his arm. Away the lance went hizzing, and reached even to the belt of the averted ancient, upon which lightly grazing, it fell to the ground. Temple neither felt the weapon touch him nor heard it fall: and Wotton might have escaped to his army, with the honour of having remitted his lance against so great a leader unrevenged, but Apollo, enraged that a javelin flung by the assistance of so foul a goddess should pollute his fountain, put on the shape of ———, and softly came to young Boyle, who then accompanied Temple: he pointed first to the lance, then to the distant modern that flung it, and commanded the young hero to take immediate revenge. Boyle, clad in a suit of armour which had been given him by all the gods, immediately advanced against the trembling foe, who now fled before him. As a young lion in the Libyan plains or Araby desert, sent by his aged sire to hunt for prey, or health, or exercise, he scours along, wishing to meet some tiger from the mountains, or a furious boar; if chance a wild ass, with brayings importune, affronts his ear, the generous beast, though loathing to distain his claws with blood so vile, yet, much provoked at the offensive noise, which Echo, foolish nymph, like her ill-judging sex, repeats much louder and with more delight than Philomela's song, he vindicates the honour of the forest, and hunts the noisy long-eared animal. So Wotton fled, so Boyle pursued. But Wotton, heavy-armed and slow of foot, began to slack his course, when his lover Bentley appeared, returning laden with the spoils of the two sleeping ancients. Boyle observed him well, and soon discovering the helmet and shield of Phalaris his friend, both which he had lately with his own hands new polished and gilt, rage sparkled in his eyes, and, leaving his pursuit after Wotton, he furiously rushed on against this new approacher. Fain would he be revenged on both; but both now fled different ways: and, as a woman in a little house, that gets a painful livelihood by spinning, if chance her geese be scattered o'er the common, she courses round the plain from side to side, compelling here and there the stragglers to the flock; they cackle loud, and flutter o'er the champaign: so Boyle pursued, so fled this pair of friends; finding at length their flight was vain, they bravely joined, and drew themselves in phalanx. First Bentley threw a spear with all his force, hoping to pierce the enemy's breast; but Pallas came unseen, and in the air took off the point, and clapped on one of lead, which, after a dead bang against the enemy's shield, fell blunted to the ground. Then Boyle, observing well his time, took up a lance of wondrous length and sharpness; and, as this pair of friends compacted stood close side to side, he wheeled him to the right, and, with unusual force, darted the weapon. Bentley saw his fate approach, and flanking down his arms close to his ribs, hoping to save his body, in went the point, passing through arm and side, nor stopped or spent its force till it had also pierced the valiant Wotton, who, going to sustain his dying friend, shared his fate. As when a skilful cook has trussed a brace of woodcocks, he with iron skewer pierces the tender sides of both, their legs and wings close pinioned to the ribs; so was this pair of friends transfixed, till down they fell, joined in their lives, joined in their deaths; so closely joined that Charon would mistake them both for one, and waft them over Styx for half his fare. Farewell, beloved, loving pair; few equals have you left behind: and happy and immortal shall you be, if all my wit and eloquence can make you.

And now * * * * * *

Desunt catera.

AN ARGUMENT TO PROVE THAT THE ABOLISHING OF CHRISTIANITY IN ENGLAND

MAY, AS THINGS NOW STAND, BE ATTENDED WITH
SOME INCONVENIENCES, AND PERHAPS NOT
PRODUCE THOSE MANY GOOD EFFECTS
PROPOSED THEREBY.

'The *Tale of a Tub* had offended the orthodox, not perhaps without reason, and Swift now tried to undo the effect he had produced in his former work by defending Christianity with the same weapon which he had before wielded against certain historical perversions of it. The tract was written and published in 1708.

THE ABOLISHING OF CHRISTIANITY IN ENGLAND

I AM very sensible what a weakness and presumption it is to reason against the general humour and disposition of the world. I remember it was, with great justice and due regard to the freedom both of the public and the press, forbidden upon several penalties to write, or discourse, or lay wagers, against the Union, even before it was confirmed by parliament; because that was looked upon as a design to oppose the current of the people, which, beside the folly of it, is a manifest breach of the fundamental law that makes this majority of opinion the voice of God. In like manner, and for the very same reasons, it may perhaps be neither safe nor prudent to argue against the abolishing of Christianity at a juncture when all parties appear so unanimously determined upon the point, as we cannot but allow from their actions, their discourses, and their writings. However, I know not how, whether from the affectation of singularity or the perverseness of human nature, but so it unhappily falls out, that I cannot be entirely of this opinion. Nay, though I were sure an order were issued for my immediate prosecution by the attorney-general, I should still confess that, in the present posture of our affairs at home or abroad, I do not yet see the absolute necessity of extirpating the Christian religion from among us.

This perhaps may appear too great a paradox even for our wise and paradoxical age to endure; therefore I shall handle it with all tenderness and with the utmost deference to that great and profound majority which is of another sentiment.

And yet the curious may please to observe how much the genius of a nation is liable to alter in half an age. I have heard it affirmed for certain, by some very old people, that the contrary opinion was, even in their memories, as much in vogue as the other is now; and that a project for the abolishing of Christianity would then have appeared as singular, and been thought as absurd, as it would be at this time to write or discourse in its defence.

Therefore I freely own that all appearances are against me. The system of the gospel, after the fate of other systems, is generally antiquated and exploded: and the mass or body of the common people, among whom it seems to have had its latest credit, are now grown as much ashamed of it as their betters; opinions, like fashions, always descending from those of quality to the middle sort, and thence to the vulgar, where at length they are dropped and vanish.

But here I would not be mistaken, and must therefore be so bold as to borrow a distinction from the writers on the other side, when they make a difference between nominal and real Trinitarians. I hope no reader imagines me so weak to stand up in the defence of real Christianity, such as used in primitive times, if we may believe the authors of those ages, to have an influence upon men's belief and actions:

to offer at the restoring of that would indeed be a wild project; it would be to dig up foundations; to destroy at one blow all the wit and half the learning of the kingdom; to break the entire frame and constitution of things; to ruin trade, extinguish arts and sciences, with the professors of them; in short, to turn our courts, exchanges, and shops into deserts; and would be full as absurd as the proposal of Horace, where he advises the Romans all in a body to leave their city, and seek a new seat in some remote part of the world, by way of cure for the corruption of their manners.

Therefore I think this caution was in itself altogether unnecessary, (which I have inserted only to prevent all possibility of cavilling,) since every candid reader will easily understand my discourse to be intended only in defence of nominal Christianity; the other having been for some time wholly laid aside by general consent, as utterly inconsistent with our present schemes of wealth and power.

But why we should therefore cast off the name and title of Christians, although the general opinion and resolution be so violent for it, I confess I cannot (with submission) apprehend, nor is the consequence necessary. However, since the undertakers propose such wonderful advantages to the nation by this project, and advance many plausible objections against the system of Christianity, I shall briefly consider the strength of both, fairly allow them their greatest weight, and offer such answers as I think most reasonable. After which, I will beg leave to show what inconveniences may possibly happen by such an innovation, in the present posture of our affairs.

First, one great advantage proposed by the abolishing of Christianity is that it would very much enlarge and establish liberty of conscience, that great bulwark of our nation, and of the Protestant religion; which is still too much limited by priestcraft, notwithstanding all the good intentions of the legislature, as we have lately found by a severe instance. For it is confidently reported that two young gentlemen of real hopes, bright wit, and profound judgment, upon a thorough examination of causes and effects, and by the mere force of natural abilities, without the least tincture of learning, having made a discovery that there was no God, and generously communicating their thoughts for the good of the public, were some time ago, by an unparalleled severity and upon I know not what obsolete law, broke for blasphemy. And as it has been wisely observed, if persecution once begins, no man alive knows how far it may reach or where it will end.

In answer to all which, with deference to wiser judgments, I think this rather shows the necessity of a nominal religion among us. Great wits love to be free with the highest objects; and if they cannot be allowed a God to revile or renounce, they will speak evil of dignities, abuse the government, and reflect upon the ministry; which I am sure few will deny to be of much more pernicious consequence, according to the saying of Tiberius, *deorum offensa diis cura*. As to the particular fact related, I think it is not fair to argue from one instance; perhaps another cannot be produced: yet (to the comfort of all those who may be apprehensive of persecution) blasphemy, we know, is freely spoken a million of times in every coffeehouse and tavern, or wherever else good company meet. It must be allowed, indeed, that to break an English free-born officer only for blasphemy was, to speak the gentlest of such an action, a very high strain of absolute power. Little can be said in excuse for the general: perhaps he was afraid it might give offence to the allies, among whom, for aught we know, it may be the custom of the country to believe a God. But if he argued, as some have done, upon a mistaken principle that an officer who is guilty of speaking blasphemy may some time or other proceed so far as to raise a mutiny, the consequence is by no means to be admitted; for surely the commander of an English army is likely to be but ill obeyed, whose soldiers fear and reverence him as little as they do a Deity.

It is farther objected against the gospel system that it obliges men to the belief of things too difficult for freethinkers and such who have shaken off the prejudices that usually cling to a confined education. To which I answer, that men should be cautious how they raise objections which reflect upon the wisdom of the nation. Is not everybody freely allowed to believe whatever he pleases, and to publish his belief to the world whenever he thinks fit, especially if it serves to strengthen the party which is in the right? Would any indifferent foreigner, who should read the trumpery lately written by Asgil, Tindal, Toland, Coward, and forty more, imagine the gospel to be our rule of faith and confirmed by parliaments? Does any man either believe, or say he believes, or desire to have it thought that he says he believes, one syllable of the matter? And is any man worse received upon that score, or does he find his want of nominal faith a disadvantage to him in the pursuit of any civil or military employment? What if there be an old dormant statute or two against him, are they not now obsolete, to a degree that Empson and Dudley themselves, if they were now alive, would find it impossible to put them in execution?

It is likewise urged that there are, by computation, in this kingdom above ten thousand parsons, whose revenues, added to those of my lords the bishops, would suffice to maintain at least two hundred young gentlemen of wit and pleasure, and freethinking, enemies to priestcraft, narrow principles, pedantry, and prejudices, who might be an ornament to the court and town: and then, again, so great a number of able (bodied) divines might be a recruit to our fleet and armies. This indeed appears to be a consideration of some weight; but then, on the other side, several things deserve to be considered likewise: as, first, whether it may not be thought necessary that in certain tracts of country, like what we call parishes, there shall be one man at least of abilities to read and write. Then it seems a wrong computation, that the revenues of the Church throughout this island would be large enough to maintain two hundred young gentlemen, or even half that number, after the present refined way of living; that is, to allow each of them such a rent as, in the modern form of speech, would make them easy. But still there is in this project a greater mischief behind; and we ought to beware of the woman's folly, who killed the hen that every morning laid her a golden egg. For pray what would become of the race of men in the next age, if we had nothing to trust to besides the scrofulous, consumptive productions furnished by our men of wit and pleasure, when, having squandered away their vigour, health and estates, they are forced, by some disagreeable marriage, to piece up their broken fortunes? Now, here are ten thousand persons reduced, by the wise regulations of Henry VIII., to the necessity of a low diet and moderate exercise ; who are the only great restorers of our breed, without which the nation would in an age or two become one great hospital.

Another advantage proposed by the abolishing of Christianity is the clear gain of one day in seven, which is now entirely lost, and consequently the kingdom one seventh less considerable in trade, business, and pleasure ; beside the loss to the public of so many stately structures, now in the hands of the clergy, which might be converted into playhouses, market-houses, exchanges, common dormitories, and other public edifices.

I hope I shall be forgiven a hard word, if I call this a perfect cavil. I readily own there has been an old custom, time out of mind, for people to assemble in the churches every Sunday, and that shops are still frequently shut, in order, as it is conceived, to preserve the memory of that ancient practice ; but how this can prove a hindrance to business or pleasure is hard to imagine. What if the men of pleasure are forced, one day in the week, to game at home instead of the chocolate-houses? are not the taverns and coffee-houses open? can there be a more convenient season for taking a dose of physic? is not that the chief day for traders to sum up the accounts of the week, and for lawyers to prepare their briefs? But I would fain know how it can be pretended that the churches are misapplied? Where are more appointments and rendezvouses of gallantry? where more care to appear in the foremost box, with greater advantage of dress? where more meetings for business? where more bargains driven of all sorts? and where so many conveniences or incitements to sleep?

There is one advantage greater than any of the foregoing proposed by the abolishing of Christianity; that it will utterly extinguish parties among us, by removing those factious distinctions of High and Low Church, of Whig and Tory, Presbyterian and Church of England, which are now so many grievous clogs upon public proceedings, and are apt to dispose men to prefer the gratifying of themselves, or depressing of their adversaries, before the most important interests of the state.

I confess, if it were certain that so great an advantage would redound to the nation by this expedient, I would submit and be silent; but will any man say that, if the words *drinking, cheating, lying, stealing,* were, by act of parliament, ejected out of the English tongue and dictionaries, we should all awake next morning chaste and temperate, honest, and just, and lovers of truth? Is this a fair consequence? Or if the physicians would forbid us to pronounce the words *gout, rheumatism,* and *stone,* would that expedient serve, like so many talismans, to destroy the diseases themselves? Are party and faction rooted in men's hearts no deeper than phrases borrowed from religion, or founded upon no firmer principles? and is our language so poor that we cannot find other terms to express them? Are envy, pride, avarice, and ambition, such ill nomenclators that they cannot furnish appellations for their owners? Will not *heydukes* and *mamalukes, mandarins* and *patshaws,* or any other words formed at pleasure, serve to distinguish those who are in the ministry from others who would be in it if they could? What, for instance, is easier than to vary the form of speech, and instead of the word Church make it a question in politics whether the Monument be in danger? Because religion was nearest at hand to furnish a few convenient phrases, is our invention so barren we can find no other? Suppose, for argument sake, that the Tories favoured Margarita, the Whigs Mrs. Tofts, and the trimmers Valentini; would not *Margaritians*, *Toftians*, and *Valentinians* be very tolerable marks of distinction? The Prasini and Veniti, two most virulent factions in Italy, began (if I remember right) by a distinction of colours in ribbons; and we might contend with as good a grace about the dignity of the blue and the green, which would serve as properly to divide the court, the parliament, and the kingdom between them, as any terms of art whatsoever borrowed from religion. And therefore I think there is little force in this objection against Christianity, or prospect of so great an advantage as is proposed in the abolishing of it.

It is again objected, as a very absurd, ridiculous custom, that a set of men should be suffered, much less employed and hired, to bawl one day in seven against the lawfulness of those methods most in use toward the pursuit of greatness, riches, and pleasure, which are the constant practice of all men alive on the other six. . But this objection is, I think, a little unworthy of so refined an age as ours. Let us argue this matter calmly: I appeal to the breast of any polite freethinker, whether, in the pursuit of gratifying a predominant passion, he has not always felt a wonderful incitement by reflecting it was a thing forbidden; and therefore we see, in order to cultivate this taste, the wisdom of the nation has taken special care that the ladies should be furnished with prohibited silks and the men with prohibited wine. And indeed it were to be wished that some other prohibitions were promoted, in order to improve the pleasures of the town; which, for want of such expedients, begin already, as I am told, to flag and grow languid, giving way daily to cruel inroads from the spleen.

It is likewise proposed as a great advantage to the public, that if we once discard the system of the gospel, all religion will of course be banished for ever; and consequently along with it those grievous prejudices of education which, under the names of *virtue, conscience, honour, justice,* and the like, are so apt to disturb the peace of human minds, and the notions whereof are so hard to be eradicated by right reason or freethinking, sometimes during the whole course of our lives.

Here, first, I observe, how difficult it is to get rid of a phrase which the world is once grown fond of, though the occasion that first produced it be entirely taken away. For several years past, if a man had but an ill-favoured nose, the deep thinkers of the age would some way or other contrive to impute the cause to the prejudice of his education. From this fountain were said to be derived all our foolish notions of justice, piety, love of our country; all our opinions of God or a future state, heaven, hell, and the like; and there might formerly perhaps have been some pretence for this charge. But so effectual care has been taken to remove those prejudices by an entire change in the methods of education, that (with honour I mention it to our polite innovators) the young gentlemen who are now on the scene seem to have not the least tincture of those infusions or string of those weeds; and, by consequence, the reason for abolishing nominal Christianity upon that pretext is wholly ceased.

For the rest, it may perhaps admit a controversy whether the banishing of all notions of religion whatsoever would be convenient for the vulgar. Not that I am in the least of opinion with those who hold religion to have been the invention of politicians to keep the lower part of the world in awe by the fear of invisible powers, unless mankind were then very different to what it is now: for I look upon the mass or body of our people here in England to be as free thinkers, that is to say, as staunch unbelievers, as any of the highest rank. But I conceive some scattered notions about a superior power to be of singular use for the common people, as furnishing excellent materials to keep children quiet when they grow peevish, and providing topics of amusement in a tedious winter night.

Lastly, it is proposed as a singular advantage, that the abolishing of Christianity will very much contribute to the uniting of Protestants, by enlarging the terms of communion, so as to take in all sorts of dissenters, who are now shut out of the pale upon account of a few ceremonies which all sides confess to be things indifferent; that this alone will effectually answer the great ends of a scheme for comprehension, by opening a large noble gate at which all bodies may enter; whereas the chaffering with dissenters, and dodging about this or the other ceremony, is but like opening a few wickets and leaving them at jar, by which no more than one can get in at a time, and that not without stooping, and sidling, and squeezing his body.

To all this I answer, that there is one darling inclination of mankind which usually affects to be a retainer to religion, though she be neither its parent, its godmother, or its friend; I mean the spirit of opposition, that lived long before Christianity, and can easily subsist without it. Let us, for instance, examine wherein the opposition of sectaries among us consists; we shall find Christianity to have no share in it at all. Does the gospel anywhere prescribe a starched, squeezed countenance, a stiff formal gait, a singularity of manners and habit, or any affected modes of speech different from the reasonable part of mankind? Yet, if Christianity did not lend its name to stand in the gap, and to employ or divert these humours, they must of necessity be spent in contraventions to the laws of the land, and disturbance of the public peace. There is a portion of enthusiasm assigned to every nation, which, if it has not proper objects to work on, will burst out and set all in a flame. If the quiet of a state can be bought by only flinging men a few ceremonies to devour, it is a purchase no wise man would refuse. Let the mastiffs amuse themselves about a sheep's skin stuffed with hay, provided it will keep them from worrying the flock. The institution of convents abroad seems in one point a strain of great wisdom; there being few irregularities in human passions that may not have recourse to vent themselves in some of those orders, which are so many retreats for the speculative, the melancholy, the proud, the silent, the politic, and the morose, to spend themselves and evaporate the noxious particles; for each of whom we in this island are forced to provide a several sect of religion, to keep them quiet; and whenever Christianity shall be abolished, the legislature must find some other expedient to employ and entertain them. For what imports it how large a gate you open, if there will be always left a number who place a pride and a merit in refusing to enter?

Having thus considered the most important objections against Christianity, and the chief advantages proposed by the abolishing thereof, I shall now, with equal deference and submission to wiser judgments as before, proceed to mention a few inconveniences that may happen, if the gospel should be repealed, which perhaps the projectors may not have sufficiently considered.

And, first, I am very sensible how much the gentlemen of wit and pleasure are apt to murmur and be choked at the sight of so many daggled-tail parsons, who happen to fall in their way and offend their eyes; but, at the same time, these wise reformers do not consider what an advantage and felicity it is for great wits to be always provided with objects of scorn and contempt, in order to exercise and improve their talents, and divert their spleen from falling on each other or on themselves; especially when all this may be done without the least imaginable danger to their persons.

And to urge another argument of a parallel nature: if Christianity were once abolished, how could the freethinkers, the strong reasoners, and the men of profound learning, be able to find another subject so calculated in all points whereon to display their abilities? What wonderful productions of wit should we be deprived of from those whose genius by continual practice has been wholly turned upon raillery and invectives against religion, and who would therefore never be able to shine or distinguish themselves upon any other subject? We are daily complaining of the great decline of wit among us, and would we take away the greatest, perhaps the only, topic we have left? Who would ever have suspected Asgil for a wit, or Toland for a philosopher, if the inexhaustible stock of Christianity had not been at hand to provide them with materials? what other subject, through all art or nature, could have produced Tindal for a profound author, or furnished him with readers? it is the wise choice of the subject that alone adorns and distinguishes the writer. For had a hundred such pens as these been employed on the side of religion, they would have immediately sunk into silence and oblivion.

Nor do I think it wholly groundless, or my fears altogether imaginary, that the abolishing Christianity may perhaps bring the Church into danger, or at least put the senate to the trouble of another securing vote. I desire I may not be mistaken; I am far from presuming to affirm or think that the Church is in danger at present, or as things now stand; but we know not how soon it may be so when the Christian religion is repealed. As plausible as this project seems, there may be a dangerous design lurking under it. Nothing can be more notorious than that the atheists, deists, socinians, anti-trinitarians, and other subdivisions of freethinkers, are persons of little zeal for the present ecclesiastical establishment; their declared opinion is for repealing the sacramental test; they are very indifferent with regard to ceremonies, nor do they hold the *jus divinum* of episcopacy; therefore this may be intended as one politic step toward altering the constitution of the Church Established, and setting up Presbytery in the stead, which I leave to be farther considered by those at the helm.

In the last place, I think nothing can be more plain than that, by this expedient, we shall run into the evil we chiefly pretend to avoid; and that the abolishment of the Christian religion will be the readiest course we can take to introduce popery. And I am the more inclined to this opinion, because we know it has been the constant practice of the jesuits to send over emissaries with instructions to personate themselves members of the several prevailing sects among us. So it is recorded that they have at sundry times appeared in the disguise of presbyterians, anabaptists, independents, and quakers, according as any of these were most in credit; so, since the fashion has been taken up of exploding religion, the popish missionaries have not been wanting to mix with the freethinkers; among whom Toland, the great oracle of the anti-Christians, is an Irish priest, the son of an Irish priest, and the most learned and ingenious author of a book called The Rights of the Christian Church, and was in a proper juncture reconciled to the Romish faith, whose true son, as appears by a hundred passages in his treatise, he still continues. Perhaps I could add some others to the number, but the fact is beyond dispute, and the reasoning they proceed by is right; for, supposing Christianity to be extinguished, the people will never be at ease till they find out some other method of worship; which will as infallibly produce superstition, as superstition will end in popery.

And therefore if, notwithstanding all I have said, it still be thought necessary to have a bill brought in for repealing Christianity, I would humbly offer an amendment, that instead of the word Christianity may be put religion in general; which, I conceive, will much better answer all the good ends proposed by the projectors of it. For, as long as we leave in being a God and his providence, with all the necessary consequences which curious and inquisitive men will be apt to draw from such premises, we do not strike at the root of the evil, though we should ever so effectually annihilate the present scheme of the gospel: for of what use is freedom of thought if it will not produce freedom of action? which is the sole end, how remote soever in appearance, of all objections against Christianity; and therefore the freethinkers consider it as a sort of edifice, wherein all the parts have such a mutual dependence on each other, that if you happen to pull out one single nail, the whole fabric must fall to the ground. This was happily expressed by him, who had heard of a text brought for proof of the Trinity, which in an ancient manuscript was differently read; he thereupon immediately took the hint, and by a sudden deduction of a long *sorites* most logically concluded: "Why, if it be as you say, I may safely drink on, and defy the parson." From which, and many the like instances easy to be produced, I think nothing can be more manifest than that the quarrel is not against any particular points of hard digestion in the Christian system, but against religion in general; which, by laying restraints on human nature, is supposed the great enemy to the freedom of thought and action.

Upon the whole, if it shall still be thought for the benefit of church and state that Christianity be abolished, I conceive, however, it may be more convenient to defer the execution to a time of peace, and not venture, in this conjuncture, to disoblige our allies; who, as it falls out, are all Christians, and many of them, by the prejudices of their education, so bigoted as to place a sort of pride in the appellation. If, upon being rejected by them, we are to trust to an alliance with the Turk, we shall find ourselves much deceived: for as he is too remote, and generally engaged in war with the Persian emperor, so his people would be more scandalised at our infidelity than our Christian neighbours. For the Turks are not only strict observers of religious worship, but, what is worse, believe a God; which is more than is required of us, even while we preserve the name of Christians.

To conclude: whatever some may think of the great advantages to trade by this favourite scheme, I do very much apprehend that, in six months time after the act is passed for the extirpation of the gospel, the Bank and East-India stock may fall at least one *per cent*. And since that is fifty times more than ever the wisdom of our age thought fit to venture for the preservation of Christianity, there is no reason we should be at so great a loss merely for the sake of destroying it.

A MEDITATION UPON A BROOMSTICK:
ACCORDING TO THE STYLE AND MANNER OF THE HONOURABLE ROBERT BOYLE'S MEDITATIONS.

Swift went to Ireland in 1699 as chaplain and secretary to Lord Berkeley, one of the Lords Justices. Lady Berkeley evinced a singular partiality for Boyle's *Meditations*, which she would ask Swift to read aloud to her of an evening. Weary of these pious platitudes, he at last ventured to substitute a meditation of his own, *On a Broomstick*, which Lady Berkeley accepted in all good faith; until the fraud being discovered by more discerning persons, Swift was relieved from further persecution at the hands of the Honourable Robert Boyle. The parody was published in 1710.

A MEDITATION UPON A BROOMSTICK

THIS single stick, which you now behold ingloriously lying in that neglected corner, I once knew in a flourishing state in a forest: it was full of sap, full of leaves, and full of boughs: but now, in vain does the busy art of man pretend to vie with nature, by tying that withered bundle of twigs to its sapless trunk : it is now, at best, but the reverse of what it was, a tree turned upside down, the branches on the earth, and the root in the air ; it is now handled by every dirty wench, condemned to do her drudgery, and, by a capricious kind of fate, destined to make other things clean and be nasty itself; at length, worn to the stumps in the service of the maids, it is either thrown out of doors, or condemned to the last use of kindling a fire. When I beheld this, I sighed, and said within myself *Surely man is a Broomstick!* Nature sent him into the world strong and lusty, in a thriving condition, wearing his own hair on his head, the proper branches of this reasoning vegetable, until the axe of intemperance has lopped off his green boughs, and left him a withered trunk : he then flies to art, and puts on a periwig, valuing himself upon an unnatural bundle of hairs (all covered with powder), that never grew on his head ; but now, should this our broomstick pretend to enter the scene, proud of those birchen spoils it never bore, and all covered with dust, though the sweepings of the finest lady's chamber, we should be apt to ridicule and despise its vanity. Partial judges that we are of our own excellences and other men's defaults!

But a broomstick, perhaps you will say, is an emblem of a tree standing on its head: and pray what is man but a topsyturvy creature, his animal faculties perpetually mounted on his rational, his head where his heels should be, grovelling on the earth! And yet, with all his faults, he sets up to be a universal reformer and correcter of abuses, a remover of grievances, rakes into every slut's corner of nature, bringing hidden corruption to the light, and raises a mighty dust where there was none before; sharing deeply all the while in the very same pollutions he pretends to sweep away: his last days are spent in slavery to women, and generally the least deserving; till, worn out to the stumps, like his brother besom, he is either kicked out of doors, or made use of to kindle flames for others to warm themselves by.

TRAVELS INTO SEVERAL REMOTE NATIONS OF THE WORLD.

BY LEMUEL GULLIVER,

FIRST A SURGEON, AND THEN A CAPTAIN OF SEVERAL SHIPS.

Gulliver's Travels were first published in Nov. 1726, but had been known to Swift's friends for at least five years previously. His own account of the motives which led to the writing of the work is found in a letter to Pope of Sept. 29, 1725. "I am now returning to the noble scene of Dublin, into the *grand monde*, for fear of burying my parts, to signalize myself among curates and vicars, and correct all corruptions crept in, relating to the weight of bread and butter, through those dominions which I govern. I have employed my time (beside ditching) in finishing, correcting, and transcribing my travels, in four parts complete, newly augmented, and intended for the press when the world shall deserve them, or rather when a printer shall be found brave enough to venture his ears. I like the scheme of our meeting after distresses and dispersions, but the chief end I propose to myself in all my labours is to vex the world rather than divert it; and if I could compass that design without hurting my own person or fortune, I would be the most indefatigable writer you have ever seen without reading. I am exceedingly pleased that you have done with translations : lord treasurer Oxford often lamented that a rascally world should lay you under a necessity of misemploying your genius for so long a time. But since you will now be so much better employed, when you think of the world, give it one lash more at my request. I have ever hated all nations, professions, and communities, and all my love is toward individuals; for instance, I hate the tribe of lawyers, but I love counsellor such-a-one and judge such-a-one : it is so with physicians, (I will not speak of my own trade,) soldiers, English, Scotch, French, and the rest. But principally I hate and detest that animal called man; although I heartily love John, Peter, Thomas, and so forth. This is the system upon which I have governed myself many years (but do not tell) and so shall I go on till I have done with them. I have got materials towards a treatise proving the falsity of that definition *animal rationale*, and to show that it should be only *rationis capax*. Upon this great foundation of misanthropy (though not in Timon's manner) the whole building of my travels is erected; and I never will have peace of mind till all honest men are of my opinion. . . . . I am daily losing friends, and neither seeking nor getting others. O if the world had but a dozen Arbuthnots in it, I would burn my travels !"

GULLIVER'S RECEPTION IN LILLIPUT

IT would not be proper, for some reasons, to trouble the reader with the particulars of our adventures in those seas: let it suffice to inform him that, in our passage from thence to the East Indies, we were driven by a violent storm to the north-west of Van Diemen's Land. By an observation we found ourselves in the latitude of 30 degrees 2 minutes south. Twelve of our crew were dead, by immoderate labour and ill food; the rest were in a very weak condition. On the 5th of November, which was the beginning of summer in those parts, the weather being very hazy, the seamen spied a rock within half a cable's length of the ship: but the wind was so strong, that we were driven directly upon it, and immediately split. Six of the crew, of whom I was one, having let down the boat into the sea, made a shift to get clear of the ship and the rock. We rowed, by my computation, about three leagues, till we were able to work no longer, being already spent with labour while we were in the ship. We therefore trusted ourselves to the mercy of the waves, and in about half an hour the boat was overset by a sudden flurry from the north. What became of my companions in the boat, as well as of those who escaped on the rock, or were left in the vessel, I cannot tell, but conclude they were all lost. For my own part, I swam as fortune directed me, and was pushed forward by wind and tide. I often let my legs drop, and could feel no bottom; but when I was almost gone, and able to struggle no longer, I found myself within my depth; and by this time the storm was much abated. The declivity was so small, that I walked near a mile before I got to the shore, which I conjectured was about eight o'clock in the evening. I then advanced forward near half a mile, but could not discover any sign of houses or inhabitants; at least I was in so weak a condition, that I did not observe them. I was extremely tired; and with that, and the heat of the weather, and about half a pint of brandy that I drank as I left the ship, I found myself much inclined to sleep. I lay down on the grass, which was very short and soft, where I slept sounder than ever I remembered to have done in my life, and, as I reckoned, about nine hours; for when I awaked it was just daylight. I attempted to rise, but was not able to stir; for, as I happened to lie on my back, I found my arms and legs were strongly fastened on each side to the ground, and my hair, which was long and thick, tied down in the same manner. I likewise felt several slender ligatures across my body, from my arm-pits to my thighs. I could only look upwards; the sun began to grow hot, and the light offended my eyes. I heard a confused noise about me, but, in the posture I lay, could see nothing except the sky. In a little time I felt something alive moving on my left leg, which, advancing gently forward over my breast, came almost up to my chin; when, bending my eyes downward as much as I could, I perceived it to be a human creature not six inches high, with a bow and arrow in his hands and a quiver at his back. In the mean time, I felt at least forty more of the same kind (as I conjectured) following the first. I was in the utmost astonishment, and roared so loud that they all ran back in a fright; and some of them, as I was afterwards told, were hurt with the falls they got by leaping from my sides upon the ground. However, they soon returned; and one of them, who ventured so far as to get a full sight of my face, lifting up his hands and eyes by way of admiration, cried out, in a shrill but distinct voice, *Hekinah degul;* the others repeated the same words several times; but I then knew not what they meant. I lay all this while, as the reader may believe, in great uneasiness. At length struggling to get loose, I had the fortune to break the strings and wrench out the pegs that fastened my left arm to the ground; for, by lifting it up to my face, I discovered the methods they had taken to bind me; and at the same time, with a violent pull, which gave me excessive pain, I a little loosened the strings that tied down my hair on the left side, so that I was just able to turn my head about two inches. But the creatures ran off a second time before I could seize them; whereupon there was a great shout in a very shrill accent, and after it ceased I heard one of them cry aloud, *Tolgo phonac;* when in an instant I felt above a hundred arrows discharged on my left hand, which pricked me like so many needles; and besides, they shot another flight into the air, as we do bombs in Europe, whereof many, I suppose, fell on my body (though I felt them not,) and some on my face, which I immediately covered with my left hand. When this shower of arrows was over, I fell a-groaning with grief and pain; and then striving again to get loose, they discharged another volley, larger than the first, and some of them attempted with spears to stick me in the sides; but, by good luck, I had on me a buff jerkin, which they could not pierce. I thought it the most prudent method to lie still; and my design was to continue so till night, when, my left hand being already loose, I could easily free myself: and as for the inhabitants, I had reason to believe I might be a match for the greatest army they could bring against me, if they were all of the same size with him that I saw. But fortune disposed otherwise of me. When the people observed I was quiet, they discharged no more arrows; but by the noise I heard, I knew their numbers increased; and about four yards from me, over against my right ear, I heard a knocking for above an hour, like that of people at work; when, turning my head that way as well as the pegs and strings would permit me, I saw a stage erected about a foot and a half from the ground, capable of holding four of the inhabitants, with two or three ladders to mount it; from whence one of them, who seemed to be a person of quality, made me a long speech, whereof I understood not one syllable. But I should have mentioned that before the principal person began his oration, he cried out three times, *Langro dehul san;* (these words and the former were afterwards repeated and explained to me;) whereupon immediately about fifty of the inhabitants came and cut the strings that fastened the left side of my head, which gave me the liberty of turning it to the right, and of observing the person and gesture of him that was to speak. He

appeared to be of a middle age, and taller than any of
the other three who attended him ; whereof one was a
page, that held up his train, and seemed to be somewhat
longer than my middle finger ; the other two stood
one on each side to support him. He acted every
part of an orator, and I could observe many periods of
threatenings, and others of promises, pity, and kindness. I answered in a few words, but in the most
submissive manner, lifting up my left hand and both
my eyes to the sun, as calling him for a witness ; and
being almost famished with hunger, having not eaten
a morsel for some hours before I left the ship, I found
the demands of nature so strong upon me, that I could
not forbear showing my impatience, perhaps against
the strict rules of decency, by putting my finger frequently to my mouth, to signify that I wanted food.
The *hurgo* (for so they call a great lord, as I afterwards
learned) understood me very well. He descended
from the stage, and commanded that several ladders
should be applied to my sides, on which above a
hundred of the inhabitants mounted, and walked
towards my mouth, laden with baskets full of meat,
which had been provided and sent thither by the king's
orders, upon the first intelligence he received of me. I
observed there was the flesh of several animals, but
could not distinguish them by the taste. There were
shoulders, legs, and loins, shaped like those of mutton,
and very well dressed, but smaller than the wings of
a lark. I eat them by two or three at a mouthful,
and took three loaves at a time, about the bigness of
musket-bullets. They supplied me as fast as they
could, showing a thousand marks of wonder and
astonishment at my bulk and appetite. I then made

another sign, that I wanted drink. They found by
my eating that a small quantity would not suffice me;
and, being a most ingenious people, they slung up,
with great dexterity, one of their largest hogsheads,
then rolled it towards my hand, and beat out the top:
I drank it off at a draught, which I might well do, for
it did not hold half a pint, and tasted like a small
wine of Burgundy, but much more delicious. They
brought me a second hogshead, which I drank in the
same manner, and made signs for more; but they had
none to give me. When I had performed these
wonders, they shouted for joy, and danced upon my
breast, repeating several times, as they did at first,
Hekinah degul. They made me a sign that I should
throw down the two hogsheads, but first warning the
people below to stand out of the way, crying aloud,
Borach mevolah; and when they saw the vessels in
the air, there was a universal shout of *Hekinah degul.*
I confess I was often tempted, while they were passing
backwards and forwards on my body, to seize forty or
fifty of the first that came in my reach, and dash them
against the ground. But the remembrance of what I
had felt, which probably might not be the worst they
could do, and the promise of honour I had made them,—
for so I interpreted my submissive behaviour,—soon
drove out these imaginations. Besides, I now considered myself as bound by the laws of hospitality to a
people who had treated me with so much expense and
magnificence. However, in my thoughts I could not
sufficiently wonder at the intrepidity of these diminutive
mortals, who durst venture to mount and walk upon
my body, while one of my hands was at liberty, without trembling at the very sight of so prodigious a

creature as I must appear to them. After some time, when they observed that I made no more demands for meat, there appeared before me a person of high rank from his imperial majesty. His excellency, having mounted on the small of my right leg, advanced forwards up to my face, with about a dozen of his retinue; and producing his credentials under the signet-royal, which he applied close to my eyes, spoke about ten minutes without any signs of anger, but with a kind of determined resolution, often pointing forwards, which as I afterwards found was towards the capital city, about half a mile distant, whither it was agreed by his majesty in council that I must be conveyed. I answered in a few words, but to no purpose, and made a sign with my hand that was loose, putting it to the other, (but over his excellency's head, for fear of hurting him or his train,) and then to my own head and body, to signify that I desired my liberty. It appeared that he understood me well enough for he shook his head by way of disapprobation, and held his hand in a posture to show that I must be carried as a prisoner. However, he made other signs, to let me understand that I should have meat and drink enough, and very good treatment. Whereupon I once more thought of attempting to break my bonds; but again, when I felt the smart of their arrows upon my face and hands, which were all in blisters, and many of the darts still sticking in them, and observing likewise that the number of my enemies increased, I gave tokens to let them know that they might do with me what they pleased. Upon this the *hurgo* and his train withdrew, with much civility and cheerful countenances.

THE INVENTORY OF WHAT WAS FOUND UPON THE MAN-MOUNTAIN

IN the mean time the emperor held frequent councils to debate what course should be taken with me; and I was afterwards assured by a particular friend, a person of great quality, who was as much in the secret as any, that the court was under many difficulties concerning me. They apprehended my breaking loose; that my diet would be very expensive, and might cause a famine. Sometimes they determined to starve me, or at least to shoot me in the face and hands with poisoned arrows, which would soon despatch me; but again they considered that the stench of so large a carcase might produce a plague in the metropolis, and probably spread through the whole kingdom. In the midst of these consultations several officers of the army went to the door of the great council-chamber, and two of them, being admitted, gave an account of my behaviour which made so favourable an impression in the breast of his majesty and the whole board in my behalf that an imperial commission was issued out, obliging all the villages, nine hundred yards round the city, to deliver in every morning six beeves, forty sheep, and other victuals;

for my sustenance; together with a proportionable quantity of bread, and wine and other liquors; for the due payment of which his majesty gave assignments upon his treasury: for this prince lives chiefly upon his own demesnes, seldom, except upon great occasions, raising any subsidies upon his subjects, who are bound to attend him in his wars at their own expense. An establishment was also made of six hundred persons to be my domestics, who had board wages allowed for their maintenance, and tents built for them very conveniently on each side of my door. It was likewise ordered that three hundred tailors should make me a suit of clothes after the fashion of the country; that six of his majesty's greatest scholars should be employed to instruct me in their language; and lastly, that the emperor's horses, and those of the nobility and troops of guards, should be frequently exercised in my sight, to accustom themselves to me. All these orders were duly put in execution; and in about three weeks I made a great progress in learning their language; during which time the emperor frequently honoured me with his visits, and was pleased to assist my masters in teaching me. We began already to converse together in some sort; and the first words I learnt were to express my desire "that he would please to give me my liberty;" which I every day repeated on my knees. His answer, as I could apprehend it, was, "that this must be a work of time, not to be thought on without the advice of his council, and that first I must *lumos kelmin pesso desmar lon emposo;*" that is, swear a peace with him and his kingdom. However, that I should be used with all kindness. And he advised me to "acquire, by my patience and discreet behaviour, the good opinion of himself and his subjects." He desired "I would not take it ill if he gave orders to certain proper officers to search me; for probably I might carry about me several weapons, which must needs be dangerous things, if they answered the bulk of so prodigious a person." I said, "his majesty should be satisfied, for I was ready to strip myself and turn up my pockets before him." This I delivered part in words and part in signs. He replied, "that by the laws of the kingdom I must be searched by two of his officers; that he knew this could not be done without my consent and assistance; and he had so good an opinion of my generosity and justice as to trust their persons in my hands; that whatever they took from me should be returned when I left the country, or paid for at the rate which I would set upon them." I took up the two officers in my hands, put them first into my coat-pockets, and then into every other pocket about me, except my two fobs and another secret pocket, which I had no mind should be searched, wherein I had some little necessaries that were of no consequence to any but myself. In one of my fobs there was a silver watch, and in the other a small quantity of gold in a purse. These gentlemen, having pen, ink, and paper about them, made an exact inventory of everything they saw; and when they had done desired I would set them down, that they might deliver it to the emperor. This inventory I afterwards translated into English, and is, word for word, as follows :—

Imprimis, in the right coat-pocket of the great man-mountain (for so I interpret the words *quinbus flestrin*), after the strictest search, we found only one great piece of coarse cloth, large enough to be a footcloth for your majesty's chief room of state. In the left pocket we saw a huge silver chest, with a cover of the same metal, which we the searchers were not able to lift. We desired it should be opened, and one of us stepping into it found himself up to the mid-leg in a sort of dust, some part whereof, flying up to our faces, set us both a-sneezing for several times together. In his right waistcoat-pocket we found a prodigious bundle of white thin substances, folded one over another, about the bigness of three men, tied with a strong cable, and marked with black figures, which we humbly conceive to be writings, every letter almost half as large as the palm of our hands. In the left there was a sort of engine, from the back of which were extended twenty long poles, resembling the palisadoes before your majesty's court, wherewith we conjecture the man-mountain combs his head; for we did not always trouble him with questions, because we found it a great difficulty to make him understand us. In the large pocket, on the right side of his middle cover (so I translate the word *ranfulo*, by which they meant my breeches), we saw a hollow pillar of iron, about the length of a man, fastened to a strong piece of timber larger than the pillar; and upon one side of the pillar were huge pieces of iron sticking out, cut into strange figures, which we know not what to make of. In the left pocket another engine of the same kind. In the smaller pocket, on the right side, were several round flat pieces of white and red metal, of different bulk; some of the white, which seemed to be silver, were so large and heavy that my comrade and I could hardly lift them. In the left pocket were two black pillars irregularly shaped; we could not, without difficulty, reach the top of them as we stood at the bottom of his pocket. One of them was covered, and seemed all of a piece; but at the upper end of the other there appeared a white round substance, about twice the bigness of our heads. Within each of these was enclosed a prodigious plate of steel; which, by our orders, we obliged him to show us, because we apprehended they might be dangerous engines. He took them out of their cases, and told us that, in his own country, his practice was to shave his beard with one of these, and cut his meat with the other. There were two pockets which we could not enter; these he called his fobs; they were two large slits cut into the top of his middle cover, but squeezed close by the pressure of his belly. Out of the right fob hung a great silver chain, with a wonderful kind of engine at the bottom. We directed him to draw out whatever was at the end of that chain, which appeared to be a globe, half silver, and half of some transparent metal; for, on the transparent side, we saw certain strange figures circularly drawn, and thought we could touch them, till we found our fingers stopped by that lucid substance. He put this engine to our ears, which made an incessant noise, like that of a water-mill; and we conjecture it is either some unknown animal, or the god that he worships; but we are more inclined to the latter opinion, because he assured us (if we understood him right, for he expressed himself very imperfectly) that he seldom did anything without consulting it. He called it his oracle, and said it pointed out the time for every action of his life. From the left fob he took out a net, almost large enough for a fisherman, but contrived to open and shut like a purse, and served him for the same use; we found therein several massy pieces of yellow metal, which, if they be real gold, must be of immense value.

"Having thus, in obedience to your majesty's commands, diligently searched all his pockets, we observed a girdle about his waist, made of the hide of some prodigious animal, from which, on the left side, hung a sword of the length of five men; and on the right, a bag or pouch divided into two cells, each cell capable of holding three of your majesty's subjects. In one of these cells were several globes, or balls, of a most ponderous metal, about the bigness of our heads, and required a strong hand to lift them; the other cell contained a heap of certain black grains, but of no great bulk or weight, for we could hold above fifty of them in the palms of our hands.

"This is an exact inventory of what we found about the body of the man-mountain, who used us with great civility, and due respect to your majesty's commission. Signed and sealed on the fourth day of the eighty-ninth moon of your majesty's auspicious reign.

"CLEFRIN FRELOCK, MARSI FRELOCK."

When this inventory was read over to the emperor, he directed me, although in very gentle terms, to deliver up the several particulars. He first called for my scimitar, which I took out, scabbard and all. In the meantime he ordered three thousand of his choicest troops (who then attended him) to surround me, at a distance, with their bows and arrows just ready to discharge; but I did not observe it, for mine eyes were wholly fixed upon his majesty. He then desired me to draw my scimitar, which, although it had got some rust by the sea-water, was in most parts exceeding bright. I did so, and immediately all the troops gave a shout between terror and surprise; for the sun shone clear, and the reflection dazzled their eyes as I waved the scimitar to and fro in my hand. His majesty, who is a most magnanimous prince, was less daunted than I could expect; he ordered me to return it into the scabbard, and cast it on the ground as gently as I could, about six feet from the end of my chain. The next thing he demanded was one of the hollow iron pillars, by which he meant my pocket pistols. I drew it out, and, at his desire, as well as I could, expressed to him the use of it; and, charging it only with powder, which by the closeness of my pouch, happened to escape wetting in the sea (an inconvenience against which all prudent mariners take special care to provide), I first cautioned the emperor not to be afraid, and then I let it off in the air. The astonishment here was much greater than at the sight of my scimitar. Hundreds fell down as if they had been struck dead; and even the emperor, although he stood his ground, could not recover himself for some time. I delivered up both my pistols in the same manner as I had done my scimitar, and then my pouch of powder and bullets; begging him that the former might be kept from fire, for it would kindle with the smallest spark, and blow up his imperial palace into the air. I likewise delivered up my watch, which the emperor was very curious to see, and commanded two of his tallest yeoman of the guards to bear it on a pole upon their shoulders, as draymen in England do a barrel of ale. He was amazed at the continual noise it made, and the motion of the minute-hand, which he could easily discern, for their sight is much more acute than ours; he asked the opinions of his learned men about it, which were various and remote, as the reader may well imagine without my repeating; although, indeed, I could not very perfectly understand them. I then gave up my silver and copper money, my purse with nine large pieces of gold and some smaller ones; my knife and razor, my comb and silver snuff-box, my handkerchief and journal-book. My scimitar, pistols, and pouch, were conveyed in carriages to his majesty's stores; but the rest of my goods were returned me.

FACTIONS IN THE STATE OF LILLIPUT

ONE morning, about a fortnight after I had obtained my liberty, Reldresal, principal secretary (as they style him) for private affairs, came to my house attended only by one servant. He ordered his coach to wait at a distance, and desired I would give him an hour's audience; which I readily consented to, on account of his quality and personal merits, as well as of the many good offices he had done me during my solicitations at court. I offered to lie down, that he might the more conveniently reach my ear; but he chose rather to let me hold him in my hand during our conversation. He began with compliments on my liberty; said, "he might pretend to some merit in it;" but, however, added, "that if it had not been for the present situation of things at court, perhaps I might not have obtained it so soon. For," said he, "as flourishing a condition as we may appear to be in to foreigners, we labour under two mighty evils: a violent faction at home, and the danger of an invasion by a most potent enemy from abroad. As to the first, you are to understand that for above seventy moons past there have been two struggling parties in this empire, under the names of *Tramecksan* and *Slamecksan*, from the high and low heels of their shoes, by which they distinguish themselves. It is alleged, indeed, that the high heels are most agreeable to our ancient constitution; but, however this be, his majesty has determined to make use only of low heels in the administration of the government and all offices in the gift of the crown, as you cannot but observe; and particularly, that his majesty's imperial heels are lower at least by a *drurr* than any of his court (*drurr* is a measure about the fourteenth part of an inch). The animosities between these two parties run so high, that they will neither eat, nor drink, nor talk with each other. We compute the *Tramecksan*, or high heels, to exceed us in number: but the power is wholly on our side. We apprehend his imperial highness, the heir to the crown, to have some tendency towards the high heels; at least, we can plainly discover that one of his heels is higher than the other, which gives him a hobble in his gait. Now, in the midst of these intestine disquiets, we are threatened with an invasion from the island of Blefuscu, which is the other great empire of the universe, almost as large and powerful as this of his majesty. For as to what we have heard you affirm, that there are other kingdoms and states in the world, inhabited by human creatures as large as yourself, our philosophers are in much doubt, and would rather conjecture that you dropped from the moon or one of the stars; because it is certain that a hundred mortals of your bulk would in a short time destroy all the fruits and cattle of his majesty's dominions: besides, our histories of six thousand moons make no mention of any other regions than the two great empires of Lilliput and Blefuscu. Which two mighty powers have, as I was going to tell you, been engaged in a most obstinate war for six-

and-thirty moons past. It began upon the following occasion: it is allowed on all hands that the primitive way of breaking eggs, before we eat them, was upon the larger end; but his present majesty's grandfather, while he was a boy, going to eat an egg, and breaking it according to the ancient practice, happened to cut one of his fingers. Whereupon the emperor his father published an edict, commanding all his subjects, upon great penalties, to break the smaller ends of their eggs. The people so highly resented this law, that our histories tell us there have been six rebellions raised on that account; wherein one emperor lost his life, and another his crown. These civil commotions were constantly fomented by the monarchs of Blefuscu; and when they were quelled, the exiles always fled for refuge to that empire. It is computed that eleven thousand persons have at several times suffered death, rather than submit to break their eggs at the smaller end. Many hundred large volumes have been published upon this controversy; but the books of the Big-endians have been long forbidden, and the whole party rendered incapable by law of holding employments. During the course of these troubles, the emperors of Blefuscu did frequently expostulate by their ambassadors, accusing us of making a schism in religion, by offending against a fundamental doctrine of our great prophet Lustrog, in the fifty-fourth chapter of the Blundecral (which is their Alcoran). This, however, is thought to be a mere strain upon the text; for the words are these: that all true believers break their eggs at the convenient end. And which is the convenient end seems in my humble opinion to be left to every man's conscience, or at least in the power

of the chief magistrate to determine. Now, the Big-
endian exiles have found so much credit in the emperor
of Blefuscu's court, and so much private assistance and
encouragement from their party here at home, that a
bloody war has been carried on between the two
empires for six-and-thirty moons, with various success;
during which time we have lost forty capital ships, and
a much greater number of smaller vessels, together
with thirty thousand of our best seamen and soldiers;
and the damage received by the enemy is reckoned
to be somewhat greater than ours. However, they
have now equipped a numerous fleet, and are just preparing to make a descent upon us: and his imperial
majesty, placing great confidence in your valour and
strength, has commanded me to lay this account of his
affairs before you."

I desired the secretary to present my humble duty to
the emperor; and to let him know " that I thought it
would not become me, who was a foreigner, to interfere
with parties; but I was ready, with the hazard of my
life, to defend his person and state against all invaders."

THE CAPTURE OF THE FLEET OF BLEFUSCU

THE empire of Blefuscu is an island situated to the north-east of Lilliput, from which it is parted only by a channel of eight hundred yards wide. I had not yet seen it, and, upon this notice of an intended invasion, I avoided appearing on that side of the coast, for fear of being discovered by some of the enemy's ships, who had received no intelligence of me ;• all intercourse between the two empires having been strictly forbidden during the war upon pain of death, and an embargo laid by our emperor upon all vessels whatsoever. I communicated to his majesty a project I had formed of seizing the enemy's whole fleet; which, as our scouts assured us, lay at anchor in the harbour, ready to sail with the first fair wind. I consulted the most experienced seamen upon the depth of the channel, which they had often plumbed ; who told me that in the middle, at high water, it was seventy *glumgluffs* deep, which is about six feet of European measure ; and the rest of it fifty *glumgluffs* at most. I walked towards the north-east coast, over against Blefuscu ; where, lying down behind a hillock, I took out my small perspective glass, and viewed the enemy's fleet at

CAPTURE OF THE FLEET OF BLEFUSCU

anchor, consisting of about fifty men-of-war, and a great number of transports: I then came back to my house, and gave orders (for which I had a warrant) for a great quantity of the strongest cable and bars of iron. The cable was about as thick as packthread, and the bars of the length and size of a knitting-needle. I trebled the cable to make it stronger, and for the same reason I twisted three of the iron bars together, bending the extremities into a hook. Having thus fixed fifty hooks to as many cables, I went back to the north-east coast, and, putting off my coat, shoes, and stockings, walked into the sea, in my leathern jerkin, about half an hour before high water. I waded with what haste I could, and swam in the middle about thirty yards, till I felt ground. I arrived at the fleet in less than half an hour. The enemy were so frighted when they saw me, that they leaped out of their ships, and swam to shore, where there could not be fewer than thirty thousand souls: I then took my tackling, and, fastening a hook to the hole at the prow of each, I tied all the cords together at the end. While I was thus employed, the enemy discharged several thousand arrows, many of which stuck in my hands and face, and, besides the excessive smart, gave me much disturbance in my work. My greatest apprehension was for mine eyes, which I should have infallibly lost, if I had not suddenly thought of an expedient. I kept, among other little necessaries, a pair of spectacles in a private pocket, which, as I observed before, had escaped the emperor's searchers. These I took out, and fastened as strongly as I could upon my nose; and, thus armed, went on boldly with my work, in spite of the enemy's arrows; many of which struck against the glasses of my spectacles, but without any other effect farther than a little to discompose them. I had now fastened all the hooks, and, taking the knot in my hand, began to pull ; but not a ship would stir, for they were all too fast held by their anchors, so that the boldest part of my enterprise remained. I therefore let go the cord, and, leaving the hooks fixed to the ships, I resolutely cut with my knife the cables that fastened the anchors, receiving about two hundred shots in my face and hands ; then I took up the knotted end of the cables, to which my hooks were tied, and with great ease drew fifty of the enemy's largest men-of-war after me.

The Blefuscudians, who had not the least imagination of what I intended, were at first confounded with astonishment. They had seen me cut the cables, and thought my design was only to let the ships run adrift, or fall foul on each other ; but when they perceived the whole fleet moving in order, and saw me pulling at the end, they set up such a scream of grief and despair, as it is almost impossible to describe or conceive. When I had got out of danger, I stopped a while to pick out the arrows that stuck in my hands and face ; and rubbed on some ointment. I then took off my spectacles, and waiting about an hour, till the tide was a little fallen, I waded through the middle with my cargo, and arrived safe at the royal port of Lilliput.

ARRIVAL IN BROBDINGNAG

I FELL into a high road, for so I took it to be, though it served to the inhabitants only as a footpath through a field of barley. Here I walked on for some time, but could see little on either side, it being now near harvest, and the corn rising at least forty feet. I was an hour walking to the end of this field, which was fenced in with a hedge of at least one hundred and twenty feet high, and the trees so lofty that I could make no computation of their altitude. There was a stile to pass from this field into the next. It had four steps, and a stone to cross over when you came to the uppermost. It was impossible for me to climb this stile, because every step was six feet high, and the upper stone about twenty. I was endeavouring to find some gap in the hedge, when I discovered one of the inhabitants in the next field, advancing towards the stile. He appeared as tall as an ordinary spire-steeple, and took about ten yards at every stride, as near as I could guess. I was struck with the utmost fear and astonishment, and ran to hide myself in the corn, whence I saw him at the top of the stile, looking back into the next field on the right hand, and heard him call in a voice many degrees louder than a speaking-trumpet; but the noise was so high in the

air that at first I certainly thought it was thunder.
Whereupon seven monsters like himself came towards
him with reaping-hooks in their hands, each hook
about the largeness of six scythes. These people
were not so well clad as the first, whose servants or
labourers they seemed to be ; for, upon some words
he spoke, they went to reap the corn in the field
where I lay. I kept from them at as great a distance as I could, but was forced to move with extreme difficulty, for the stalks of the corn were sometimes not above a foot distant, so that I could hardly
squeeze my body betwixt them. However, I made a
shift to go forward, till I came to a part of the field
where the corn had been laid by the rain and wind.
Here it was impossible for me to advance a step ; for
the stalks were so interwoven that I could not creep
through, and the beards of the fallen ears so strong
and pointed, that they pierced through my clothes
into my flesh. At the same time I heard the reapers
not above a hundred yards behind me. Being quite
dispirited with toil, and wholly overcome by grief and
despair, I lay down between two ridges, and heartily
wished I might there end my days. I bemoaned my
desolate widow and fatherless children. I lamented
my own folly and wilfulness, in attempting a second
voyage against the advice of all my friends and relations. In this terrible agitation of mind, I could
not forbear thinking of Lilliput, whose inhabitants
looked upon me as the greatest prodigy that ever appeared in the world ; where I was able to draw an
imperial fleet in my hand, and perform those other
actions which will be recorded for ever in the chronicles
of that empire, while posterity shall hardly believe

them, although attested by millions. I reflected what a mortification it must prove to me to appear as inconsiderable in this nation, as one single Lilliputian would be among us. But this I conceived was to be the least of my misfortunes: for, as human creatures are observed to be more savage and cruel in proportion to their bulk, what could I expect but to be a morsel in the mouth of the first among these enormous barbarians that should happen to seize me? Undoubtedly philosophers are in the right, when they tell us that nothing is great or little otherwise than by comparison. It might have pleased fortune to let the Lilliputians find some nation where the people were as diminutive with respect to them, as they were to me. And who knows but that even this prodigious race of mortals might be equally overmatched in some distant part of the world whereof we have yet no discovery?

Scared and confounded as I was, I could not forbear going on with these reflections, when one of the reapers, approaching within ten yards of the ridge where I lay, made me apprehend that with the next step I should be squashed to death under his foot, or cut in two with his reaping-hook. And therefore, when he was again about to move, I screamed as loud as fear could make me: whereupon the huge creature trod short, and, looking round about under him for some time, at last espied me as I lay on the ground. He considered a while, with the caution of one who endeavours to lay hold on a small dangerous animal in such a manner that it shall not be able either to scratch or to bite him, as I myself have sometimes done with a weasel in England. At length he ventured to take me behind, by the middle, between his fore-finger and thumb, and brought me within three yards of his eyes, that he might behold my shape more perfectly. I guessed his meaning, and my good fortune gave me so much presence of mind, that I resolved not to struggle in the least as he held me in the air above sixty feet from the ground, (although he grievously pinched my sides,) for fear I should slip through his fingers. All I ventured was to raise mine eyes towards the sun, and place my hands together in a supplicating posture, and to speak some words in an humble, melancholy tone, suitable to the condition I then was in: for I apprehended every moment that he would dash me against the ground, as we usually do any little hateful animal which we have a mind to destroy. But my good star would have it that he appeared pleased with my voice and gestures, and began to look upon me as a curiosity, much wondering to hear me pronounce articulate words, although he could not understand them. In the mean time I was not able to forbear groaning and shedding tears, and turning my head towards my sides; letting him know, as well as I could, how cruelly I was hurt by the pressure of his thumb and finger. He seemed to apprehend my meaning; for lifting up the lappet of his coat, he put me gently into it, and immediately ran along with me to his master, who was a substantial farmer, and the same person I had first seen in the field.

The farmer, having (as I suppose by their talk) received such an account of me as his servant could give him, took a piece of a small straw, about the size of a walking staff, and therewith lifted up the lappets of my coat; which it seems he thought to be some kind of covering that nature had given me. He blew my hairs aside to take a better view of my face. He called his hinds about him, and asked them (as I afterwards learned) whether they had ever seen in the fields any little creature that resembled me. He then placed me softly on the ground upon all four, but I got immediately up, and walked slowly backwards and forwards, to let those people see I had no intent to run away. They all sat down in a circle about me, the better to observe my motions. I pulled off my hat, and made a low bow towards the farmer. I fell on my knees, and lifted up my hands and eyes, and spoke several words as loud as I could. I took a purse of gold out of my pocket, and humbly presented it to him. He received it on the palm of his hand, then applied it close to his eye to see what it was, and afterwards turned it several times with the point of a pin, which he took out of his sleeve, but could make nothing of it. Whereupon I made a sign that he should place his hand on the ground. I then took the purse, and, opening it, poured all the gold into his palm. There were six Spanish pieces of four pistoles each, besides twenty or thirty smaller coins. I saw him wet the tip of his little finger upon his tongue, and take up one of my largest pieces, and then another; but he seemed to be wholly ignorant what they were. He made me a sign to put them again into my purse, and the purse again into my pocket, which, after offering it to him several times, I thought it best to do.

The farmer by this time was convinced I must be a rational creature. He spoke often to me, but the sound of his voice pierced my ears like that of a water-mill, yet his words were articulate enough. I answered as loud as I could in several languages, and he often laid his ear within two yards of me; but all in vain, for we were wholly unintelligible to each other. He then sent his servants to their work, and, taking his handkerchief out of his pocket, he doubled and spread it on his left hand, which he placed flat on the ground with the palm upward, making me a sign to step into it; as I could easily do, for it was not above a foot in thickness. I thought it my part to obey; and, for fear of falling, laid myself at full length upon the handkerchief, with the remainder of which he lapped me up to the head for farther security, and in this manner carried me home to his house. There he called his wife, and showed me to her; but she screamed and ran back, as women in England do at the sight of a toad or a spider. However, when she had awhile seen my behaviour, and how well I observed the signs her husband made, she was soon reconciled, and by degrees grew extremely tender of me.

It was about twelve at noon, and a servant brought in dinner. It was only one substantial dish of meat, fit for the plain condition of an husbandman, in a dish of about four and twenty feet diameter. The company were the farmer and his wife, three children, and an old grandmother. When they were sat down, the farmer placed me at some distance from him on the table, which was thirty feet high from the floor. I was in a terrible fright, and kept as far as I could from the edge, for fear of falling. The wife minced a bit of meat, then crumbled some bread on a trencher, and placed it before me. I made her a low bow, took out my knife and fork, and fell to eat, which gave them exceeding delight. The mistress sent her maid for a small dram-cup, which held about two gallons, and filled it with drink; I took up the vessel with much difficulty in both hands, and in a most respectful manner drank to her ladyship's health, expressing the words as loud as I could in English; which made the company laugh so heartily, that I was almost deafened with the noise. This liquor tasted like a small cider, and was not unpleasant. Then the master made me a sign to come to his trencher side; but as I walked on the table, being in great surprise all the time, as the indulgent reader will easily conceive and excuse, I happened to stumble against a crust, and fell flat on my face, but received no hurt. I got up immediately, and observing the good people to be in much concern, I took my hat, which I held under my arm out of good manners, and waving it over my head, made three huzzas, to show I had got no mischief by my fall. But advancing forward towards my master (as I shall henceforth call him), his youngest son, who sat next to him, an arch boy of about ten years old, took me up by the legs, and held me so high in the air, that I trembled every limb; but his father snatched me from him, and at the same time gave him such a box on the left ear as would have felled an European troop of horse to the earth, ordering him to be taken from the table. But being afraid the boy might owe me a spite, and well remembering how mischievous all children among us naturally are to sparrows, rabbits, young kittens, and puppy-dogs, I fell on my knees, and, pointing to the boy, made my master to understand as well as I could that I desired his son might be pardoned. The father complied, and the lad took his seat again; whereupon I went to him and kissed his hand, which my master took, and made him stroke me gently with it.

In the midst of dinner, my mistress's favourite cat leaped into her lap. I heard a noise behind me like that of a dozen stocking-weavers at work; and, turning my head, I found it proceeded from the purring of that animal, who seemed to be three times larger than an ox, as I computed by the view of her head and one of her paws, while her mistress was feeding and stroking her. The fierceness of this creature's countenance altogether discomposed me; though I stood at the farther end of the table, about fifty feet off, and although my mistress held her fast, for fear she might give a spring and seize me in her talons. But it happened there was no danger; for the cat took not the least notice of me, when my master placed me within three yards of her. And, as I have been always told, and found true by experience in my travels, that flying or discovering fear before a fierce animal is a certain way to make it pursue or attack you, so I resolved in this dangerous juncture to show no manner of concern. I walked with intrepidity five or six times before the very head of the cat, and came within half a yard of her; whereupon she drew herself back, as if she were more afraid of me. I had less apprehension concerning the dogs, whereof three or four came into the room, as it is usual in farmers' houses: one of which was a mastiff equal in bulk to four elephants, and a greyhound somewhat taller than the mastiff, but not so large.

THE KING OF BROBDINGNAG'S INQUIRY INTO THE STATE OF ENGLAND

THE king, who was a prince of excellent understanding, would frequently order that I should be brought in my box, and set upon the table in his closet : he would then command me to bring one of my chairs out of the box, and sit down within three yards' distance, upon the top of the cabinet, which brought me almost to a level with his face. In this manner I had several conversations with him. I one day took the freedom to tell his majesty, "that the contempt he discovered towards Europe, and the rest of the world, did not seem answerable to those excellent qualities of mind that he was master of : that reason did not extend itself with the bulk of the body; on the contrary, we observed in our country that the tallest persons were usually the least provided with it; that, among other animals, bees and ants had the reputation of more industry, art, and sagacity, than many of the larger kinds : and that, as inconsiderable as he took me to be, I hoped I might live to do his majesty some signal service." The king heard me with attention, and began to conceive a much better opinion of me than he had ever before. He desired "I would give him as exact an account of the government of England as I possibly could; because, as fond as princes commonly are of their own customs, (for so he conjectured of other monarchs by my former discourses,) he should be glad to hear of anything that might deserve imitation."

Imagine with thyself, courteous reader, how often I then wished for the tongue of Demosthenes or Cicero, that might have enabled me to celebrate the praise of my own dear native country in a style equal to its merits and felicity.

I began my discourse by informing his majesty that our dominions consisted of two islands, which composed three mighty kingdoms, under one sovereign; besides our plantations in America. I dwelt long upon the fertility of our soil, and the temperature of our climate. I then spoke at large upon the constitution of an English parliament; partly made up of an illustrious body, called the House of Peers, persons of the noblest blood and of the most ancient and ample patrimonies. I described that extraordinary care always taken of their education in arts and arms, to qualify them for being counsellors both to the king and kingdom; to have a share in the legislature; to be members of the highest court of judicature, whence there can be no appeal; and to be champions always ready for the defence of their prince and country, by their valour, conduct, and fidelity. That these were the ornament and bulwark of the kingdom, worthy followers of their most renowned ancestors, whose honour had been the reward of their virtue, from which their posterity were never once known to degenerate. To these were joined several holy persons, as part of that assembly, under the title of bishops; whose peculiar business it is to take care of religion, and of those who instruct the people therein. These were searched and sought out through the whole nation, by the prince and his wisest counsellors, among such of the priesthood as were most deservedly distinguished by the sanctity of their lives and the depth of their erudition; who were indeed the spiritual fathers of the clergy and the people.

That the other part of the parliament consisted of an assembly called the House of Commons, who were all principal gentlemen, freely picked and culled out by the people themselves, for their great abilities and love of their country, to represent the wisdom of the whole nation. And that these two bodies made up the most august assembly in Europe; to whom, in conjunction with the prince, the whole legislature is committed.

I then descended to the courts of justice; over which the judges, those venerable sages and interpreters of the law, presided, for determining the disputed rights and properties of men, as well as for the punishment of vice and protection of innocence. I mentioned the prudent management of our treasury, the valour and achievements of our forces by sea and land. I computed the number of our people, by reckoning how many millions there might be of each religious sect, or political party, among us. I did not omit even our sports and pastimes, or any other particular which I thought might redound to the honour of my country. And I finished all with a brief historical account of affairs and events in England for about a hundred years past.

This conversation was not ended under five audiences, each of several hours; and the king heard the whole with great attention, frequently taking notes of what I spoke, as well as memorandums of what questions he intended to ask me.

When I had put an end to these long discourses, his majesty in a sixth audience, consulting his notes, proposed many doubts, queries, and objections upon every article. He asked : "What methods were used to cultivate the minds and bodies of our young nobility, and in what kind of business they commonly spent the first and teachable part of their lives? What course was taken to supply that assembly when any noble family became extinct? What qualifications were necessary in those who were to be created new lords; whether the humour of the prince, a sum of money to a court lady or a prime minister, or a design of strengthening a party opposite to the public interest, ever happened to be motives in those advancements? What share of knowledge those lords had in the laws of their country, and how they came by it, so as to enable them to decide the properties of their fellow-subjects in the last resort? Whether they were always so free from avarice, partialities, or want, that a bribe, or some other sinister view, could have no place among them? Whether those holy lords I spoke of were always promoted to that rank upon account of their knowledge in religious matters, and the sanctity of their lives; had never been compliers with the times while they were common priests; or slavish prostitute chaplains to some noblemen, whose opinions they continued servilely to follow after they were admitted into that assembly?"

He then desired to know "What arts were practised in electing those whom I called commoners. Whether a stranger, with a strong purse, might not influence the vulgar voters to choose him before their own landlord, or the most considerable gentleman in the neighbourhood? How it came to pass that people were so violently bent upon getting into this assembly, which I allowed to be a great trouble and expense, often to the ruin of their families, without any salary or pension, because this appeared such an exalted strain of virtue and public spirit, that his majesty seemed to doubt it might possibly not be always sincere?" And he desired to know "Whether such zealous gentlemen could have any views of refunding themselves for the charges and trouble they were at, by sacrificing the public good to the designs of a weak and vicious prince, in conjunction with a corrupted ministry?" He multiplied his questions, and sifted me thoroughly upon every part of this head; proposing numberless inquiries and objections which I think it not prudent or convenient to repeat.

Upon what I said in relation to our courts of justice, his majesty desired to be satisfied in several points: and this I was the better able to do, having been formerly almost ruined by a long suit in Chancery, which was decreed for me with costs. He asked: "What time was usually spent in determining between right and wrong, and what degree of expense? Whether advocates and orators had liberty to plead in causes manifestly known to be unjust, vexatious, or oppressive? Whether party in religion or politics were observed to be of any weight in the scale of justice? Whether those pleading orators were persons educated in the general knowledge of equity, or only in provincial, national, and other local customs? Whether they or their judges had any part in penning those laws which they assumed the liberty of interpreting and glossing upon at their pleasure? Whether they had ever, at different times, pleaded for and against the same cause, and cited precedents to prove contrary opinions? Whether they were a rich or a poor corporation? Whether they received any pecuniary reward for pleading or delivering their opinions? And, particularly, whether they were ever admitted as members in the lower senate?"

He fell next upon the management of our treasury; and said "He thought my memory had failed me, because I computed our taxes at about five or six millions a-year, and when I came to mention the issues, he found they sometimes amounted to more than double; for the notes he had taken were very particular in this point, because he hoped, as he told me, that the knowledge of our conduct might be useful to him, and he could not be deceived in his calculations. But, if what I told him were true, he was still at a loss how a kingdom could run out of its estate like a private person." He asked me "Who were our creditors, and where we found money to pay them?" He wondered to hear me talk of such chargeable and expensive wars; "that certainly we must be a quarrelsome people, or live among very bad neighbours, and that our generals must needs be richer than our kings." He asked "What business we had out of our own islands, unless upon the score of trade or treaty, or to defend the coasts with our fleet?" Above all, he was amazed to hear me talk of a mercenary standing army, in the midst of peace, and among a free people. He said: "If we were governed by our own consent, in the persons of our representatives, he could not imagine of whom we were afraid, or against whom we were to fight; and would hear my opinion, whether a private man's house might not better be defended by himself, his children, and family, than by half a dozen rascals picked up at a venture in the streets for small wages, who might get a hundred times more by cutting their throats?"

He laughed at my "odd kind of arithmetic," as he was pleased to call it, "in reckoning the numbers of our people by a computation drawn from the several sects among us in religion and politics." He said "He knew no reason why those who entertain opinions prejudicial to the public should be obliged to change, or should not be obliged to conceal them. And as it was tyranny in any government to require the first, so it was weakness not to enforce the second; for a man may be allowed to keep poisons in his closet, but not to vend them about for cordials."

He observed "That among the diversions of our nobility and gentry I had mentioned gaming: he desired to know, at what age this entertainment was usually taken up, and when it was laid down; how much of their time it employed; whether it ever went so high as to affect their fortunes; whether mean, vicious people, by their dexterity in that art, might not arrive at great riches, and sometimes keep our very nobles in dependence, as well as habituate them to vile companions, wholly take them from the improvement of their minds, and force them by the losses they received to learn and practise that infamous dexterity upon others."

He was perfectly astonished with the historical account I gave him of our affairs during the last century; protesting "It was only a heap of conspiracies, rebellions, murders, massacres, revolutions, banishments, the very worst effects that avarice, faction, hypocrisy, perfidiousness, cruelty, rage, madness, hatred, envy, lust, malice, and ambition, could produce."

His majesty, in another audience, was at the pains to recapitulate the sum of all I had spoken; compared the questions he made with the answers I had given; then taking me into his hands, and stroking me gently, delivered himself in these words, which I shall never forget, nor the manner he spoke them in : " My little friend Grildrig, you have made a most admirable panegyric upon your country; you have clearly proved that ignorance, idleness, and vice, are the proper ingredients for qualifying a legislator; that laws are best explained, interpreted, and applied, by those whose interest and abilities lie in perverting, confounding, and eluding them. I observe among you some lines of an institution which, in its original, might have been tolerable; but these half erased, and the rest wholly blurred and blotted by corruptions. It does not appear, from all you have said, how any one perfection is required toward the procurement of any one station among you; much less that men are ennobled on account of their virtue, that priests are advanced for their piety or learning, soldiers for their conduct or valour, judges for their integrity, senators for the love of their country, or counsellors for their wisdom. As for yourself," continued the king, "who have spent the greatest part of your life in travelling, I am well disposed to hope you may hitherto have escaped many vices of your country. But, by what I have gathered from your own relation, and the answers I have with much pains wringed and extorted from you, I cannot but conclude the bulk of your natives to be the most pernicious race of little odious vermin that nature ever suffered to crawl upon the surface of the earth." . . .

But great allowances should be given to a king who lives wholly secluded from the rest of the world, and must therefore be altogether unacquainted with the manners and customs that prevail in other nations: the want of which knowledge will ever produce many prejudices, and a certain narrowness of thinking, from which we, and the politer countries of Europe, are wholly exempted. And it would be hard indeed, if so remote a prince's notions of virtue and vice were to be offered as a standard for all mankind.

II

THE HUMOURS OF THE LAPUTIANS

At my alighting, I was surrounded with a crowd of people, but those who stood nearest seemed to be of better quality. They beheld me with all the marks and circumstances of wonder; neither indeed was I much in their debt, having never till then seen a race of mortals so singular in their shapes, habits, and countenances. Their heads were all reclined, either to the right or the left: one of their eyes turned inwards, and the other directly up to the zenith. Their outward garments were adorned with the figures of suns, moons, and stars, interwoven with those of fiddles, flutes, harps, trumpets, guitars, harpsichords, and many other instruments of music unknown to us in Europe. I observed here and there many in the habit of servants, with a blown bladder fastened like a flail to the end of a stick which they carried in their hands. In each bladder was a small quantity of dried pease, or little pebbles, as I was afterwards informed. With these bladders they now and then flapped the mouths and ears of those who stood near them, of which practice I could not then conceive the meaning. It seems the minds of these people are so taken up with intense speculations, that they neither can speak, nor attend to the discourses of others, without being roused by some external taction upon the organs of speech and hearing; for which reason, those persons who are able to afford it always keep a flapper (the original is *climenole*,) in their family, as one of their domestics, nor ever walk abroad or make visits without him. And the business of this officer is, when two, three, or more persons are in company, gently to strike with his bladder the mouth of him who is to speak, and the right ear of him or them to whom the speaker addresses himself. This flapper is likewise employed diligently to attend his master in his walks, and upon occasion to give him a soft flap on his eyes, because he is always so wrapped up in cogitation, that he is in manifest danger of falling down every precipice, and bouncing his head against every post: and in the streets of justling others or being justled himself into the kennel.

It was necessary to give the reader this information, without which he would be at the same loss with me to understand the proceedings of these people, as they conducted me up the stairs to the top of the island, and from thence to the royal palace. While we were ascending they forgot several times what they were about, and left me to myself, till their memories were again roused by their flappers; for they appeared altogether unmoved by the sight of my foreign habit and countenance, and by the shouts of the vulgar, whose thoughts and minds were more disengaged.

At last we entered the palace, and proceeded into the chamber of presence, where I saw the king seated on his throne, attended on each side by persons of prime quality. Before the throne was a large table filled with globes, and spheres, and mathematical instruments of all kinds. His majesty took not the least notice of us, although our entrance was not without sufficient noise, by the concourse of all persons belonging to the court. But he was then deep in a problem, and we attended at least an hour, before he could solve it. There stood by him on each side a young page with flaps in their hands, and when they saw he was at leisure, one of them gently struck his mouth, and the other his right ear; at which he startled like one awaked on the sudden, and, looking towards me and the company I was in, recollected the occasion of our coming, whereof he had been informed before. He spoke some words, whereupon immediately a young man with a flap came up to my side, and flapped me gently on the right ear; but I made signs as well as I could that I had no occasion for such an instrument; which, as I afterwards found, gave his majesty and the whole court a very mean opinion of my understanding. The king, as far as I could conjecture, asked me several questions, and I addressed myself to him in all the languages I had. When it was found I could neither understand nor be understood, I was conducted by his order to an apartment in his palace, (this prince being distinguished above all his predecessors for his hospitality to strangers,) where two servants were appointed to attend me. My dinner was brought, and four persons of quality, whom I remembered to have seen very near the king's person, did me the honour to dine with me. We had two courses, of three dishes each. In the first course there was a shoulder of mutton cut into an equilateral triangle, a piece of beef into a rhomboides, and a pudding into a cycloid. The second course was two ducks trussed up in the form of fiddles, sausages and puddings resembling flutes and hautboys, and a breast of veal in the shape of a harp. The servants cut our bread into cones, cylinders, parallelograms, and several other mathematical figures. . . .

Those to whom the king had entrusted me observing how ill I was clad, ordered a tailor to come next morning and take measure for a suit of clothes. This operator did his office after a different manner from those of his trade in Europe. He first took my altitude by a quadrant, and then with rule and compasses described the dimensions and outlines of my whole body; all which he entered upon paper, and in six days brought my clothes, very ill made, and quite out of shape, by happening to mistake a figure in the calculation. But my comfort was that I observed such accidents very frequent and little regarded.

THE ACADEMY OF LAGADO

This academy is not an entire single building, but a continuation of several houses on both sides of a street, which, growing waste, was purchased and applied to that use.

I was received very kindly by the warden, and went for many days to the academy. Every room has in it one or more projectors; and I believe I could not be in fewer than five hundred rooms.

The first man I saw was of a meagre aspect, with sooty hands and face, his hair and beard long, ragged, and singed in several places. His clothes, shirt, and skin, were all of the same colour. He had been eight years upon a project for extracting sun-beams out of cucumbers, which were to be put in phials hermetically sealed, and let out to warm the air in raw inclement summers. He told me he did not doubt that in eight years more he should be able to supply the governor's gardens with sunshine at a reasonable rate; but he complained that his stock was low, and entreated me to give him "something as an encouragement to ingenuity, especially since this had been a very dear season for cucumbers." I made him a small present, for my lord had furnished me with money on purpose, because he knew their practice of begging from all who go to see them. . . .

There was a most ingenious architect, who had contrived a new method for building houses, by beginning at the roof and working downward to the foundation; which he justified to me by the like practice of those two prudent insects, the bee and the spider.

There was a man born blind, who had several apprentices in his own condition: their employment was to mix colours for painters, which their master taught them to distinguish by feeling and smelling. It was indeed my misfortune to find them at that time not very perfect in their lessons, and the professor himself happened to be generally mistaken. This artist is much encouraged and esteemed by the whole fraternity.

In another apartment, I was highly pleased with a projector who had found a device of ploughing the ground with hogs, to save the charges of ploughs, cattle, and labour. The method is this: In an acre of ground, you bury, at six inches' distance and eight deep, a quantity of acorns, dates, chestnuts, and other mast or vegetables whereof these animals are fondest; then you drive six hundred or more of them into the field, where in a few days they will root up the whole ground in search of their food, and make it fit for sowing; it is true, upon experiment they found the charge and trouble very great, and they had little or no crop. However, it is not doubted that this invention may be capable of great improvement. . . .

We next went to the school of languages, where three professors sat in consultation upon improving that of their own country.

The first project was to shorten discourse, by cutting polysyllables into one, and leaving out verbs and participles, because, in reality all things imaginable are but nouns.

The other project was a scheme for entirely abolishing all words whatsoever, and this was urged as a great advantage in point of health, as well as brevity. For it is plain, that every word we speak is, in some degree, a diminution of our lungs by corrosion, and consequently contributes to the shortening of our lives. An expedient was therefore offered, "that since words are only names for things, it would be more convenient for all men to carry about them such things as were necessary to express a particular business they are to discourse on." And this invention would certainly have taken place, to the great ease as well as health of the subject, if the women, in conjunction with the vulgar and illiterate, had not threatened to raise a rebellion, unless they might be allowed the liberty to speak with their tongues, after the manner of their forefathers; such constant irreconcilable enemies to science are the common people. However, many of the most learned and wise adhere to the new scheme of expressing themselves by things, which has only this inconvenience attending it, that if a man's business be very great, and of various kinds, he must be obliged in proportion to carry a greater bundle of things upon his back, unless he can afford one or two strong servants to attend him. I have often beheld two of these sages almost sinking under the weight of their packs, like pedlars among us; who, when they meet in the street, would lay down their loads, open their sacks, and hold conversation for an hour together, then put up their implements, help each other to resume their burdens, and take their leave.

But for short conversations, a man may carry implements in his pockets, and under his arms, enough to supply him: and in his house he cannot be at a loss. Therefore the room where company meet who practise this art is full of all things ready at hand, requisite to furnish matter for this kind of artificial converse.

Another great advantage proposed by this invention was, that it would serve as a universal language to be understood in all civilized nations, whose goods and utensils are generally of the same kind, or nearly resembling, so that their uses might easily be comprehended. And thus ambassadors would be qualified to treat with foreign princes, or ministers of state, to whose tongues they were utter strangers. . . .

In the school of political projectors I was but ill entertained; the professors appearing, in my judgment, wholly out of their senses; which is a scene that never fails to make me melancholy. These unhappy people were proposing schemes for persuading monarchs to choose favourites upon the score of their wisdom, capacity, and virtue; of teaching ministers to consult the public good; of rewarding merit, great abilities, and eminent services; of instructing princes to know their true interest, by placing it on the same foundation with that of their people; of choosing for employments persons qualified to exercise them; with many other wild impossible chimeras, that never entered before into the heart of man to conceive; and confirmed in me the old observation, "That there is nothing so extravagant and irrational, which some philosophers have not maintained for truth."

But, however, I shall so far do justice to this part of the academy, as to acknowledge that all of them were not so visionary. There was a most ingenious doctor who seemed to be perfectly versed in the whole nature and system of government. This illustrious person had very usefully employed his studies in finding out effectual remedies for all diseases and corruptions to which the several kinds of public administration are subject, by the vices or infirmities of those who govern, as well as by the licentiousness of those who are to obey. For instance, whereas all writers and reasoners have agreed that there is a strict universal resemblance between the natural and the political body; can there be anything more evident than that the health of both must be preserved, and the diseases cured, by the same prescriptions? It is allowed, that senates and great councils are often troubled with redundant, ebullient, and other peccant humours; with many diseases of the head, and more of the heart; with strong convulsions, with grievous contractions of the nerves and sinews in both hands, but especially the right; with spleen, flatus, vertigoes, and deliriums; with scrofulous tumours, full of fetid purulent matter; with sour frothy ructations; with canine appetites, and crudeness of digestion, besides many others needless to mention. This doctor, therefore, proposed, that "Upon the meeting of the senate certain physicians should attend at the three first days of their sitting, and at the close of each day's debate feel the pulses of every senator; after which, having maturely considered and consulted upon the nature of the several maladies and the methods of cure, they should, on the fourth day, return to the senate-house, attended by their apothecaries stored with proper medicines; and, before the members sat, administer to each of them lenitives, aperitives, abstersives, corrosives, restringents, palliatives, laxatives, cephalalgics, icterics, apophlegmatics, acoustics, as their several cases required ; and, according as these medicines should operate, repeat, alter, or omit them at the next meeting."

This project could not be of any great expense to the public, and might, in my poor opinion, be of much use for the despatch of business, in those countries where senates have any share in the legislative power ; beget unanimity, shorten debates, open a few mouths which are now closed, and close many more which are now open ; curb the petulancy of the young, and correct the positiveness of the old ; rouse the stupid, and damp the pert.

Again : because it is a general complaint that the favourites of princes are troubled with short and weak memories, the same doctor proposed "That whoever attended a first minister, after having told his business with the utmost brevity and in the plainest words, should at his departure give the said minister a tweak by the nose, or a kick on the belly, or tread on his corns, or lug him thrice by both ears, or run a pin into his breech, or pinch his arm black and blue, to prevent forgetfulness : and at every levee day repeat the same operation, till the business were done, or absolutely refused."

He likewise directed, "That every senator in the great council of a nation, after he had delivered his opinion, and argued in the defence of it, should be obliged to give his vote directly contrary ; because, if that were done, the result would infallibly terminate in the good of the public."

When parties in a state are violent, he offered a wonderful contrivance to reconcile them. The method is this: you take a hundred leaders of each party; you dispose them into couples of such whose heads are nearest of a size; then let two nice operators saw off the occiput of each couple at the same time, in such a manner that the brain may be equally divided. Let the occiputs thus cut off be interchanged, applying each to the head of his opposite party-man. It seems, indeed, to be a work that requires some exactness; but the professor assured us "That if it were dexterously performed, the cure would be infallible." For he argued thus: "That the two half brains, being left to debate the matter between themselves within the space of one skull, would soon come to a good understanding, and produce that moderation, as well as regularity of thinking, so much to be wished for in the heads of those who imagine they come into the world only to watch and govern its motion: and as to the difference of brains, in quantity or quality, among those who are directors in faction," the doctor assured us, from his own knowledge, "that it was a perfect trifle."

I heard a very warm debate between two professors, about the most commodious and effectual ways and means of raising money without grieving the subject. The first affirmed "The justest method would be, to lay a certain tax upon vices and folly; and the sum fixed upon every man to be rated, after the fairest manner, by a jury of his neighbours." The second was of an opinion directly contrary: "to tax those qualities of body and mind for which men chiefly value themselves; the rate to be more or less according to the degrees of excelling; the decision whereof should be left entirely to their own breast." The highest tax was upon men who are the greatest favourites of the other sex, and the assessments according to the number and nature of the favours they have received; for which they are allowed to be their own vouchers. Wit, valour, and politeness, were likewise proposed to be largely taxed, and collected in the same manner, by every person's giving his own word for the quantum of what he possessed. But as to honour, justice, wisdom and learning, they should not be taxed at all; because they are qualifications of so singular a kind, that no man will either allow them in his neighbour, or value them in himself.

The women were proposed to be taxed according to their beauty and skill in dressing; wherein they had the same privilege with the men, to be determined by their own judgment. But constancy, good sense, and good nature, were not rated, because they would not bear the charge of collecting.

To keep senators in the interest of the crown, it was proposed that the members should raffle for employments; every man first taking an oath and giving security that he would vote for the court, whether he won or not; after which, the losers had, in their turn, the liberty of raffling upon the next vacancy. Thus hope and expectation would be kept alive; none would complain of broken promises, but impute their disappointments wholly to fortune, whose shoulders are broader and stronger than those of a ministry.

A PARTICULAR ACCOUNT OF THE STRULDBRUGS

ONE day, in much good company, I was asked by a person of quality "Whether I had seen any of their *struldbrugs*, or immortals." I said "I had not;" and desired he would explain to me "what he meant by such an appellation applied to a mortal creature." He told me "That sometimes, though very rarely, a child happened to be born in a family with a red circular spot in the forehead, directly over the left eyebrow, which was an infallible mark that it should never die. The spot," as he described it, "was about the compass of a silver threepence, but in the course of time grew larger, and changed its colour; for at twelve years old it became green, so continued till five-and-twenty, then turning to a deep blue; at five-and-forty it grew coal-black, and as large as an English shilling, but never admitted any farther alteration." He said "These births were so rare, that he did not believe that there could be above eleven hundred *struldbrugs*, of both sexes, in the whole kingdom, of which he computed above fifty in the metropolis, and among the rest a young girl born about three years ago; that these productions were not peculiar to any family, but a mere effect of chance ; and the children of the *struldbrugs* themselves were equally mortal with the rest of the people." . . .

He said "They commonly acted like mortals, till about thirty years old, after which by degrees they grew melancholy and dejected, increasing in both till they came to fourscore. This he learned from their own confession : for otherwise, there not being above two or three of that species born in an age, they were too few to form a general observation by. When they came to fourscore years, which is reckoned the extremity of living in this country, they had not only all the follies and infirmities of other old men, but many more which arose from the dreadful prospect of never dying. They were not only opinionative, peevish, covetous, morose, vain, talkative, but incapable of friendship, and dead to all natural affection, which never descended below their grandchildren. Envy and impotent desires are their prevailing passions. But those objects against which their envy seems principally directed, are the vices of the younger sort, and the deaths of the old. By reflecting on the former, they find themselves cut off from all possibility of pleasure ; and whenever they see a funeral, they lament and repine that others are gone to a harbour of rest to which they themselves never can hope to arrive. They have no remembrance of anything but what they learned and observed in their youth and middle age ; and even that is very imperfect. And for the truth or particulars of any fact, it is safer to depend on common tradition, than upon their best recollections. The least miserable among them appear to be those who turn to dotage and entirely lose their memories; these meet with more pity and assistance, because they want many bad qualities which abound in others.

"If a *struldbrug* happen to marry one of his own kind, the marriage is dissolved of course, by the courtesy of the kingdom, as soon as the younger of the two comes to be fourscore. For the law thinks it a reasonable indulgence that those who are condemned, without any fault of their own, to a perpetual continuance in the world, should not have their misery doubled by the load of a wife.

"As soon as they have completed the term of eighty years, they are looked on as dead in law; their heirs immediately succeed to their estates; only a small pittance is reserved for their support; and the poor ones are maintained at the public charge. After that period they are held incapable of any employment of trust or profit; they cannot purchase lands or take leases; neither are they allowed to be witnesses in any cause either civil or criminal, not even for the decision of meers and bounds.

"At ninety they lose their teeth and hair; they have at that age no distinction of taste, but eat and drink whatever they can get, without relish or appetite. The diseases they were subject to still continue, without increasing or diminishing. In talking they forget the common appellation of things, and the names of persons, even of those who are their nearest friends and relations. For the same reason they never can amuse themselves with reading, because their memory will not serve to carry them from the beginning of a sentence to the end; and by this defect they are deprived of the only entertainment whereof they might otherwise be capable.

"The language of this country being always upon the flux, the *struldbrugs* of one age do not understand those of another; neither are they able, after two hundred years, to hold any conversation, farther than by a few general words, with their neighbours the mortals; and thus they lie under the disadvantage of living like foreigners in their own country."

This was the account given me of the *struldbrugs*, as near as I can remember. I afterwards saw five or six of different ages, the youngest not above two hundred years old, who were brought to me at several times by some of my friends; but although they were told "That I was a great traveller, and had seen all the world," they had not the least curiosity to ask me a question; only desired "I would give them *slumskudask*, or a token of remembrance;" which is a modest way of begging, to avoid the law, that strictly forbids it, because they are provided for by the public, although indeed with a very scanty allowance.

They are despised and hated by all sorts of people. When one of them is born, it is reckoned ominous, and their birth is recorded very particularly; so that you may know their age by consulting the register, which however has not been kept above a thousand years past, or at least has been destroyed by time or public disturbances. But the usual way of computing how old they are, is by asking them what kings or great persons they can remember, and then consulting history; for infallibly the last prince in their mind did not begin his reign after they were fourscore years old.

They were the most mortifying sight I ever beheld; and the women more horrible than the men. Besides the usual deformities in extreme old age, they acquired an additional ghastliness, in proportion to their number of years, which is not to be described ; and among half a dozen, I soon distinguished which was the eldest, although there was not above a century or two between them

THE GRAY HOUYHNHNM

THE horse started a little when he came near me, but soon recovering himself, looked full in my face with manifest tokens of wonder. He viewed my hands and feet, walking round me several times. I would have pursued my journey, but he placed himself directly in the way, yet looking with very mild aspect, never offering the least violence. We stood gazing at each other for some time; at last I took the boldness to reach my hand towards his neck, with a design to stroke it, using the common style and whistle of jockeys when they are going to handle a strange horse. But this animal seemed to receive my civilities with disdain, shook his head and bent his brows, softly raising up his right fore-foot to remove my hand. Then he neighed three or four times, but in so different a cadence, that I almost began to think he was speaking to himself in some language of his own.

While he and I were thus employed, another horse came up; who applying himself to the first in a very formal manner, they gently struck each other's right hoof before, neighing several times by turns, and varying the sound, which seemed to be almost articulate. They went some paces off, as if it were to confer together, walking side by side, backward and forward, like persons deliberating upon some affair of weight, but often turning their eyes towards me, as it were to watch that I might not·escape. I was amazed to see such actions and behaviour in brute beasts, and concluded with myself, that if the inhabitants of this country were endued with a proportionable degree of reason, they must needs be the wisest people upon earth. This thought gave me so much comfort, that I resolved to go forward until I could discover some house or village, or meet with any of the natives, leaving the two horses to discourse together as they pleased. But the first, who was a dapple gray, observing me to steal off, neighed after me in so expressive a tone, that I fancied myself to understand what he meant; whereupon I turned back and came near him, to expect his farther commands; but concealing my fear as much as I could, for I began to be in some pain how this adventure might terminate: and the reader will easily believe I did not much like my present situation.

The two horses came up close to me, looking with great earnestness upon my face and hands. The gray steed rubbed my hat all round with his right fore-hoof, and discomposed it so much, that I was forced to adjust it better by taking it off and settling it again; whereat both he and his companion, who was a brown bay, appeared to be much surprised: the latter felt the lappet of my coat, and finding it to hang loose about me, they both looked with new signs of wonder. He stroked my right hand, seeming to admire the softness and colour; but he squeezed it so hard between his hoof and his pastern, that I was forced to roar; after which, they both touched it with all possible tenderness. They were under great perplexity about my shoes and stockings, which they felt very often, neighing to each other, and using various gestures, not unlike those of a philosopher when he would attempt to solve some new and difficult phenomenon.

Upon the whole, the behaviour of these animals was so orderly and rational, so acute and judicious, that I at last concluded they must needs be magicians who had thus metamorphosed themselves upon some design, and, seeing a stranger in the way, resolved to divert themselves with him; or perhaps were really amazed at the sight of a man so very different in habit, feature, and complexion, from those who might probably live in so remote a climate. Upon the strength of this reasoning, I ventured to address them in the following manner : " Gentlemen, if you be conjurors, as I have good cause to believe, you can understand my language; therefore I make bold to let your worships know that I am a poor distressed Englishman, driven by his misfortunes upon your coast; and I entreat one of you to let me ride upon his back, as if he were a real horse, to some house or village where I can be relieved. In return of which favour, I will make you a present of this knife and bracelet " (taking them out of my pocket). The two creatures stood silent while I spoke, seeming to listen with great attention; and when I had ended they neighed frequently towards each other, as if they were engaged in serious conversation. I plainly observed that their language expressed the passions very well; and the words might, with little pains, be resolved into an alphabet more easily than the Chinese.

I could frequently distinguish the word *Yahoo*, which was repeated by each of them several times;

and although it was impossible for me to conjecture what it meant, yet, while the two horses were busy in conversation, I endeavoured to practise this word upon my tongue; and, as soon as they were silent, I boldly pronounced *Yahoo* in a loud voice, imitating at the same time, as near as I could, the neighing of a horse; at which they were both visibly surprised, and the gray repeated the same word twice, as if he meant to teach me the right accent; wherein I spoke after him as well as I could, and found myself perceivably to improve every time, though very far from any degree of perfection. Then the bay tried me with a second word much harder to be pronounced, but reducing it to the English orthography, may be spelt thus, *Houyhnhnm*. I did not succeed in this so well as in the former: but after two or three farther trials I had better fortune, and they both appeared amazed at my capacity.

After some farther discourse, which I then conjectured might relate to me, the two friends took their leaves with the same compliment of striking each other's hoof, and the gray made me signs that I should walk before him; wherein I thought it prudent to comply, till I could find a better director. When I offered to slacken my pace, he would cry *hhuun hhuun*. I guessed his meaning, and gave him to understand as well as I could, "that I was weary, and not able to walk faster;" upon which he would stand a while to let me rest.

Having travelled about three miles, we came to a long kind of building made of timber stuck in the ground and wattled across; the roof was low and covered with straw. I now began to be a little comforted, and took out some toys which travellers usually carry for presents to the savage Indians of America and other parts, in hopes the people of the house would be thereby encouraged to receive me kindly. The horse made me a sign to go in first. It was a large room, with a smooth clay floor, and a rack and manger extending the whole length on one side. There were three nags and two mares, not eating, but some of them sitting down upon their hams; which I very much wondered at, but wondered more to see the rest employed in domestic business: these seemed but ordinary cattle. However, this confirmed my first opinion, that a people who could so far civilize brute animals must needs excel in wisdom all the nations of the world. The gray came in just after, and thereby prevented any ill treatment which the others might have given me. He neighed to them several times in a style of authority, and received answers.

Beyond this room there were three others reaching the length of the house, to which you passed through three doors, opposite to each other, in the manner of a vista. We went through the second room towards the third. Here the gray walked in first, beckoning me to attend: I waited in the second room, and got ready my presents for the master and mistress of the house; they were two knives, three bracelets of false pearl, a small looking-glass, and a bead necklace. The horse neighed three or four times, and I waited to hear some answers in a human voice; but I heard no other returns than in the same dialect, only one or two a little shriller than his. I began to think that this house must belong to some person of great note among them, because there appeared so much ceremony before I could gain admittance. But that a man of quality should be served all by horses, was beyond my comprehension. I feared my brain was disturbed by my sufferings and misfortunes. I roused myself, and looked about me in the room where I was left alone ; this was furnished like the first, only after a more elegant manner. I rubbed my eyes often, but the same objects still occurred : I pinched my arms and sides to awake myself, hoping I might be in a dream. I then absolutely concluded that all these appearances could be nothing else but necromancy and magic. But I had no time to pursue these reflections, for the gray horse came to the door, and made me a sign to follow him into the third room ; where I saw a very comely mare, together with a colt and foal, sitting on their haunches upon mats of straw not unartfully made, and perfectly neat and clean.

The mare, soon after my entrance, rose from her mat, and coming up close, after having nicely observed my hands and face, gave me a most contemptuous look ; and turning to the horse, I heard the word *Yahoo* often repeated betwixt them, the meaning of which word I could not then comprehend, although it was the first I had learned to pronounce. But I was soon better informed, to my everlasting mortification ; for the horse beckoning to me with his head, and repeating the *hhuun, hhuun,* as he did upon the road, which I understood was to attend him, led me out into a kind of court where was another building at some distance from the house. Here we entered, and I saw three detestable creatures, feeding upon roots and the flesh of some animals, which I afterwards found to be that of asses and dogs and now and then a cow dead by accident or disease. They were all tied by the neck with strong withes fastened to a beam ; they held their food between the claws of their fore-feet, and tore it with their teeth.

The master horse ordered a sorrel nag, one of his servants, to untie the largest of these animals, and take him into the yard. The beast and I were brought close together, and our countenances diligently compared both by master and servant, who thereupon repeated several times the word *Yahoo.* My horror and astonishment are not to be described, when I observed in this abominable animal a perfect human figure : the face of it indeed was flat and broad, the nose depressed, the lips large, and the mouth wide ; but these differences are common to all savage nations, where the lineaments of the countenance are distorted by the natives suffering their infants to lie grovelling on the earth, or by carrying them on their backs nuzzling with their face against the mother's shoulders. The fore-feet of the *Yahoo* differed from my hands in nothing else but the length of the nails, the coarseness and brownness of the palms, and the hairiness on the backs. There was the same resemblance between our feet, with the same differences, which I knew very well, though the horses did not, because of my shoes and stockings ; the same in every part of our bodies, except as to hairiness and colour, which I have already described.

THE VIRTUES OF THE HOUYHNHNMS

HAVING lived three years in this country, the reader, I suppose, will expect that I should, like other travellers, give him some account of the manners and customs of its inhabitants, which it was indeed my principal study to learn.

As these noble *Houyhnhnms* are endowed by nature with a general disposition to all virtues, and have no conceptions or ideas of what is evil in a rational creature, so their grand maxim is to cultivate reason and to be wholly governed by it. Neither is reason among them a point problematical, as with us, where men can argue with plausibility on both sides of the question; but strikes you with immediate conviction, as it must needs do where it is not mingled, obscured, or discoloured, by passion and interest. I remember it was with extreme difficulty that I could bring my master to understand the meaning of the word *opinion*, or how a point could be disputable; because reason taught us to affirm or deny only where we are certain; and beyond our knowledge we cannot do either: so that controversies, wranglings, disputes, and positiveness, in false or dubious propositions, are evils unknown among the *Houyhnhnms*. In the like manner, when I used to explain to him our several systems of natural philosophy, he would laugh "that a creature pretending to reason should value itself upon the knowledge of other people's conjectures, and in things where that knowledge, if it were certain, could be of no use." Wherein he agreed entirely with the sentiments of Socrates, as Plato delivers them; which I mention as the highest honour I can do to that prince of philosophers. I have often since reflected what destruction such doctrine would make in the libraries of Europe, and how many paths to fame would be then shut up in the learned world.

Friendship and benevolence are the two principal virtues among the *Houyhnhnms;* and these not confined to particular objects, but universal to the whole race: for a stranger from the remotest part is equally treated with the nearest neighbour, and, wherever he goes, looks upon himself as at home. They preserve decency and civility in the highest degrees, but are altogether ignorant of ceremony. They have no fondness for their colts or foals, but the care they take in educating them proceeds entirely from the dictates of reason. And I observed my master to show the same affection to his neighbour's issue, that he had for his own. They will have it that nature teaches them to love the whole species, and it is reason only that makes a distinction of persons where there is a superior degree of virtue.

When the matron *Houyhnhnms* have produced one of each sex, they no longer accompany with their consorts, except they lose one of their issue by some casualty, which very seldom happens. This caution is necessary to prevent the country from being overburdened with numbers. But the race of inferior

Houyhnhnms, bred up to be servants, is not so strictly limited upon this article; these are allowed to produce three of each sex, to be domestics in the noble families.

In their marriages they are exactly careful to choose such colours as will not make any disagreeable mixture in the breed. Strength is chiefly valued in the male, and comeliness in the female; not upon the account of love, but to preserve the race from degenerating; for where a female happens to excel in strength, a consort is chosen with regard to comeliness.

Courtship, love, presents, jointures, settlements, have no place in their thoughts, or terms whereby to express them in their language. The young couple meet and are joined, merely because it is the determination of their parents and friends; it is what they see done every day, and they look upon it as one of the necessary actions of a reasonable being. But the violation of marriage, or any other unchastity, was never heard of; and the married pair pass their lives with the same friendship and mutual benevolence that they bear to all others of the same species who come in their way, without jealousy, fondness, quarrelling, or discontent.

In educating the youth of both sexes, their method is admirable, and highly deserves our imitation. These are not suffered to taste a grain of oats, except upon certain days, till eighteen years old; nor milk, but very rarely; and in summer they graze two hours in the morning, and as many in the evening, which their parents likewise observe: but the servants are not allowed above half that time, and a great part of their grass is brought home, which they eat at the most convenient hours, when they can be best spared from work.

Temperance, industry, exercise, and cleanliness, are the lessons equally enjoined to the young ones of both sexes; and my master thought it monstrous in us to give the females a different kind of education from the males, except in articles of domestic management; whereby, as he truly observed, one half of our natives were good for nothing but bringing children into the world; and to trust the care of our children to such useless animals, he said, was yet a greater instance of brutality.

ENGLISH POLITICAL
TRACTS.

The *Examiner*, a weekly political broadside of the same size as the *Tatler*, was started by St. John in 1710 as the organ of the Tory party, but at first with small success. "Addison had brought into the field his *Whig Examiner* with such damaging effect that the ministry were in ill case if better advocacy for them could not be found." Then Swift undertook the defence, and thirty-three consecutive *Examiners*, from the fourteenth (Nov. 2, 1710) to the forty-sixth (June 14th 1711), inclusive, were written by him. They were the "leading articles" of the day, and provided for the first time a statesmanlike exposition of the ministerial policy.

The Conduct of the Allies was written and published in Nov. 1711. This tract was intended to make Marlborough unpopular and prepare the way for a peace, by opening the eyes of the people to the cost of the war, the venality of the General and of the Allies, and the interested motives of its upholders, the "monied men;" and by showing how other powers were profiting at England's expense. It produced a tremendous effect. "The people, who had been amused with bonfires and triumphal processions, and looked with idolatry on the general and his friends, who, as they thought, had made England the arbitress of nations, were confounded between shame and rage, when they found that 'mines had been exhausted and millions destroyed,' to secure the Dutch, or aggrandize the emperor, without any advantage to ourselves; that we had been bribing our neighbours to fight their own quarrel; and that amongst our enemies we might number our allies."—*Johnson*. The extract here given, which forms but a tenth part of the tract, occurs near the end. Swift has urged his three-headed indictment against the war party and the Allies, and proceeds to show to what a pass the country has been brought by their policy.

THE EXAMINER

No. 15.

THURSDAY, NOVEMBER 9, 1710.

*E quibus hi vacuas implent sermonibus aures,
Hi narrata ferunt alio : mensuraque ficti
Crescit, et auditis aliquid novus adjicit auctor.
Illic Credulitas, illic temerarius Error,
Vanaque Lætitia est, consternatique Timores,
Seditioque recens, dubioque auctore Susurri.*

With idle tales this fills our empty ears ;
The next reports what from the first he hears :
The rolling fictions grow in strength and size,
Each author adding to the former lies.
Here vain credulity, with new desires,
Leads us astray, and groundless joy inspires ;
The dubious whispers tumults fresh design'd,
And chilling fears astound the anxious mind.

I AM prevailed on, through the importunity of friends, to interrupt the scheme I had begun in my last paper, by an Essay upon the Art of Political Lying. We are told the devil is the father of lies, and was a liar from the beginning ; so that, beyond contradiction, the invention is old : and, which is more, his first Essay of it was purely political, employed in undermining the authority of his prince, and seducing a third part of the subjects from their obedience: for which he was driven down from heaven, where (as Milton expresses it) he had been viceroy of a great western province; and forced to exercise his talent in inferior regions among other fallen spirits, poor or deluded men, whom he still daily tempts to his own sin, and will ever do so, till he be chained in the bottomless pit.

But although the devil be the father of lies, he seems, like other great inventors, to have lost much of his reputation by the continual improvements that have been made upon him.

Who first reduced lying into an art, and adapted it to politics, is not so clear from history, although I have made some diligent inquiries. I shall therefore consider it only according to the modern system, as it has been cultivated these twenty years past in the southern part of our own island.

The poets tell us that, after the giants were overthrown by the gods, the earth in revenge produced her last offspring, which was Fame. And the fable is thus interpreted: that when tumults and seditions are quieted, rumours and false reports are plentifully spread through a nation. So that, by this account, lying is the last relief of a routed, earth-born, rebellious party in a state. But here the moderns have made great additions, applying this art to the gaining of power and preserving it, as well as revenging themselves after they have lost it; as the same instruments are made use of by animals to feed themselves when they are hungry, and to bite those that tread upon them.

But the same genealogy cannot always be admitted

for political lying; I shall therefore desire to refine upon it, by adding some circumstances of its birth and parents. A political lie is sometimes born out of a discarded statesman's head, and thence delivered to be nursed and dandled by the rabble. Sometimes it is produced a monster, and licked into shape: at other times it comes into the world completely formed, and is spoiled in the licking. It is often born an infant in the regular way, and requires time to mature it; and often it sees the light in its full growth, but dwindles away by degrees. Sometimes it is of noble birth, and sometimes the spawn of a stock-jobber. Here it screams aloud at the opening of the womb, and there it is delivered with a whisper. I know a lie that now disturbs half the kingdom with its noise, [of] which, although too proud and great at present to own its parents, I can remember its whisperhood. To conclude the nativity of this monster; when it comes into the world without a sting it is still-born; and whenever it loses its sting it dies.

No wonder if an infant so miraculous in its birth should be destined for great adventures; and accordingly we see it has been the guardian spirit of a prevailing party for almost twenty years. It can conquer kingdoms without fighting, and sometimes with the loss of a battle. It gives and resumes employments; can sink a mountain to a mole-hill, and raise a mole-hill to a mountain; has presided for many years at committees of elections; can wash a blackmoor white; make a saint of an atheist, and a patriot of a profligate; can furnish foreign ministers with intelligence, and raise or let fall the credit of the nation. This goddess flies with a huge looking-glass in her hands, to dazzle the crowd, and make them see, according as she turns it, their ruin in their interest, and their interest in their ruin. In this glass you will behold your best friends, clad in coats powdered with *fleurs de lis* and triple crowns; their girdles hung round with chains, and beads, and wooden shoes; and your worst enemies adorned with the ensigns of liberty, property, indulgence, moderation, and a cornucopia in their hands. Her large wings, like those of a flying-fish, are of no use but while they are moist; she therefore dips them in mud, and, soaring aloft, scatters it in the eyes of the multitude, flying with great swiftness; but at every turn is forced to stoop in dirty ways for new supplies.

I have been sometimes thinking, if a man had the art of the second sight for seeing lies, as they have in Scotland for seeing spirits, how admirably he might entertain himself in this town, by observing the different shapes, sizes, and colours of those swarms of lies which buzz about the heads of some people, like flies about a horse's ears in summer; or those legions hovering every afternoon in Exchange-alley, enough to darken the air; or over a club of discontented grandees, and thence sent down in cargoes to be scattered at elections.

There is one essential point wherein a political liar differs from others of the faculty, that he ought to have but a short memory, which is necessary according to the various occasions he meets with every hour of differing from himself and swearing to both sides of a contradiction, as he finds the persons disposed with whom he has to deal. In describing the virtues and vices of mankind, it is convenient, upon every article, to have some eminent person in our eye, from whom we copy our description. I have strictly observed this rule, and my imagination this minute represents before me a certain great man famous for this talent, to the constant practice of which he owes his twenty years' reputation of the most skilful head in England for the management of nice affairs. The superiority of his genius consists in nothing else but an inexhaustible fund of political lies, which he plentifully distributes every minute he speaks, and by an unparalleled generosity forgets, and consequently contradicts, the next half-hour. He never yet considered whether any proposition were true or false, but whether it were convenient for the present minute or company to affirm or deny it; so that, if you think fit to refine upon him by interpreting everything he says, as we do dreams, by the contrary, you are still to seek, and will find yourself equally deceived whether you believe or not: the only remedy is to suppose that you have heard some inarticulate sounds, without any meaning at all; and besides, that will take off the horror you might be apt to conceive at the oaths wherewith he perpetually tags both ends of every proposition; although, at the same time, I think he cannot with any justice be taxed with perjury when he invokes God and Christ, because he has often fairly given public notice to the world that he believes in neither.

Some people may think that such an accomplishment as this can be of no great use to the owner, or his party, after it has been often practised and is become notorious; but they are widely mistaken. Few lies carry the inventor's mark, and the most prostitute enemy to truth may spread a thousand without being known for the author: besides, as the vilest writer has his readers, so the greatest liar has his believers; and it often happens that, if a lie be believed only for an hour, it has done its work, and there is no farther occasion for it. Falsehood flies, and truth comes limping after it, so that when men come to be undeceived it is too late; the jest is over, and the tale has had its effect: like a man who has thought of a good repartee when the discourse is changed or the company parted; or like a physician who has found out an infallible medicine after the patient is dead.

Considering that natural disposition in many men to lie, and in multitudes to believe, I have been perplexed what to do with that maxim so frequent in everybody's mouth, that truth will at last prevail. Here has this island of ours, for the greatest part of twenty years, lain under the influence of such counsels and persons, whose principle and interest it was to corrupt our manners, blind our understanding, drain our wealth, and in time destroy our constitution both in church and state, and we at last were brought to the very brink of ruin; yet, by the means of perpetual misrepresentations, have never been able to distinguish between our enemies and friends. We have seen a great part of the nation's money got into the hands of those who, by their birth, education, and merit, could pretend no higher than to wear our liveries; while others, who, by their credit, quality, and fortune, were only able to give reputation and success to the Revolution, were not only laid aside as dangerous and useless, but loaded with the scandal of Jacobites, men of arbitrary principles, and pensioners to France; while truth, who is said to lie in a well, seemed now to be buried there under a heap of stones. But I remember it was a usual complaint among the Whigs, that the bulk of the landed men was not in their interests, which some of the wisest looked on as an ill omen; and we saw it was with the utmost difficulty that they could preserve a majority, while the court and ministry were on their side, till they had learned those admirable expedients for deciding elections and influencing distant boroughs by powerful motives from the city. But all this was mere force and constraint, however upheld by most dexterous artifice and management, until the people began to apprehend their properties, their religion, and the monarchy itself in danger; when we saw them greedily laying hold on the first occasion to interpose. But of this mighty change in the dispositions of the people I shall discourse more at large in some following paper: wherein I shall endeavour to undeceive or discover those deluded or deluding persons who hope or pretend it is only a short madness in the vulgar, from which they may soon recover; whereas, I believe it will appear to be very different in its causes, its symptoms, and its consequences; and prove a great example to illustrate the maxim I lately mentioned, that truth (however sometimes late) will at last prevail.

THE EXAMINER

No. 16.

Thursday, November 16, 1710.

> ———*Medioque ut limite curras,*
> *Icare, ait, moneo: ne si demissior ibis,*
> *Unda gravet pennas; si celsior, ignis adurat.*

> ———My boy, take care
> To wing thy course along the middle air:
> If low, the surges wet thy flagging plumes;
> If high, the sun the melting wax consumes.

It must be avowed that for some years past there have been few things more wanted in England than such a paper as this ought to be: and such I will endeavour to make it as long as it shall be found of any use, without entering into the violences of either party. Considering the many grievous misrepresentations of persons and things, it is highly requisite at this juncture that the people throughout the kingdom should, if possible, be set right in their opinions by some impartial hand, which has never been yet attempted; those who have hitherto undertaken it being, upon every account, the least qualified of all human kind for such work.

We live here under a limited monarchy, and under the doctrine and discipline of an excellent church. We are unhappily divided into two parties, both which pretend a mighty zeal for our religion and government, only they disagree about the means. The evils we must fence against are, on one side, fanaticism and infidelity in religion, and anarchy, under the name of a commonwealth, in government; on the other side, popery, slavery, and the pretender from France. Now, to inform and direct us in our sentiments upon these weighty points, here are, on one side, two stupid illiterate scribblers, both of them fanatics by profession, I mean the *Review* and *Observator;* on the other side, we have an open nonjuror, whose character and person, as well as learning and good sense, discovered upon other subjects, do indeed deserve respect and esteem; but his *Rehearsal* and the rest of his political papers are yet more pernicious than those of the former two. If the generality of the people know not how to talk or think until they have read their lesson in the papers of the week, what a misfortune is it that their duty should be conveyed to them through such vehicles as those! For, let some gentlemen think what they please, I cannot but suspect that the two worthies I first mentioned have, in a degree, done mischief among us; the mock authoritative manner of the one, and the insipid mirth of the other, however insupportable to reasonable ears, being of a level with great numbers among the lowest part of mankind. Neither was the author of the *Rehearsal*, while he continued that paper, less infectious to many persons of better figure, who, perhaps, were as well qualified, and much less prejudiced, to judge for themselves.

It was this reason that moved me to take the matter out of those rough as well as those dirty hands; to let the remote and uninstructed part of the nation see that they have been misled on both sides by mad ridiculous extremes, at a wide distance on each side of the truth; while the right path is so broad and plain as to be easily kept if they were once put into it.

Farther, I had lately entered on a resolution to take little notice of other papers, unless it were such where the malice and falsehood had so great a mixture of wit and spirit as would make them dangerous; which, in the present circle of scribblers, from twelve-pence to a halfpenny, I could easily foresee would not very frequently occur. But here again I am forced to dispense with my resolution, although it be only to tell my reader what measures I am likely to take on such occasions for the future. I was told that the paper called the *Observator* was twice filled last week with remarks upon a late *Examiner*. These I read with the first opportunity, and, to speak in the news-writers' phrase, they gave me occasion for many speculations. I observed with singular pleasure the nature of those things which the owners of them usually call answers, and with what dexterity this matchless author had fallen into the whole art and cant of them. To transcribe here and there three or four detached lines of least weight in a discourse, and by a foolish comment mistake every syllable of the meaning, is what I have known many, of a superior class to this formidable adversary, entitle an Answer. This is what he has exactly done, in about thrice as many words as my whole discourse; which is so mighty an advantage over me, that I shall by no means engage in so unequal a combat; but, as far as I can judge of my own temper, entirely dismiss him for the future; heartily wishing he had a match exactly of his own size to meddle with, who should only have the odds of truth and honesty, which, as I take it, would be an effectual way to silence him for ever. Upon this occasion I cannot forbear a short story of a fanatic farmer, who lived in my neighbourhood, and was so great a disputant in religion that the servants in all the families thereabouts reported how he had confuted the bishop and all his clergy. I had then a footman who was fond of reading the Bible; and I borrowed a comment for him, which he studied so close that in a month or two I thought him a match for the farmer. They disputed at several houses, with a ring of servants and other people always about them; where Ned explained his texts so full and clear to the capacity of his audience, and showed the insignificancy of his adversary's cant to the meanest understanding, that he got the whole country on his side, and the farmer was cured of his itch of disputation for ever after.

The worst of it is, that this sort of outrageous party-writers I have spoken of above are like a couple of makebates, who inflame small quarrels by a thousand stories, and, by keeping friends at a distance, hinder them from coming to a good understanding, as they certainly would if they were suffered to meet and debate between themselves; for let any one examine a reasonable honest man, of either side, upon those opinions in religion and government which both parties daily buffet each other about, he shall hardly find one material point in difference between them. I would be glad to ask a question about two great men of the late ministry, how they came to be Whigs? and by what figure of speech half a dozen others, lately put into great employments, can be called Tories? I doubt whoever would suit the definition to the persons must make it directly contrary to what we understood it at the time of the Revolution.

In order to remove these misapprehensions among us, I believe it will be necessary, upon occasion, to detect the malice and falsehood of some popular maxims, which those idiots scatter from the press twice a-week, and draw a hundred absurd consequences from them.

For example, I have heard it often objected, as a great piece of insolence in the clergy and others, to say or hint that the church was in danger, when it was voted otherwise in parliament some years ago ; and the queen herself, in her last speech, did openly condemn all such insinuations. Notwithstanding which, I did then and do still believe the church has, since that vote, been in very imminent danger ; and I think I might then have said so without the least offence to her majesty or either of the two Houses. The queen's words, as near as I can remember, mentioned the church being in danger from her administration ; and whoever says or thinks that deserves, in my opinion, to be hanged for a traitor ; but that the church and state may be both in danger, under the best princes that ever reigned, and without the least guilt of theirs, is such a truth as a man must be a great stranger to history and common sense to doubt. The wisest prince on earth may be forced by the necessity of his affairs and the present power of an unruly faction, or deceived by the craft of ill-designing men. One or two ministers, most in his confidence, may at first have good intentions, but grow corrupted by time, by avarice, by love, by ambition, and have fairer terms offered them to gratify their passions or interests from one set of men than another, until they are too far involved for a retreat, and so be forced to take seven spirits more wicked than themselves. This is a very possible case; and will not the last state of such men be worse than the first? that is to say, will not the public, which was safe at first, grow in danger by such proceedings as these? And shall a faithful subject, who foresees and trembles at the consequences, be called disaffected because he delivers his opinion, although the prince declares, as he justly may, that the danger is not owing to his administration? or shall the prince himself be blamed when, in such a juncture, he puts his affairs into other hands, with the universal applause of his people? As to the vote against those who should affirm the church was in danger, I think it likewise referred to danger from or under the queen's administration; for I neither have it by me, nor can suddenly have recourse to it; but, if it were otherwise, I know not how it can refer to any dangers but what were past, or at that time present; or how it could affect the future, unless the senators were all inspired, or at least that majority which voted it: neither do I see it is any crime, farther than ill manners, to differ in opinion from a majority of either or both Houses; and that ill manners, I must confess, I have been often guilty of for some years past, although I hope I never shall again.

Another topic of great use to these weekly inflamers is the young pretender in France, to whom their whole party is in a high measure indebted for all their greatness; and whenever it lies in their power they may perhaps return their acknowledgments, as, out of their zeal for frequent revolutions, they were ready to do to his supposed father, which is a piece of secret history that I hope will one day see the light; and I am sure it shall if ever I am master of it, without regarding whose ears may tingle. But at present the word *pretender* is a term of art in their profession. A secretary of state cannot desire leave to resign, but the pretender is at bottom; the queen cannot dissolve a parliament, but it is a plot to dethrone herself and bring in the pretender; half-a-score stock-jobbers are playing the knave in Exchange-alley, and there goes the pretender with a sponge. One would be apt to think they bawl out the pretender so often to take off the terror, or tell so many lies about him to slacken our caution, that when he is really coming, by their connivance, we may not believe them, as the boy served the shepherds about the coming of the wolf; or perhaps they scare us with the pretender because they think he may be like some diseases that come with a fright. Do they not believe that the queen's present ministry love her majesty at least as well as some loved the church? And why is it not as great a mark of disaffection now to say the queen is in danger, as it was some months ago to affirm the same of the church? Suppose it be a false opinion that the queen's right is hereditary and indefeasible; yet how is it possible that those who hold and believe such a doctrine can be in the pretender's interest? His title is weakened by every argument that strengthens hers: it is as plain as the words of an act of parliament can make it that her present majesty is heir to the survivor of the late king and queen, her sister: is not that an hereditary right? What need we explain it any farther? I have known an article of faith expounded in much looser and more general terms, and that by an author whose opinions are very much followed by a certain party. Suppose we go farther, and examine the word *indefeasible*, with which some writers of late have made themselves so merry; I confess it is hard to conceive how any law which the supreme power makes may not by the same power be repealed; so that I shall not determine whether the queen's right be indefeasible or not. But this I will maintain, that whoever affirms it is so is not guilty of a crime; for in that settlement of the crown after the Revolution, where her present majesty is named in remainder, there are (as near as I can remember) these remarkable words, "to which we bind ourselves and our posterity for ever." Lawyers may explain this, or call them words of form, as they please; and reasoners may argue that such an obligation is against the nature of government; but a plain reader, who takes the words in their natural meaning, may be excused in thinking a right so confirmed is indefeasible; and if there be an absurdity in such an opinion, he is not to answer for it.

P.S. When this paper was going to the press, the printer brought me two more *Observators*, wholly taken up in my *Examiner* upon lying, which I was at the pains to read; and they are just such an answer as the two others I have mentioned. This is all I have to say on that matter.

THE CONDUCT OF THE ALLIES

It is the folly of too many to mistake the echo of a London coffeehouse for the voice of the kingdom. The city coffeehouses have been for some years filled with people whose fortunes depend upon the Bank, East India, or some other stock. Every new fund to these is like a new mortgage to a usurer, whose compassion for a young heir is exactly the same with that of a stock-jobber to the landed gentry. At the court end of the town, the like places of resort are frequented either by men out of place, and consequently enemies to the present ministry, or by officers of the army: no wonder, then, if the general cry in all such meetings be against any peace, either with Spain or without, which in other words is no more than this, that discontented men desire another change of ministry; that soldiers would be glad to keep their commissions; and that the creditors have money still, and would have the debtors borrow on at the old extorting rate while they have any security to give.

Now, to give the most ignorant reader some idea of our present circumstances, without troubling him or myself with computations in form: everybody knows that our land and malt tax amount annually to about two millions and a half. All other branches of the revenue are mortgaged to pay interest for what we have already borrowed. The yearly charge of the war is usually about six millions, to make up which sum we are forced to take up on the credit of new funds about three millions and a half. This last year the computed charge of the war came to above a million more than all the funds the parliament could contrive were sufficient to pay interest for, and so we have been forced to divide a deficiency of twelve hundred thousand pounds among the several branches of our expense. This is a demonstration that, if the war be to last another campaign, it will be impossible to find funds for supplying it without mortgaging the malt tax, or by some other method equally desperate.

If the peace be made this winter, we are then to consider what circumstances we shall be in toward paying a debt of about fifty millions, which is a fourth part of the purchase of the whole island if it were to be sold.

Towards clearing ourselves of this monstrous incumbrance, some of these annuities will expire or pay off the principal in thirty, forty, or a hundred years; the bulk of the debt must be lessened gradually by the best management we can, out of what will remain of the land and malt taxes, after paying guards and garrisons, and maintaining and supplying our fleet in the time of peace. I have not skill enough to compute what will be left, after these necessary charges, toward annually clearing so vast a debt, but believe it must be very little; however, it is plain that both these taxes must be continued, as well for supporting the government, as because we have no other means for paying off the principal. And so likewise must all the other funds remain for paying the interest. How long a time this must require, how steady an administration, and how undisturbed a state of affairs both at home and abroad, let others determine.

However, some people think all this very reasonable, and that, since the struggle has been for peace and safety, posterity, which is to partake of the benefit, ought to share in the expense ; as if at the breaking out of this war there had been such a conjuncture of affairs as never happened before, nor would ever happen again. It is wonderful that our ancestors, in all their wars, should never fall under such a necessity ; that we meet no examples of it in Greece and Rome ; that no other nation in Europe ever knew anything like it, except Spain, about a hundred and twenty years ago, when they drew it upon themselves by their own folly and have suffered for it ever since ; no doubt we shall teach posterity wisdom, but they will be apt to think the purchase too dear, and I wish they may stand to the bargain we have made in their names.

It is easy to entail debts on succeeding ages, and to hope they will be able and willing to pay them ; but how to ensure peace for any term of years is difficulty enough to apprehend. Will human nature ever cease to have the same passions, princes to entertain designs of interest or ambition, and occasions of quarrel to arise ? May not we ourselves, by the variety of events and incidents which happen in the world, be under a necessity of recovering towns out of the very hands of those for whom we are now ruining our country to take them ? Neither can it be said that those states with whom we may probably differ will be in as bad a condition as ourselves ; for by the circumstances of our situation, and the impositions of our allies, we are more exhausted than either they or the enemy : and by the nature of our government, the corruption of our manners, and the opposition of factions, we shall be more slow in recovering.

It will no doubt be a mighty comfort to our grandchildren, when they see a few rags hung up in Westminster Hall, which cost a hundred millions, whereof they are paying the arrears, to boast as beggars do that their grandfathers were rich and great.

I have often reflected on that mistaken notion of credit so boasted of by the advocates of the late ministry: was not all that credit built upon funds raised by the landed men whom they now so much hate and despise? Is not the greatest part of those funds raised from the growth and product of land? Must not the whole debt be entirely paid, and our fleets and garrisons be maintained, by the land and malt tax after a peace? If they call it credit to run ten millions in debt without parliamentary security, by which the public is defrauded of almost half, I must think such credit to be dangerous, illegal, and perhaps treasonable. Neither has anything gone farther to ruin the nation than their boasted credit. For my own part, when I saw this false credit sink upon the change of the ministry, I was singular enough to conceive it a good omen. It seemed as if the young extravagant heir had got a new steward, and was resolved to look into his estate before things grew desperate, which made the usurers forbear feeding him with money as they used to do.

Since the moneyed men are so fond of war, I should be glad they would furnish out one campaign at their own charge: it is not above six or seven millions; and I dare engage to make it out that when they have done this, instead of contributing equal to the landed men, they will have their full principal and interest at six per cent. remaining of all the money they ever lent to the government.

Without this resource, or some other equally miraculous, it is impossible for us to continue the war upon the same foot. I have already observed that the last funds of interest fell short above a million, although the persons most conversant in ways and means employed their utmost invention; so that of necessity we must be still more defective next campaign. But perhaps our allies will make up this deficiency on our side by great efforts on their own? Quite the contrary: both the emperor and Holland failed this year in several articles, and signified to us some time ago that they cannot keep up to the same proportions in the next. We have gained a noble barrier for the latter, and they have nothing more to demand or desire. The emperor, however sanguine he may now affect to appear, will I suppose be satisfied with Naples, Sicily, Milan, and his other acquisitions, rather than engage in a long, hopeless war for the recovery of Spain, to which his allies the Dutch will neither give their assistance nor consent. So that, since we have done their business, since they have no farther service for our arms, and we have no more money to give them, and lastly, since we neither desire any recompense nor expect any thanks, we ought in pity to be dismissed and have leave to shift for ourselves. They are ripe for a peace to enjoy and cultivate what we have conquered for them; and so are we to recover, if possible, the effects of their hardships upon us. The first overtures from France are made to England upon safe and honourable terms : we, who bore the burden of the war, ought in reason to have the greatest share in making the peace. If we do not hearken to a peace, others certainly will, and get the advantage of us there, as they have done in the war. We know the Dutch have perpetually threatened us that they would enter into separate measures of a peace ; and by the strength of that argument, as well as by other powerful motives, prevailed on those who were then at the helm to comply with them on any terms, rather than put an end to a war which every year brought them such great accessions to their wealth and power. Whoever falls off, a peace will follow, and then we must be content with such conditions as our allies, out of their great concern for our safety and interest, will please to choose. They have no farther occasion for fighting, they have gained their point, and they now tell us it is our war ; so that in common justice it ought to be our peace.

All we can propose by the desperate steps of pawning our land or malt tax, or erecting a general excise, is only to raise a fund of interest for running us annually four millions farther in debt, without any prospect of ending the war so well as we can do at present. And when we have sunk the only unengaged revenues we had left, our encumbrances must of necessity remain perpetual.

We have hitherto lived upon expedients which in time will certainly destroy any constitution, whether civil or natural ; and there was no country in Christendom had less occasion for them than ours. We have dieted a healthy body into a consumption, by plying it with physic instead of food. Art will help us no longer ;

and if we cannot recover by letting the remains of nature work, we must inevitably die.

What arts have been used to possess the people with a strong delusion that Britain must infallibly be ruined without the recovery of Spain to the house of Austria; making the safety of a great and powerful kingdom, as ours was then, to depend upon an event which, after a war of miraculous successes, proves impracticable! As if princes and great ministers could find no way of settling the public tranquillity without changing the possessions of kingdoms, and forcing sovereigns upon a people against their inclinations. Is there no security for the island of Britain unless a king of Spain be dethroned by the hands of his grandfather? Has the enemy no cautionary towns and seaports to give us for securing trade? Can he not deliver us possession of such places as would put him in a worse condition whenever he should perfidiously renew the war? The present king of France has but few years to live by the course of nature, and doubtless would desire to end his days in peace. Grandfathers, in private families, are not observed to have great influence on their grandsons, and I believe they have much less among princes; however, when the authority of a parent is gone, is it likely that Philip will be directed by a brother against his own interest and that of his subjects? Have not those two realms their separate maxims of policy, which must operate in the times of peace? These at least are probabilities, and cheaper at least by six millions a-year than recovering Spain or continuing the war, both which seem absolutely impossible.

But the common question is, if we must now surrender Spain, what have we been fighting for all this while? The answer is ready : we have been fighting for the ruin of the public interest and the advancement of a private. We have been fighting to raise the wealth and grandeur of a particular family, to enrich usurers and stock-jobbers, and to cultivate the pernicious designs of a faction by destroying the landed interest. The nation begins now to think these blessings are not worth fighting for any longer, and therefore desires a peace.

But the advocates on the other side cry out that we might have had a better peace than is now in agitation, above two years ago. Supposing this to be true, I do assert that, by parity of reason, we must expect one just so much the worse about two years hence. If those in power could then have given us a better peace, more is their infamy and guilt that they did it not. Why did they insist upon conditions which they were certain would never be granted? We allow it was in their power to have put a good end to the war, and left the nation in some hope of recovering itself. And this is what we charge them with, as answerable to God, their country, and posterity,—that the bleeding condition of their fellow subjects was a feather in the balance with their private ends.

A PROPOSAL FOR CORRECTING, IMPROVING, AND ASCERTAINING THE ENGLISH TONGUE

IN A LETTER TO THE MOST HONOURABLE ROBERT EARL OF OXFORD AND MORTIMER, LORD HIGH TREASURER OF GREAT BRITAIN

This letter was addressed to Lord Oxford in February, 1711-12, and printed in the following May. It is the only composition to which Swift put his name, and is also interesting as an early attempt to import the principle of the Académie Française into England. Some of the historical parallels have been omitted, together with part of the too effusive panegyric upon Harley, in order to bring the piece within due compass.

A PROPOSAL FOR CORRECTING, IMPROVING, AND ASCERTAINING THE ENGLISH TONGUE

THE period wherein the English tongue received most improvement I take to commence with the beginning of queen Elizabeth's reign, and to conclude with the great Rebellion in forty-two. It is true, there was a very ill taste, both of style and wit, which prevailed under king James I. ; but that seems to have been corrected in the first years of his successor, who, among many other qualifications of an excellent prince, was a great patron of learning. From the civil war to this present time, I am apt to doubt whether the corruptions in our language have not at least equalled the refinements of it ; and these corruptions very few of the best authors in our age have wholly escaped. During the usurpation, such an infusion of enthusiastic jargon prevailed in every writing, as was not shaken off in many years after. To this succeeded that licentiousness which entered with the Restoration, and, from infecting our religion and morals, fell to corrupt our language ; which last was not likely to be much improved by those who at that time made up the court of king Charles II. ; either such who had followed him in his banishment, or who had been altogether conversant in the dialect of those fanatic times ; or young men who had been educated in the same country: so that the court, which used to be the standard of propriety and correctness of speech, was then, and I think has ever since continued, the worst school in England for that accomplishment; and so will remain till better care be taken in the education of our young nobility, that they may set out into the world with some foundation of literature, in order to qualify them for patterns of politeness. The consequence of this defect upon our language may appear from the plays and other compositions written for entertainment within fifty years past, filled with a succession of affected phrases and new conceited words, either borrowed from the current style of the court, or from those who, under the character of men of wit and pleasure, pretended to give the law. Many of these refinements have already been long antiquated, and are now hardly intelligible; which is no wonder, when they were the product only of ignorance and caprice.

I have never known this great town without one or more dunces of figure, who had credit enough to give rise to some new word, and propagate it in most conversations, though it had neither humour nor significancy. If it struck the present taste, it was soon transferred into the plays and current scribbles of the week, and became an addition to our language; while the men of wit and learning, instead of early obviating such corruptions, were too often seduced to imitate and comply with them.

There is another set of men who have contributed very much to the spoiling of the English tongue; I mean the poets from the time of the Restoration.

These gentlemen, although they could not be insensible how much our language was already overstocked with monosyllables, yet, to save time and pains, introduced that barbarous custom of abbreviating words to fit them to the measure of their verses ; and this they have frequently done so very injudiciously as to form such harsh unharmonious sounds that none but a northern ear could endure. They have joined the most obdurate consonants with one intervening vowel, only to shorten a syllable ; and their taste in time became so depraved, that what was at first a poetical license not to be justified, they made their choice, alleging that the words pronounced at length sounded faint and languid. This was a pretence to take up the same custom in prose ; so that most of the books we see now-a-days are full of those manglings and abbreviations. Instances of this abuse are innumerable : what does your lordship think of the words *drudg'd, disturb'd, rebuk'd, fledg'd*, and a thousand others everywhere to be met with in prose as well as verse? where, by leaving out a vowel to save a syllable, we form so jarring a sound, and so difficult to utter, that I have often wondered how it could ever obtain.

Another cause (and perhaps borrowed from the former) which has contributed not a little to the maiming of our language, is a foolish opinion, advanced of late years, that we ought to spell exactly as we speak ; which, besides the obvious inconvenience of utterly destroying our etymology, would be a thing we should never see an end of. Not only the several towns and counties of England have a different way of pronouncing, but even here in London they clip their words after one manner about the court, another in the city, and a third in the suburbs; and, in a few years, it is probable, will all differ from themselves, as fancy or fashion shall direct; all which, reduced to writing, would entirely confound orthography. Yet many people are so fond of this conceit that it is sometimes a difficult matter to read modern books and pamphlets, where the words are so curtailed and varied from their original spelling, that whoever has been used to plain English will hardly know them by sight.

Several young men at the universities, terribly possessed with the fear of pedantry, run into a worse extreme, and think all politeness to consist in reading the daily trash sent down to them from hence; this they call knowing the world and reading men and manners. Thus furnished, they come up to town, reckon all their errors for accomplishments, borrow the newest set of phrases; and if they take a pen into their hands, all the odd words they have picked up in a coffeehouse or a gaming ordinary are produced as flowers of style, and the orthography refined to the utmost. To this we owe those monstrous productions which, under the name of Trips, Spies, Amusements, and other conceited appellations, have overrun us for some years past. To this we owe that strange race of wits who tell us they write to the humour of the age. And I wish I could say these quaint fopperies were wholly absent from graver subjects. In short, I would undertake to show your lordship several pieces where the beauties of this kind are so predominant, that, with all your skill in languages, you could never be able to read or understand them.

But I am very much mistaken if many of these false

refinements among us do not arise from a principle which would quite destroy their credit, if it were well understood and considered. For I am afraid, my lord, that, with all the real good qualities of our country, we are naturally not very polite. This perpetual disposition to shorten our words by retrenching the vowels is nothing else but a tendency to lapse into the barbarity of those northern nations from whom we are descended, and whose languages labour all under the same defect. For it is worthy our observation that the Spaniards, the French, and the Italians, although derived from the same northern ancestors with ourselves, are with the utmost difficulty taught to pronounce our words; which the Swedes and Danes, as well as the Germans and the Dutch, attain to with ease, because our syllables resemble theirs in the roughness and frequency of consonants. Now, as we struggle with an ill climate to improve the nobler kinds of fruits, are at the expense of walls to receive and reverberate the faint rays of the sun, and fence against the northern blast, we sometimes, by the help of a good soil, equal the production of warmer countries, who have no need to be at so much cost and care. It is the same thing with respect to the politer arts among us; and the same defect of heat, which gives a fierceness to our natures, may contribute to that roughness of our language, which bears some analogy to the harsh fruit of colder countries. For I do not reckon that we want a genius more than the rest of our neighbours: but your lordship will be of my opinion, that we ought to struggle with these natural disadvantages as much as we can, and be careful whom we employ whenever we design to correct them; which is a work that has hitherto been assumed by the least qualified hands. So that; if the choice had been left to me, I would rather have trusted the refinement of our language, as far as it relates to sound, to the judgment of the women, than of illiterate court fops, half-witted poets, and university boys. For it is plain that women, in their manner of corrupting words, do naturally discard the consonants as we do the vowels. What I am going to tell your lordship appears very trifling: that more than once, where some of both sexes were in company, I have persuaded two or three of each to take a pen, and write down a number of letters joined together, just as it came into their heads; and upon reading this gibberish we have found that which the men had wrote, by the frequent encountering of rough consonants, to sound like High Dutch; and the other, by the women, like Italian, abounding in vowels and liquids. Now, though I would by no means give ladies the trouble of advising us in the reformation of our language, yet I cannot help thinking that, since they have been left out of all meetings, except parties at play or where worse designs are carried on, our conversation has very much degenerated.

In order to reform our language, I conceive, my lord, that a free judicious choice should be made of such persons as are generally allowed to be best qualified for such a work, without any regard to quality, party, or profession. These, to a certain number at least, should assemble at some appointed time and place, and fix on rules by which they design to proceed. What methods they will take is not for me to prescribe. Your lordship, and other persons in great employments, might please to be of the number: and I am afraid such a society would want your instruction and example as much as your protection; for I have, not without a little envy, observed of late the style of some great ministers very much to exceed that of any other productions.

The persons who are to undertake this work will have the example of the French before them, to imitate where these have proceeded right, and to avoid their mistakes. Beside the grammar part, wherein we are allowed to be very defective, they will observe many gross improprieties, which, however authorized by practice and grown familiar, ought to be discarded. They will find many words that deserve to be utterly thrown out of our language; many more to be corrected; and perhaps not a few, long since antiquated, which ought to be restored on account of their energy and sound.

But what I have most at heart is that some method should be thought on for ascertaining and fixing our language for ever, after such alterations are made in it as shall be thought requisite. For I am of opinion it is better a language should not be wholly perfect, than that it should be perpetually changing; and we must give over at one time, or at length infallibly change for the worse; as the Romans did, when they began to quit their simplicity of style for affected refinements, such as we meet in Tacitus and other authors; which ended by degrees in many barbarities, even before the Goths had invaded Italy.

The fame of our writers is usually confined to these two islands; and it is hard it should be limited in time, as much as place, by the perpetual variations of our speech. It is your lordship's observation, that if it were not for the Bible and Common Prayer Book in the vulgar tongue, we should hardly be able to understand anything that was written among us a hundred years ago; which is certainly true: for those books, being perpetually read in churches, have proved a kind of standard for language, especially to the common people. And I doubt whether the alterations since introduced have added much to the beauty or strength of the English tongue, though they have taken off a great deal from that simplicity which is one of the greatest perfections in any language. You, my lord, who are so conversant in the sacred writings, and so great a judge of them in their originals, will agree that no translation our country ever yet produced has come up to that of the Old and New Testament: and by the many beautiful passages which I have often had the honour to hear your lordship cite from thence, I am persuaded that the translators of the Bible were masters of an English style much fitter for that work than any we see in our present writings; which I take to be owing to the simplicity that runs through the whole. Then, as to the greatest part of our liturgy, compiled long before the translation of the Bible now in use, and little altered since, there seems to be in it as great strains of true sublime eloquence as are anywhere to be found in our language; which every man of good taste will observe in the communion service, that of burial, and other parts.

But when I say that I would have our language, after it is duly correct, always to last, I do not mean that it should never be enlarged. Provided that no word, which a society shall give a sanction to, be afterwards antiquated and exploded, they may have liberty to receive whatever new ones they shall find occasion for; because then the old books will yet be always valuable according to their intrinsic worth, and not thrown aside on account of unintelligible words and phrases, which appear harsh and uncouth only because they are out of fashion. Had the Roman tongue continued vulgar in that city till this time, it would have been absolutely necessary, from the mighty changes that have been made in law and religion, from the many terms of art required in trade and in war, from the new inventions that have happened in the world, from the vast spreading of navigation and commerce, with many other obvious circumstances, to have made great additions to that language; yet the ancients would still have been read and understood with pleasure and ease. The Greek tongue received many enlargements between the time of Homer and that of Plutarch, yet the former author was probably as well understood in Trajan's time as the latter. What Horace says of words going off and perishing like leaves, the new ones coming in their place, is a misfortune he laments, rather than a thing he approves; but I cannot see why this should be absolutely necessary, or, if it were, what would have become of his *monumentum acre perennius*.

As barbarous and ignorant as we were in former centuries, there was more effectual care taken by our ancestors to preserve the memory of times and persons, than we find in this age of learning and politeness, as we are pleased to call it. The rude Latin of the monks is still very intelligible; whereas, had their records been delivered down only in the vulgar tongue, so barren and so barbarous, so subject to continual succeeding changes, they could not now be understood unless by antiquaries who make it their study to expound them. And we must at this day have been content with such poor abstracts of our English story as laborious men of low genius would think fit to give us; and even these, in the next age, would be likewise swallowed up in succeeding collections. If things go on at this rate, all I can promise your lordship is, that about two hundred years hence some painful compiler, who will be at the trouble of studying old language, may inform the world that, in the reign of queen Anne, Robert earl of Oxford, a very wise and excellent man, was made high treasurer, and saved his country, which in those days was almost ruined by a foreign war and a domestic faction. Thus much he may be able to pick out, and willing to transfer into his new history; but the rest of your character, which I or any other writer may now value ourselves by drawing, and the particular account of the great things done under your ministry, for which you are already so celebrated in most parts of Europe, will probably be dropped, on account of the antiquated style and manner they are delivered in.

How, then, shall any man who has a genius for history equal to the best of the ancients be able to undertake such a work with spirit and cheerfulness, when he considers that he will be read with pleasure but a very few years, and in an age or two shall hardly be understood without an interpreter? This is like employing an excellent statuary to work upon mouldering stone. Those who apply their studies to preserve the memory of others will always have some concern for their own;

and I believe it is for this reason that so few writers among us of any distinction have turned their thoughts to such a discouraging employment; for the best English historian must lie under this mortification, that, when his style grows antiquated, he will be only considered as a tedious relater of facts, and perhaps consulted in his turn, among other neglected authors, to furnish materials for some future collector.

I doubt your lordship is but ill entertained with a few scattered thoughts upon a subject that deserves to be treated with ability and care. However, I must beg leave to add a few words more, perhaps not altogether foreign to the same matter. I know not whether that which I am going to say may pass for caution, advice, or reproach; any of which will be justly thought very improper from one in my station to one in yours. However, I must venture to affirm, that if genius and learning be not encouraged under your lordship's administration, you are the most inexcusable person alive. All your other virtues, my lord, will be defective without this; your affability, candour, and good nature; that perpetual agreeableness of conversation, so disengaged in the midst of such a weight of business and opposition; even your justice, prudence, and magnanimity, will shine less bright without it. Your lordship is universally allowed to possess a very large portion in most parts of literature; and to this you owe the cultivating of those many virtues which otherwise would have been less adorned or in lower perfection. Neither can you acquit yourself of these obligations without letting the arts, in their turn, share your influence and protection : besides, who knows but some true genius may happen to arise under your ministry, *exortus ut æthereus sol.* Every age might perhaps produce one or two of these to adorn it, if they were not sunk under the censure and obloquy of plodding, servile, imitating pedants. I do not mean, by a true genius, any bold writer who breaks through the rules of decency to distinguish himself by the singularity of his opinions; but one who, upon a deserving subject, is able to open new scenes, and discover a vein of true and noble thinking, which never entered into any imagination before; every stroke of whose pen is worth all the paper blotted by hundreds of others in the compass of their lives. I know, my lord, your friends will offer in your defence that in your private capacity you never refused your purse and credit to the service and support of learned or ingenious men; and that, ever since you have been in public employment, you have constantly bestowed your favours to the most deserving persons. But I desire your lordship not to be deceived; we never will admit of these excuses, nor will allow your private liberality, as great as it is, to atone for your excessive public thrift. But here again, I am afraid, most good subjects will interpose in your defence, by alleging the desperate condition you found the nation in, and the necessity there was for so able and faithful a steward to retrieve it, if possible, by the utmost frugality. We grant all this, my lord; but then it ought likewise to be considered that you have already saved several millions to the public, and that what we ask is too inconsiderable to break into any rules of the strictest good husbandry. The French king bestows about half-a-dozen pensions to learned men in several parts of Europe, and perhaps a dozen in his own kingdom; which in the whole do probably not amount to half the income of many a private commoner in England, yet have more contributed to the glory of that prince than any million he has otherwise employed. For learning, like all true merit, is easily satisfied; while the false and counterfeit is perpetually craving, and never thinks it has enough. The smallest favour given by a great prince as a mark of esteem to reward the endowments of the mind, never fails to be returned with praise and gratitude, and loudly celebrated to the world.

TRACTS RELATING TO
IRELAND

A project was set on foot in 1720 for the establishing of a national bank in Dublin. Swift took it for a variety of the stock-jobbing schemes which the South Sea Bubble had made over-familiar, and wrote several skits upon the subject, including the *Swearer's Bank*, with the result that the project was rejected in parliament.

The seven *Drapier's Letters*, which were published at intervals in 1724, were the first of Swift's writings to exercise that powerful influence over the people of Ireland which he long afterwards retained. Their precise object, the rejection of a copper coinage supposed to be base, and known to be uttered by a party "job," presents little of permanent interest, though the fraud, if such it was, stirred the vials of Swift's wrath tempest-high. The real importance of these *Letters* lies in their effect upon the Irish nation. For the first time an Irish public opinion was brought to bear upon the distant Government. The *Drapier's Letters* won the day; Wood's Halfpence were countermanded; and the Dean, with an ineffectual offer of £300 for the discovery of the Drapier upon his head, became the idol of his countrymen and the terror of the lord-lieutenant. But the *Letters* are not wholly busied with halfpence. In the fourth, along with some of Swift's best manner in the treatment of the threat about the fire-balls, we come upon a noble vindication of Irish liberty and a strenuous repudiation of the doctrine of dependence. It was in this fourth letter that the Government found matter for prosecution, but no jury could be induced to bring a true bill even against the printer; and as for betraying the Dean, the popular feeling was expressed in the scriptural saying, then on everyone's lips, "Shall Jonathan die who hath wrought this great salvation in Israel"?

The *Modest Proposal* was written and published in 1729, when people in Ireland were starving in thousands and the dead lay unburied at the doors. It gives the essence of Swift's feeling about Ireland, and is "one of the most tremendous pieces of satire in existence. Swift is burning with a passion, the glow of which makes other passions look cold, as it is said that some bright lights cause other illuminating objects to cast a shadow. Yet his face is absolutely grave, and he details his plan as calmly as a modern projector suggesting the importation of Australian meat. The superficial coolness may be revolting to tender-hearted people, and has indeed led to condemnation of the supposed ferocity of the author almost as surprising as the criticisms which can see in it nothing but an exquisite piece of humour. It is, in truth, fearful to read even now. Yet we can forgive and even sympathize when we take it for what it really is—the most complete expression of burning indignation against intolerable wrongs."—*Leslie Stephen.*

THE SWEARER'S BANK

OR PARLIAMENTARY SECURITY FOR ESTABLISHING A NEW BANK IN IRELAND, WHEREIN THE MEDICAL USE OF OATHS IS CONSIDERED

Si populus vult decipi, decipiatur.

"TO believe everything that is said by a certain set of men, and to doubt of nothing they relate, though ever so improbable," is a maxim that has contributed as much, for the time, to the support of Irish banks as it ever did to the Popish religion; and they are not wholly beholden to the latter for their foundation, but they have the happiness to have the same patron saint; for Ignorance, the reputed mother of the devotion of one, seems to bear the same affectionate relation to the credit of the other.

To subscribe to banks, without knowing the scheme or design of them, is not unlike to some gentlemen's signing addresses without knowing the contents of them: to engage in a bank that has neither act of parliament, charter, nor lands to support it, is like sending a ship to sea without a bottom; to expect a coach and six by the former, would be as ridiculous as to hope a return by the latter.

It was well known some time ago that our banks would be included in the bubble-bill; and it was believed those chimeras would necessarily vanish with the first easterly wind that should inform the town of the royal assent.

It was very mortifying to several gentlemen who dreamed of nothing but easy chariots, on the arrival of the fatal packet, to slip out of them into their walking shoes. But should those banks, as it is vainly imagined, be so fortunate as to obtain a charter, and purchase lands; yet, on any run on them in a time of invasion, there would be so many starving proprietors, reviving their old pretensions to land and a bellyful, that the subscribers would be unwilling upon any call to part with their money, not knowing what might happen; so that in a rebellion, where the success was doubtful, the bank would infallibly break.

Since so many gentlemen of this town have had the courage, without any security, to appear in the same paper with a million or two; it is hoped, when they are made sensible of their safety, that they will be prevailed to trust themselves in a neat skin of parchment, with a single one.

To encourage them, the undertaker proposes the erecting of a bank on parliamentary security, and such security as no revolution or change of times can effect

To take away all jealousy of any private view of the undertaker, he assures the world that he is now in a garret, in a very thin waistcoat, studying the public good; having given an undeniable pledge of his love to his country by pawning his coat in order to defray the expense of the press.

It is very well known that, by an act of parliament to prevent profane swearing, the person so offending, on

THE SWEARER'S BANK

oath made before a magistrate, forfeits a shilling, which may be levied with little difficulty.

It is almost unnecessary to mention that this is become a pet vice among us; and though age renders us unfit for other vices, yet this, where it takes hold, never leaves us but with our speech.

So vast a revenue might be raised by the execution of this act, that I have often wondered, in a scarcity of funds, that methods have not been taken to make it serviceable to the public.

I dare venture to say, if this act was well executed in England, the revenue of it, applied to the navy, would make the English fleet a terror to all Europe.

It is computed by geographers that there are 2,000,000 in this kingdom (of Ireland), of which number there may be said to be 1,000,000 of swearing souls.

It is thought there may be 5000 gentlemen; every gentleman, taking one with another, may afford to swear an oath every day, which will yearly produce 1,825,000 oaths; which number of shillings makes the yearly sum of £91,250.

The farmers of this kingdom, who are computed to be 10,000, are able to spend yearly 500,000 oaths, which gives £25,000; and it is conjectured that, from the bulk of the people, £20,000 or £25,000 may be yearly collected.

These computations are very modest, since it is evident that there is a much greater consumption of oaths in this kingdom, and consequently a much greater sum might be yearly raised.

That it may be collected with ease and regularity, it is proposed to settle informers in great towns in proportion to the number of inhabitants, and to have riding-officers in the country; and since nothing brings a greater contempt on any profession than poverty, it is determined to settle very handsome salaries on the gentlemen that are employed by the bank, that they may, by a generosity of living, reconcile men to an office that has lain under so much scandal of late as to be undertaken by none but curates, clerks of meeting-houses, and broken tradesmen. . . .

It is very probable that £20,000 will be necessary to defray all expenses of servants, salaries, etc. However, there will be the clear yearly sum of £100,000, which may very justly claim a million subscription.

It is determined to lay out the remaining unapplied profits, which will be very considerable, toward the erecting and maintaining of charity schools. A design so beneficial to the public, and especially to the protestant interest of this kingdom, has met with so much encouragement from several great patriots in England, that they have engaged to procure an act to secure the sole benefit of informing on this swearing act to the agents and servants of this new bank. Several of my friends pretend to demonstrate, that this bank will in time vie with the South Sea Company: they insist, that the army dispend as many oaths yearly as will produce £100,000 nett.

There are computed to be 100 pretty fellows in this town that swear fifty oaths a-head daily; some of them would think it hard to be stinted to a hundred: this very branch would produce a vast sum yearly.

The fairs of this kingdom will bring in a vast revenue; the oaths of a little Connaught one, as well as they could be numbered by two persons, amounted to three thousand. It is true that it would be impossible to turn all of them into ready money, for a shilling is so great a duty on swearing, that if it was carefully exacted the common people might as well pretend to drink wine as to swear, and an oath would be as rare among them as a clean shirt.

A servant that I employed to accompany the militia their last muster day had scored down, in the compass of eight hours, three hundred oaths; but, as the putting of the act in execution on those days would only fill the stocks with porters, and pawn-shops with muskets and swords, and as it would be matter of great joy to papists and disaffected persons to see our militia swear themselves out of their guns and swords; it is resolved that no advantage shall be taken of any militiaman's swearing while he is under arms; nor shall any advantage be taken of any man's swearing in the Four Courts, provided he is at hearing in the exchequer, or has just paid off an attorney's bill.

The medicinal use of oaths is what the undertaker would by no means discourage, especially where it is necessary to help the lungs to throw off any distilling humour. On certificate of a course of swearing prescribed by any physician, a permit will be given to the patient by the proper officer of the bank, paying no more than sixpence. It is expected that a scheme of so much advantage to the public will meet with more encouragement than their chimerical banks; and the undertaker hopes, that as he has spent a considerable fortune in bringing this scheme to bear, he may have the satisfaction to see it take place for the public good, though he should have the fate of most projectors, to be undone.

THE DRAPIER'S LETTERS

LETTER THE FOURTH

TO THE WHOLE PEOPLE OF IRELAND

Oct. 23, 1724.

My dear Countrymen,

Having already written three letters upon so disagreeable a subject as Mr. Wood and his halfpence, I conceived my task was at an end; but I find that cordials must be frequently applied to weak constitutions, political as well as natural. A people long used to hardships lose by degrees the very notions of liberty. They look upon themselves as creatures at mercy, and that all impositions laid on them by a stronger hand are, in the phrase of the Report, legal and obligatory. Hence proceed that poverty and lowness of spirit to which a kingdom may be subject, as well as a particular person. And when Esau came fainting from the field at the point to die, it is no wonder that he sold his birthright for a mess of pottage.

I thought I had sufficiently shown to all who could want instruction by what methods they might safely proceed, whenever this coin should be offered to them; and I believe there has not been for many ages an example of any kingdom so firmly united in a point of great importance, as this of ours is at present against that detestable fraud. But however, it so happens that some weak people begin to be alarmed anew by rumours industriously spread. Wood prescribes to the newsmongers in London what they are to write. In one of their papers, published here by some obscure printer, and certainly with a bad design, we are told "That the papists in Ireland have entered into an association against his coin," although it be notoriously known that they never once offered to stir in the matter; so that the two houses of parliament, the privy-council, the great number of corporations, the lord mayor and aldermen of Dublin, the grand juries and principal gentlemen of several counties, are stigmatized in a lump under the name of "papists."

This impostor and his crew do likewise give out, that by refusing to receive his dross for sterling we "dispute the king's prerogative, are grown ripe for rebellion, and ready to shake off the dependency of Ireland upon the crown of England." To countenance which reports he has published a paragraph in another newspaper, to let us know that "the lord-lieutenant is ordered to come over immediately to settle his halfpence."

I entreat you, my dear countrymen, not to be under the least concern upon these and the like rumours, which are no more than the last howls of a dog dissected alive, as I hope he has sufficiently been. These calumnies are the only reserve that is left him. For surely our continued and (almost) unexampled loyalty will never be called in question, for not suffering ourselves to be robbed of all that we have by one obscure ironmonger.

As to disputing the king's prerogative, give me leave to explain to those who are ignorant what the meaning of that word *prerogative* is.

The kings of these realms enjoy several powers, wherein the laws have not interposed. So they can make war and peace without the consent of parliament—and this is a very great prerogative: but if the parliament does not approve of the war, the king must bear the charge of it out of his own purse—and this is a great check on the crown. So the king has a prerogative to coin money without consent of parliament; but he cannot compel the subject to take that money except it be sterling gold or silver, because herein he is limited by law. Some princes have, indeed, extended their prerogative farther than the law allowed them; wherein, however, the lawyers of succeeding ages, as fond as they are of precedents, have never dared to justify them. But to say the truth, it is only of late times that prerogative has been fixed and ascertained; for whoever reads the history of England will find that some former kings, and those none of the worst, have upon several occasions ventured to control the laws, with very little ceremony or scruple, even later than the days of queen Elizabeth. In her reign that pernicious counsel of sending base money hither very narrowly failed of losing the kingdom—being complained of by the lord-deputy, the council, and the whole body of the English here; so that soon after her death it was recalled by her successor, and lawful money paid in exchange.

Having thus given you some notion of what is meant by "the king's prerogative," as far as a tradesman can be thought capable of explaining it, I will only add the opinion of the great lord Bacon : "That, as God governs the world by the settled laws of nature, which he has made, and never transcends those laws but upon high important occasions, so among earthly princes those are the wisest and the best who govern by the known laws of the country, and seldomest make use of their prerogative."

Now here you may see that the vile accusation of Wood and his accomplices, charging us with disputing the king's prerogative by refusing his brass, can have no place—because compelling the subject to take any coin which is not sterling is no part of the king's prerogative, and I am very confident if it were so we should be the last of his people to dispute it ; as well from that inviolable loyalty we have always paid to his majesty as from the treatment we might, in such a case, justly expect from some who seem to think we have neither common sense nor common senses. But God be thanked, the best of them are only our fellow-subjects and not our masters. One great merit I am sure we have, which those of English birth can have no pretence to—that our ancestors reduced this kingdom to the obedience of England ; for which we have been rewarded with a worse climate,—the privilege of being governed by laws to which we do not consent,—a ruined trade,—a house of peers without jurisdiction,—almost an incapacity for all employments,—and the dread of Wood's halfpence.

But we are so far from disputing the king's prerogative in coining, that we own he has power to give a patent to any man for setting his royal image and superscription upon whatever materials he pleases, and liberty to the patentee to offer them in any country from England to Japan; only attended with one small limitation—that nobody alive is obliged to take them.

Upon these considerations, I was ever against all recourse to England for a remedy against the present impending evil; especially when I observed that the addresses of both houses, after long expectance, produced nothing but a REPORT, altogether in favour of Wood; upon which I made some observations in a former letter, and might at least have made as many more, for it is a paper of as singular a nature as I ever beheld.

But I mistake; for before this Report was made, his majesty's most gracious answer to the house of lords was sent over, and printed; wherein are these words, granting the patent for coining halfpence and farthings, AGREEABLE TO THE PRACTICE OF HIS ROYAL PREDECESSORS, &c. That king Charles II. and king James II. (AND THEY ONLY) did grant patents for this purpose is indisputable, and I have shown it at large. Their patents were passed under the great seal of Ireland, by references to Ireland; the copper to be coined in Ireland; the patentee was bound, on demand, to receive his coin back in Ireland, and pay silver and gold in return. Wood's patent was made under the great seal of England; the brass coined in England; not the least reference made to Ireland; the sum immense, and the patentee under no obligation to receive it again and give good money for it. This I only mention, because in my private thoughts I have sometimes made a query whether the penner of those words in his majesty's most gracious answer, "agreeable to the practice of his royal predecessors," had maturely considered the several circumstances which, in my poor opinion, seem to make a difference.

Let me now say something concerning the other great cause of some people's fear, as Wood has taught the London newswriter to express it, that his excellency the lord-lieutenant is coming over to settle Wood's halfpence.

We know very well, that the lords-lieutenants, for several years past, have not thought this kingdom worthy the honour of their residence longer than was absolutely necessary for the king's business, which consequently wanted no speed in the dispatch. And therefore it naturally fell into most men's thoughts that a new governor, coming at an unusual time, must portend some unusual business to be done; especially if the common report be true, that the parliament, prorogued to I know not when, is by a new summons revoking that prorogation to assemble soon after the arrival; for which extraordinary proceeding the lawyers on the other side the water have by great good fortune found two precedents.

All this being granted, it can never enter into my head, that so little a creature as Wood could find credit enough with the king and his ministers, to have the lord-lieutenant of Ireland sent hither in a hurry upon his errand.

For let us take the whole matter nakedly as it lies before us, without the refinements of some people, with which we have nothing to do. Here is a patent granted under the great seal of England, upon false suggestions, to one William Wood, for coining copper halfpence for Ireland. The parliament here, upon apprehensions of the worst consequences from the said patent, address the king to have it recalled. This is refused; and a committee of the privy-council report to his majesty that Wood has performed the conditions of his patent. He then is left to do the best he can with his halfpence, no man being obliged to receive them; the people here, being likewise left to themselves, unite as one man, resolving they will have nothing to do with his ware.

By this plain account of the fact it is manifest, that the king and his ministry are wholly out of the case, and the matter is left to be disputed between him and us. Will any man, therefore, attempt to persuade me that a lord-lieutenant is to be dispatched over in great haste before the ordinary time, and a parliament summoned by anticipating a prorogation, merely to put a hundred thousand pounds into the pocket of a sharper, by the ruin of a most loyal kingdom?

But supposing all this to be true, by what arguments could a lord-lieutenant prevail on the same parliament, which addressed with so much zeal and earnestness against this evil, to pass it into a law? I am sure their opinion of Wood and his project is not mended since their last prorogation; and supposing those methods should be used which detractors tell us have been sometimes put in practice for gaining votes, it is well known that in this kingdom there are few employments to be given; and if there were more it is as well known to whose share they must fall.

But, because great numbers of you are altogether ignorant of the affairs of your country, I will tell you some reasons why there are so few employments to be disposed of in this kingdom.

All considerable offices for life are here possessed by

those to whom the reversions were granted; and these have been generally followers of the chief governors, or persons who had interest in the court of England. So the lord Berkeley of Stratton holds the great office of master of the rolls; the lord Palmerstown is first remembrancer, worth near £2000 per annum. One Dodington, secretary to the earl of Pembroke, begged the reversion of clerk of the pells, worth £2500 a-year, which he now enjoys by the death of the lord Newtown. Mr. Southwell is secretary of state, and the earl of Burlington lord high treasurer of Ireland, by inheritance. These are only a few among many others which I have been told of, but cannot remember. Nay, the reversion of several employments during pleasure is granted the same way. This, among many others, is a circumstance whereby the kingdom of Ireland is distinguished from all other nations upon earth, and makes it so difficult an affair to get into a civil employ, that Mr. Addison was forced to purchase an old obscure place, called keeper of the records in Birmingham's tower, of £10 a-year, and to get a salary of £400 annexed to it, though all the records there are not worth half-a-crown either for curiosity or use. And we lately saw a favourite secretary descend to be master of the revels, which by his credit and extortion he has made pretty considerable. I say nothing of the under-treasurership, worth about £9000 a-year, nor of the commissioners of the revenue, four of whom generally live in England, for I think none of these are granted in reversion. But the jest is that I have known upon occasion some of these absent officers as keen against the interest of Ireland as if they had never been indebted to her for a single groat.

I confess I have been sometimes tempted to wish that this project of Wood's might succeed; because I reflected with some pleasure what a jolly crew it would bring over among us of lords and squires and pensioners of both sexes, and officers civil and military, where we should live together as merry and sociable as beggars, only with this one abatement, that we should neither have meat to feed nor manufactures to clothe us, unless we could be content to prance about in coats of mail or eat brass as ostriches do iron.

I return from this digression to that which gave me the occasion of making it. And I believe you are now convinced that if the parliament of Ireland were as temptable as any other assembly within a mile of Christendom (which God forbid!), yet the managers must of necessity fail for want of tools to work with. But I will yet go one step farther, by supposing that a hundred new employments were erected on purpose to gratify compliers; yet still an insuperable difficulty would remain. For it happens, I know not how, that money is neither Whig nor Tory—neither of town nor country party; and it is not improbable, that a gentleman would rather choose to live upon his own estate, which brings him gold and silver, than with the addition of an employment, when his rents and salary must both be paid in Wood's brass at above 80 per cent. discount.

For these and many other reasons I am confident you need not be under the least apprehension from the sudden expectation of the lord-lieutenant, while we continue in our present hearty disposition, to alter which no suitable temptation can possibly be offered. And if, as I have often asserted from the best authority, the law has not left a power in the crown to force any money, except sterling, upon the subject, much less can the crown devolve such a power upon another.

This I speak with the utmost respect to the person and dignity of his excellency the lord Carteret, whose character was lately given me by a gentleman that has known him from his first appearance in the world. That gentleman describes him as a young nobleman of great accomplishments, excellent learning, regular in his life, and of much spirit and vivacity. He has since, as I have heard, been employed abroad; was principal secretary of state; and is now, about the thirty-seventh year of his age, appointed lord-lieutenant of Ireland. From such a governor this kingdom may reasonably hope for as much prosperity as, under so many discouragements, it can be capable of receiving.

It is true, indeed, that within the memory of man there have been governors of so much dexterity as to carry points of terrible consequence to this kingdom by their power with those who are in office; and by their arts in managing or deluding others with oaths, affability, and even with dinners. If Wood's brass had in those times been upon the anvil, it is obvious enough to conceive what methods would have been taken. Depending persons would have been told in plain terms, "that it was a service expected from them, under the pain of the public business being put into more complying hands." Others would be allured by promises. To the country gentlemen, beside good words, burgundy, and closeting, it might perhaps have been hinted, "how kindly it would be taken to comply with a royal patent, although it were not compulsory; that if any inconveniences ensued, it might be made up with other graces or favours hereafter; that gentlemen ought to consider whether it were prudent or safe to disgust England. They would be desired to think of some good bills for encouraging of trade and setting the poor to work; some further acts against popery, and for uniting protestants." There would be solemn engagements, "that we should never be troubled with above £40,000 in his coin, and all of the best and weightiest sort, for which we should only give our manufactures in exchange, and keep our gold and silver at home." Perhaps a seasonable report of some invasion would have been spread in the most proper juncture; which is a great smoother of rubs in public proceedings; and we should have been told "that this was no time to create differences when the kingdom was in danger."

These, I say, and the like methods would, in corrupt times, have been taken to let in this deluge of brass among us; and I am confident, even then would not have succeeded; much less under the administration of so excellent a person as the lord Carteret, and in a country where the people of all ranks, parties, and denominations, are convinced to a man that the utter undoing of themselves and their posterity for ever will be dated from the admission of that execrable coin; that if it once enters, it can be no more confined to a small or moderate quantity than a plague can be confined to a few families; and that no equivalent can be given by any earthly power, any more than a dead carcase can be recovered to life by a cordial.

There is one comfortable circumstance in this universal opposition to Mr. Wood, that the people sent over hither from England, to fill up our vacancies, ecclesiastical, civil, and military, are all on our side.

Money, the great divider of the world, has, by a strange revolution, been a great uniter of a most divided people. Who would leave £100 a-year in England (a country of freedom) to be paid £1000 in Ireland out of Wood's exchequer? The gentleman they have lately made primate would never quit his seat in an English house of lords, and his preferments at Oxford and Bristol, worth £1200 a-year, for four times the denomination here but not half the value; therefore, I expect to hear he will be as good an Irishman, at least upon this one article, as any of his brethren, or even of us who have had the misfortune to be born in this island. For those who in the common phrase do not come hither to learn the language would never change a better country for a worse, to receive brass instead of gold.

Another slander spread by Wood and his emissaries is "that by opposing him we discover an inclination to throw off our dependence upon the crown of England." Pray observe how important a person is this same William Wood, and how the public weal of two kingdoms is involved in his private interest. First, all those who refuse to take his coin are papists; for he tells us, "that none but papists are associated against him." Secondly, "they dispute the king's prerogative." Thirdly, "they are ripe for rebellion." And, fourthly, "they are going to shake off their dependence upon the crown of England;" that is to say, they are going to choose another king; for there can be no other meaning in this expression, however some may pretend to strain it.

And this gives me an opportunity of explaining to those who are ignorant another point, which has often swelled in my breast.* Those who come over hither to us from England, and some weak people among ourselves, whenever in discourse we make mention of liberty and property, shake their heads, and tell us that "Ireland is a depending kingdom;" as if they would seem by this phrase to intend that the people of Ireland are in some state of slavery or dependence different from those of England; whereas a depending kingdom is a modern term of art, unknown, as I have heard, to all ancient civilians and writers upon government; and Ireland is, on the contrary, called in some statutes "an imperial crown," as held only from God; which is as high a style as any kingdom is capable of receiving. Therefore, by this expression, "a depending kingdom," there is no more to be understood than that, by a statute made here in the 33rd year of Henry VIII., the king and his successors are to be kings imperial of this realm, as united and knit to the imperial crown of England. I have looked over all the English and Irish statutes without finding any law that makes Ireland depend upon England, any more than England does upon Ireland. We have indeed obliged ourselves to have the same king with them; and consequently they are obliged to have the same king with us. For the law was made by our own parliament; and our ancestors then were not such fools (whatever they were in the preceding reign) to bring themselves under I know not what dependence, which is now talked of without any ground of law, reason, or common sense.

Let whoever thinks otherwise, I, M.B., drapier, desire to be excepted; for I declare, next under God, I depend only on the king my sovereign and on the laws of my own country. And I am so far from depending upon the people of England, that if they should ever rebel against my sovereign (which God forbid!) I would be ready, at the first command from his majesty, to take arms against them, as some of my countrymen did against theirs at Preston. And if such a rebellion should prove so successful as to fix the Pretender on the throne of England, I would venture to transgress that statute so far as to lose every drop of my blood to hinder him from being king of Ireland.

It is true, indeed, that within the memory of man the parliaments of England have sometimes assumed the power of binding this kingdom by laws enacted there; wherein they were at first openly opposed (as far as truth, reason, and justice, are capable of opposing) by the famous Mr. Molyneux, an English gentleman born here, as well as by several of the greatest patriots and best Whigs in England; but the love and torrent of power prevailed. Indeed the arguments on both sides were invincible. For in reason, all government without the consent of the governed is the very definition of slavery; but in fact, eleven men well armed will certainly subdue one single man in his shirt. But I have done; for those who have used power to cramp liberty have gone so far as to resent even the liberty of complaining; although a man upon the rack was never known to be refused the liberty of roaring as loud as he thought fit.

And as we are apt to sink too much under unreasonable fears, so we are too soon inclined to be raised by groundless hopes, according to the nature of all consumptive bodies like ours. Thus it has been given about for several days past that somebody in England empowered a second somebody to write to a third somebody here to assure us that we should no more be troubled with these halfpence. And this is reported to have been done by the same person who is said to have sworn some months ago "that he would ram them down our throats," though I doubt they would stick in our stomachs; but whichever of these reports be true or false, it is no concern of ours. For in this point we have nothing to do with English ministers, and I should be sorry to leave it in their power to redress this grievance or to enforce it, for the report of the committee has given me a surfeit. The remedy is wholly in your own hands, and therefore I have digressed a little in order to refresh and continue that spirit so seasonably raised among you, and to let you see that, by the laws of GOD, of NATURE, of NATIONS, and of your COUNTRY, you ARE and OUGHT to be as FREE a people as your brethren in England.

If the pamphlets published at London by Wood and his journeymen, in defence of his cause, were reprinted here, and our countrymen could be persuaded to read them, they would convince you of his wicked design more than all I shall ever be able to say. In short, I make him a perfect saint in comparison of what he appears to be from the writings of those whom he hires to justify his project. But he is so far master of the field (let others guess the reason) that no London printer dare publish any paper written in favour of Ireland; and here, nobody as yet has been so bold as to publish anything in favour of him.

There was a few days ago a pamphlet sent me of near fifty pages, written in favour of Mr. Wood and his coinage, printed in London : it is not worth answering, because probably it will never be published here. But it gave me occasion to reflect upon an unhappiness we lie under, that the people of England are utterly ignorant of our case ; which however is no wonder, since it is a point they do not in the least concern themselves about, further than perhaps as a subject of discourse in a coffee-house when they have nothing else to talk of. For I have reason to believe that no minister ever gave himself the trouble of reading any papers written in our defence, because I suppose their opinions are already determined, and are formed wholly upon the reports of Wood and his accomplices ; else it would be impossible that any man could have the impudence to write such a pamphlet as I have mentioned.

Our neighbours, whose understandings are just upon a level with ours (which perhaps are none of the brightest), have a strong contempt for most nations, but especially for Ireland. They look upon us as a sort of savage Irish whom our ancestors conquered several hundred years ago. And if I should describe the Britons to you as they were in Cæsar's time, when they painted their bodies or clothed themselves with the skins of beasts, I should act full as reasonably as they do. However, they are so far to be excused in relation to the present subject, that hearing only one side of the cause, and having neither opportunity nor curiosity to examine the other, they believe a lie merely for their ease ; and conclude, because Mr. Wood pretends to power, he has also reason on his side. . . .

But although our arguments are not suffered to be printed in England, yet the consequence will be of little moment. Let Wood endeavour to persuade the people there that we ought to receive his coin; and let me convince our people here that they ought to reject it, under pain of our utter undoing; and then let him do his best and his worst.

Before I conclude, I must beg leave in all humility to tell Mr. Wood, that he is guilty of great indiscretion, by causing so honourable a name as that of Mr. Walpole to be mentioned so often and in such a manner upon this occasion. A short paper printed at Bristol, and reprinted here, reports Mr. Wood to say, "that he wonders at the impudence and insolence of the Irish in refusing his coin, and what he will do when Mr. Walpole comes to town." Where, by the way, he is mistaken; for it is the true English people of Ireland who refuse it, although we take it for granted that the Irish will do so too whenever they are asked. In another printed paper of his contriving, it is roundly expressed, "that Mr. Walpole will cram his brass down our throats." Sometimes it is given out "that we must either take those halfpence or eat our brogues:" and in another Newsletter, but of yesterday, we read, "that the same great man has sworn to make us swallow his coin in fireballs."

This brings to my mind the known story of a Scotchman, who, receiving the sentence of death with all the circumstances of hanging, beheading, quartering, embowelling, and the like, cried out, " What need all this cookery?" And I think we have reason to ask the same question; for if we believe Wood, here is a dinner getting ready for us, and you see the bill of fare; and I am sorry the drink was forgot, which might easily be supplied with melted lead and flaming pitch.

What vile words are these to put into the mouth of a great counsellor, in high trust with his majesty and looked upon as a prime-minister! If Mr. Wood has no better a manner of representing his patrons, when I come to be a great man he shall never be suffered to attend at my levee. This is not the style of a great minister; it savours too much of the kettle and the furnace, and came entirely out of Wood's forge.

As for the threat of making us eat our brogues, we need not be in pain; for if his coin should pass, that unpolite covering for the feet would no longer be a national reproach; because then we should have neither shoe nor brogue left in the kingdom. But here the falsehood of Mr. Wood is fairly detected; for I am confident Mr. Walpole never heard of a brogue in his whole life.

As to "swallowing these halfpence in fire-balls," it is a story equally improbable. For to execute this operation, the whole stock of Mr. Wood's coin and metal must be melted down, and moulded into hollow balls with wild-fire, no bigger than a reasonable throat may be able to swallow. Now, the metal he has prepared, and already coined, will amount to at least fifty millions of halfpence, to be swallowed by a million and a half of people: so that, allowing two halfpence to each ball, there will be about seventeen balls of wild-fire a-piece to be swallowed by every person in the kingdom; and to administer this dose, there cannot be conveniently fewer than fifty thousand operators, allowing one operator to every thirty; which, considering the squeamishness of some stomachs, and the peevishness of young children, is but reasonable. Now, under correction of better judgments, I think the trouble and charge of such an experiment would exceed the profit; and therefore I take this report to be spurious, or at least only a new scheme of Mr. Wood himself; which, to make it pass the better in Ireland, he would father upon a minister of state.

But I will now demonstrate beyond all contradiction, that Mr. Walpole is against this project of Mr. Wood and is an entire friend to Ireland, only by this one invincible argument; that he has the universal opinion of being a wise man, an able minister, and in all his proceedings pursuing the true interest of the king his master; and that as his integrity is above all corruption, so is his fortune above all temptation. I reckon, therefore, we are perfectly safe from that corner, and shall never be under the necessity of contending with so formidable a power, but be left to possess our brogues and potatoes in peace, as remote from thunder as we are from Jupiter.

I am, my dear countrymen, your loving fellow-subject, fellow-sufferer, and humble servant, M. B.

A MODEST PROPOSAL

FOR PREVENTING THE CHILDREN OF POOR PEOPLE
IN IRELAND FROM BEING A BURDEN TO THEIR
PARENTS OR COUNTRY, AND FOR MAKING THEM
BENEFICIAL TO THE PUBLIC

IT is a melancholy object to those who walk through this great town, or travel in the country, when they see the streets, the roads, and cabin doors, crowded with beggars of the female sex, followed by three, four, or six children, all in rags, and importuning every passenger for an alms. These mothers, instead of being able to work for their honest livelihood, are forced to employ all their time in strolling to beg sustenance for their helpless infants; who, as they grow up, either turn thieves for want of work, or leave their dear native country to fight for the Pretender in Spain, or sell themselves to the Barbadoes.

I think it is agreed by all parties that this prodigious number of children in the arms, or on the backs, or at the heels, of their mothers, and frequently of their fathers, is in the present deplorable state of the kingdom a very great additional grievance; and therefore whoever could find out a fair, cheap, and easy method of making these children sound useful members of the commonwealth, would deserve so well of the public as to have his statue set up for a preserver of the nation.

But my intention is very far from being confined to provide only for the children of professed beggars; it is of a much greater extent, and shall take in the whole number of infants at a certain age who are born of parents in effect as little able to support them as those who demand our charity in the streets.

As to my own part, having turned my thoughts for many years upon this important subject, and maturely weighed the several schemes of our projectors, I have always found them grossly mistaken in their computation. It is true, a child just dropped from its dam may be supported by her milk for a solar year, with little other nourishment; at most not above the value of 2*s*., which the mother may certainly get, or the value in scraps, by her lawful occupation of begging; and it is exactly at one year old that I propose to provide for them in such a manner as, instead of being a charge upon their parents or the parish, or wanting food and raiment for the rest of their lives, they shall on the contrary contribute to the feeding, and partly to the clothing, of many thousands.

There is likewise another great advantage in my scheme; that it will prevent that horrid practice of women murdering their children, alas, too frequent among us, sacrificing the poor innocent babes, I doubt, more to avoid the expense than the shame; which would move tears and pity in the most savage and inhuman breast.

The number of souls in this kingdom being usually reckoned one million and a half, of these I calculate there may be about 200,000 couple whose wives are breeders; from which number I subtract 30,000 couple who are able to maintain their own children, although I apprehend there cannot be so many, under the present distresses of the kingdom; but this being granted, there will remain 170,000 breeders. I again subtract 50,000 for those whose children die by accident or disease within the year. There only remain 120,000 children of poor parents annually born. The question therefore is, how this number shall be reared and provided for? which, as I have already said, under the present situation of affairs is utterly impossible by all the methods hitherto proposed. For we can neither employ them in handicraft nor agriculture; we neither build houses (I mean in the country) nor cultivate land; they can very seldom pick up a livelihood by stealing, till they arrive at six years old, except where they are of towardly parts; although I confess they learn the rudiments much earlier; during which time they can, however, be properly looked upon only as probationers; as I have been informed by a principal gentleman in the county of Cavan, who protested to me that he never knew above one or two instances under the age of six, even in a part of the kingdom so renowned for the quickest proficiency in that art.

I am assured by our merchants that a boy or a girl before twelve years old is no saleable commodity; and even when they come to this age they will not yield above £3, or £3 2s. 6d. at most, on the Exchange; which cannot turn to account either to the parents or kingdom, the charge of nutriment and rags having been at least four times that value.

I shall now therefore humbly propose my own

thoughts, which I hope will not be liable to the least objection.

I have been assured by a very knowing American of my acquaintance in London, that a young healthy child, well nursed, is at a year old a most delicious, nourishing, and wholesome food, whether stewed, roasted, baked, or boiled; and I make no doubt that it will equally serve in a fricassee or a ragout.

I do therefore humbly offer it to public consideration that of the 120,000 children already computed, 20,000 may be reserved for breed, whereof only one-fourth part to be males; which is more than we allow to sheep, black cattle, or swine. That the remaining 100,000 may, at a year old, be offered in sale to the persons of quality and fortune through the kingdom; always advising the mother to let them suck plentifully in the last month, so as to render them plump and fat for a good table. A child will make two dishes at an entertainment for friends; and when the family dines alone, the fore or hind quarter will make a reasonable dish, and, seasoned with a little pepper or salt, will be very good boiled on the fourth day, especially in winter.

I have reckoned upon a medium that a child just born will weigh 12 pounds, and in a solar year, if tolerably nursed, will increase to 28 pounds.

I grant this food will be somewhat dear, and therefore very proper for landlords, who, as they have already devoured most of the parents, seem to have the best title to the children.

Infant's flesh will be in season throughout the year, but more plentifully in March, and a little before and after: for we are told by a grave author, an eminent

French physician, that, fish being a prolific diet, there are more children born in Roman Catholic countries about nine months after Lent than at any other season ; therefore, reckoning a year after Lent, the markets will be more glutted than usual, because the number of popish infants is at least three to one in this kingdom : and therefore it will have one other collateral advantage, by lessening the number of papists among us.

I have already computed the charge of nursing a beggar's child (in which list I reckon all cottagers, labourers, and four-fifths of the farmers) to be about 2*s.* per annum, rags included ; and I believe no gentleman would repine to give 10*s.* for the carcase of a good fat child, which, as I have said, will make four dishes of excellent nutritive meat, when he has only some particular friend or his own family to dine with him. Thus the squire will learn to be a good landlord, and grow popular among his tenants ; the mother will have 8*s.* net profit, and be fit for work till she produces another child.

Those who are more thrifty (as I must confess the times require) may flay the carcase ; the skin of which, artificially dressed, will make admirable gloves for ladies, and summer boots for fine gentlemen.

As to our city of Dublin, shambles may be appointed for this purpose in the most convenient parts of it, and butchers, we may be assured, will not be wanting ; although I rather recommend buying the children alive than dressing them hot from the knife as we do roasting pigs.

A very worthy person, a true lover of his country, and whose virtues I highly esteem, was lately pleased, in discoursing on this matter, to offer a refinement upon my scheme. He said that many gentlemen of this kingdom having of late destroyed their deer, he conceived that the want of venison might be well supplied by the bodies of young lads and maidens, not exceeding fourteen years of age, nor under twelve; so great a number of both sexes in every country being now ready to starve for want of work and service; and these to be disposed of by their parents if alive, or otherwise by their nearest relations. But, with due deference to so excellent a friend and so deserving a patriot, I cannot be altogether in his sentiments; for as to the males, my American acquaintance assured me, from frequent experience, that their flesh was generally tough and lean, like that of our schoolboys, by continual exercise, and their taste disagreeable; and to fatten them would not answer the charge: and besides, it is not improbable that some scrupulous people might be apt to censure such a practice, (although indeed very unjustly,) as a little bordering upon cruelty; which, I confess, has always been with me the strongest objection against any project, how well soever intended.

But, in order to justify my friend, he confessed that this expedient was put into his head by the famous Psalmanazar, a native of the island Formosa, who came thence to London above twenty years ago, and in conversation told my friend that in his country, when any young person happened to be put to death, the executioner sold the carcase to persons of quality as a prime dainty; and that in his time the body of a plump girl of fifteen, who was crucified for an attempt to poison the emperor, was sold to his imperial majesty's prime minister of state and other great mandarins of the court, in joints from the gibbet, at 400 crowns. Neither, indeed, can I deny that if the same use were made of several plump young girls in this town, who, without one single groat to their fortunes, cannot stir abroad without a chair, and appear at playhouse and assemblies in foreign fineries which they never will pay for, the kingdom would not be the worse.

Some persons of a desponding spirit are in great concern about that vast number of poor people who are aged, diseased, or maimed; and I have been desired to employ my thoughts what course may be taken to ease the nation of so grievous an encumbrance. But I am not in the least pain upon that matter, because it is very well known that they are every day dying and rotting by cold and famine, and filth and vermin, as fast as can be reasonably expected. And as to the young labourers, they are now in almost as hopeful a condition; they cannot get work, and consequently pine away for want of nourishment, to a degree that if at any time they are accidentally hired to common labour, they have not strength to perform it; and thus the country and themselves are happily delivered from the evils to come.

I have too long digressed, and therefore shall return to my subject. I think the advantages by the proposal which I have made are obvious and many, as well as of the highest importance.

For, first, as I have already observed, it would greatly lessen the number of papists, with whom we are yearly overrun, being the principal breeders of the nation, as well as our most dangerous enemies; and who stay at home on purpose to deliver the kingdom to the Pretender, hoping to take their advantage by the absence of so many good protestants, who have chosen rather to leave their country than stay at home and pay tithes against their conscience to an episcopal curate.

Secondly, The poorer tenants will have something valuable of their own, which by law may be made liable to distress, and help to pay their landlord's rent; their corn and cattle being already seized, and money a thing unknown.

Thirdly, Whereas the maintenance of 100,000 children, from two years old and upward, cannot be computed at less than 10s. a-piece per annum, the nation's stock will be thereby increased £50,000 per annum, besides the profit of a new dish introduced to the tables of all gentlemen of fortune in the kingdom who have any refinement in taste. And the money will circulate among ourselves, the goods being entirely of our own growth and manufacture.

Fourthly, The constant breeders, beside the gain of 8s. sterling per annum by the sale of their children, will be rid of the charge of maintaining them after the first year.

Fifthly, This food would likewise bring great custom to taverns; where the vintners will certainly be so prudent as to procure the best receipts for dressing it to perfection, and consequently have their houses frequented by all the fine gentlemen, who justly value themselves upon their knowledge in good eating: and a skilful cook, who understands how to oblige his guests, will contrive to make it as expensive as they please.

Sixthly, This would be a great inducement to

marriage, which all wise nations have either encouraged by rewards, or enforced by laws and penalties. It would increase the care and tenderness of mothers towards their children, when they were sure of a settlement for life to the poor babes, provided in some sort by the public, to their annual profit or expense. We should see an honest emulation among the married women, which of them could bring the fattest child to the market.

Many other advantages might be enumerated. For instance, the addition of some thousand carcases in our exportation of barreled beef, the propagation of swine's flesh, and improvement in the art of making good bacon, so much wanted among us by the great destruction of pigs, too frequent at our table ; which are in no way comparable in taste or magnificence to a well grown, fat, yearling child, which, roasted whole, will make a considerable figure at a lord mayor's feast or any other public entertainment. But this and many others I omit, being studious of brevity.

Supposing that 1000 families in this city would be constant customers for infant's flesh, beside others who might have it at merry-meetings, particularly at weddings and christenings, I compute that Dublin would take off annually about 20,000 carcases ; and the rest of the kingdom (where probably they will be sold somewhat cheaper) the remaining 80,000.

I can think of no one objection that will possibly be raised against this proposal, unless it should be urged that the number of people will be thereby much lessened in the kingdom. This I freely own, and it was indeed one principal design in offering it to the world. I desire the reader will observe, that I calculate my remedy for this one individual kingdom of Ireland, and for no other that ever was, is, or I think ever can be, upon earth. Therefore let no man talk to me of other expedients : of taxing our absentees at 5*s.* a pound ; of using neither clothes nor household furniture except what is of our own growth and manufacture ; of utterly rejecting the materials and instruments that promote foreign luxury ; of curing the expensiveness of pride, vanity, idleness, and gaming, in our women ; of introducing a vein of parsimony, prudence, and temperance ; of learning to love our country, in the want of which we differ even from Laplanders and the inhabitants of Topinamboo ; of quitting our animosities and factions, nor acting any longer like the Jews, who were murdering one another at the very moment their city was taken ; of being a little cautious not to sell our country and conscience for nothing ; of teaching landlords to have at least one degree of mercy toward their tenants ; lastly, of putting a spirit of honesty, industry, and skill into our shopkeepers ; who, if a resolution could now be taken to buy only our native goods, would immediately unite to cheat and exact upon us in the price, the measure, and the goodness, nor could ever yet be brought to make one fair proposal of just dealing, though often and earnestly invited to it.

Therefore I repeat, let no man talk to me of these and the like expedients, till he has at least some glimpse of hope that there will be ever some hearty and sincere attempt to put them in practice.

But as to myself, having been wearied out for many years with offering vain, idle, visionary thoughts, and at length utterly despairing of success, I fortunately fell upon this proposal ; which, as it is wholly new, so it has something solid and real, of no expense and little trouble, full in our own power, and whereby we can incur no danger in disobliging England. For this kind of commodity will not bear exportation, the flesh being of too tender a consistence to admit a long continuance in salt ; although perhaps I could name a country which would be glad to eat up our whole nation without it.

After all, I am not so violently bent upon my own opinion, as to reject any offer, proposed by wise men, which shall be found equally innocent, cheap, easy, and effectual. But before something of that kind shall be advanced in contradiction to my scheme, and offering a better, I desire the author or authors will be pleased naturally to consider two points. First, as things now stand, how they will be able to find food and raiment for 100,000 useless mouths and backs. And secondly, there being a round million of creatures in human figure throughout this kingdom, whose whole subsistence put into a common stock would leave them in debt £2,000,000 sterling, adding those who are beggars by profession to the bulk of farmers, cottagers, and labourers, with the wives and children, who are beggars in effect : I desire those politicians who dislike my overture, and may perhaps be so bold as to attempt an answer, that they will first ask the parents of these mortals, whether they would not at this day think it a great happiness to have been sold for food at a year old in the manner I prescribe, and thereby have avoided such a perpetual scene of misfortunes as they have since gone through by the oppression of landlords, the impossibility of paying rent without money or trade, the want of common sustenance, with neither house nor clothes to cover them from the inclemencies of the weather, and the most inevitable prospect of entailing the like or greater miseries upon their breed for ever.

I profess, in the sincerity of my heart, that I have not the least personal interest in endeavouring to promote this necessary work ; having no other motive than the public good of my country, by advancing our trade, providing for infants, relieving the poor, and giving some pleasure to the rich.

A COMPLETE COLLECTION OF GENTEEL AND INGENIOUS CONVERSATION,

ACCORDING TO THE MOST POLITE MODE AND METHOD, NOW USED AT COURT, AND IN THE BEST COMPANIES OF ENGLAND. IN THREE DIALOGUES. BY SIMON WAGSTAFF, ESQ.

"I am got eight miles from our famous metropolis to a country parson's, to whom I gave a city living such as an English chaplain would leap at. I retired thither for the public good, having two great works in hand; one to reduce the whole politeness, wit, humour, and style of England into a short system for the use of all persons of quality, and particularly the maids of honour....." *Swift to Gay and the Duchess of Queensberry*, Aug. 28, 1731. Swift presented the manuscript to Mrs. Barber,—"one of four poetesses in this town, and all citizens' wives; but she has the vogue of being the best,"—who was then in great poverty, to make what she could by its publication (1738). The first half of the Introduction, and part of the first Dialogue, sufficiently explain this caricature of the "small talk" of the day.

POLITE CONVERSATION.

INTRODUCTION

AS my life has been chiefly spent in consulting the honour and welfare of my country for more than forty years past, not without answerable success, if the world and my friends have not flattered me, so there is no point wherein I have so much laboured as that of improving and polishing all parts of conversation between persons of quality, whether they meet by accident or invitation, at meals, tea, or visits, mornings, noon, or evenings.

I have passed perhaps more time than any other man of my age and country in visits and assemblies, where the polite persons of both sexes distinguish themselves; and could not without much grief observe how frequently both gentlemen and ladies are at a loss for questions, answers, replies, and rejoinders. However, my concern was much abated when I found that these defects were not occasioned by any want of materials, but because those materials were not in every hand : for instance, one lady can give an answer better than ask a question : one gentleman is happy at a reply; another excels in a rejoinder : one can revive a languishing conversation by a sudden surprising sentence; another is more dexterous in seconding; a third can fill up the gap with laughing, or commending what has been said: thus fresh hints may be started, and the ball of the discourse kept up.

But, alas! this is too seldom the case, even in the most select companies. How often do we see at court, at public visiting days, at great men's levees, and other places of general meeting, that the conversation falls and drops to nothing, like a fire without supply of fuel! This is what we all ought to lament; and against this dangerous evil I take upon me to affirm, that I have in the following papers provided an infallible remedy.

It was in the year 1695, and the sixth of his late majesty king William III., of ever-glorious and immortal memory, who rescued three kingdoms from popery and slavery, when, being about the age of six-and-thirty, my judgment mature, of good reputation in the world, and well acquainted with the best families in town, I determined to spend five mornings, to dine four times, pass three afternoons, and six evenings every week in the house of the most polite families, of which I would confine myself to fifty; only changing as the masters or ladies died, or left the town, or grew out of vogue or sunk in their fortunes, or (which to me was of the highest moment) became disaffected to the government; which practice I have followed ever since to this very day; except when I happened to be sick, or in the spleen upon cloudy weather; and except when I entertained four of each sex at my own lodgings once in a month, by way of retaliation.

I always kept a large table-book in my pocket; and as soon as I left the company I immediately entered the choicest expressions that passed during the visit: which, returning home, I transcribed in a fair hand, but somewhat enlarged ; and had made the greatest part of my collection in twelve years, but not digested into any method, for this I found was a work of infinite labour, and what required the nicest judgment, and consequently could not be brought to any degree of perfection in less than sixteen years more.

Herein I resolved to exceed the advice of Horace, a Roman poet, which I have read in Mr. Creech's admirable translation, that an author should keep his works nine years in his closet before he ventured to publish them : and, finding that I still received some additional flowers of wit and language, although in a very small number, I determined to defer the publication, to pursue my design, and exhaust (if possible) the whole subject, that I might present a complete system to the world : for I am convinced, by long experience, that the critics will be as severe as their old envy against me can make them : I foresee they will object, that I have inserted many answers and replies, which are neither witty, humorous, polite, nor authentic, and have omitted others that would have been highly useful, as well as entertaining. But let them come to particulars, and I will boldly engage to confute their malice.

For these last six or seven years I have not been able to add above nine valuable sentences to enrich my collection : from whence I conclude that what remains will amount only to a trifle. However, if, after the publication of this work, any lady or gentleman, when they have read it, shall find the least thing of importance omitted, I desire they will please to supply my defects by communicating to me their discoveries; and their letters may be directed to Simon Wagstaff, esq., at his lodgings next door to the Gloucester-head in St. James's street, paying the postage. In return of which favour, I shall make honourable mention of their names in a short preface to the second edition.

In the mean time, I cannot but with some pride and much pleasure congratulate with my dear country, which has outdone all the nations of Europe, in advancing the whole art of conversation to the greatest height it is capable of reaching; and, therefore, being entirely convinced that the collection I now offer to the public is full and complete, I may at the same time boldly affirm that the whole genius, humour, politeness, and eloquence of England are summed up in it; nor is the treasure small, wherein are to be found at least a thousand shining questions, answers, repartees, replies, and rejoinders, fitted to adorn every kind of discourse that an assembly of English ladies and gentlemen, met together for their mutual entertainment, can possibly want: especially when the several flowers shall be set off and improved by the speakers, with every circumstance of preface and circumlocution, in proper terms, and attended with praise, laughter, or admiration.

There is a natural involuntary distortion of the muscles, which is the anatomical cause of laughter: but there is another cause of laughter, which decency requires, and is the undoubted mark of a good taste, as well as of a polite obliging behaviour; neither is this to be acquired without much observation, long practice, and sound judgment; I did therefore once intend, for the ease of the learner, to set down, in all parts of the following dialogues, certain marks, asterisks, or *nota benes* (in English, mark-wells) after most questions, and every reply or answer ; directing exactly the moment when one, two, or all the company are to laugh : but, having duly considered that this expedient would too much enlarge the bulk of the volume, and consequently the price, and likewise that something ought to be left for ingenious readers to find out, I have determined to leave that whole affair, although of great importance, to their own discretion.

The reader must learn by all means to distinguish between proverbs and those polite speeches which beautify conversation ; for, as to the former, I utterly reject them out of all ingenious discourse. I acknowledge, indeed, that there may possibly be found in this treatise a few sayings, among so great a number of smart turns of wit and humour as I have produced, which have a proverbial air ; however, I hope it will be considered that even these were not originally proverbs, but the genuine productions of superior wits, to embellish and support conversation ; whence, with great impropriety as well as plagiarism, (if you will forgive a hard word,) they have most injuriously been transferred into proverbial maxims ; and therefore, in justice, ought to be resumed out of vulgar hands, to adorn the drawing-rooms of princes both male and female, the levees of great ministers, as well as the toilet and tea-table of the ladies.

I can faithfully assure the reader that there is not one single witty phrase in this whole collection which has not received the stamp and approbation of at least one hundred years, and how much longer it is hard to determine ; he may therefore be secure to find them all genuine, sterling, and authentic.

But, before this elaborate treatise can become of universal use and ornament to my native country, two points, that will require much time and much application, are absolutely necessary.

For, first, whatever person would aspire to be completely witty, smart, humorous, and polite, must, by hard labour, be able to retain in his memory every single sentence contained in this work, so as never to be once at a loss in applying the right answers, questions, repartees, and the like, immediately, and without study or hesitation.

And, secondly, after a lady or gentleman has so well overcome this difficulty as never to be at a loss upon any emergency, the true management of every feature, and almost every limb, is equally necessary; without which an infinite number of absurdities will inevitably ensue. For instance, there is hardly a polite sentence in the following dialogues which does not absolutely require some peculiar graceful motion in the eyes, or nose, or mouth, or forehead, or chin, or suitable toss of the head, with certain offices assigned to each hand; and in ladies, the whole exercise of the fan, fitted to the energy of every word they deliver; by no means omitting the various turns and cadence of the voice, the twistings, and movements, and different postures of the body, the several kinds and gradations of laughter, which the ladies must daily practise by the looking-glass, and consult upon them with their waiting-maids.

My readers will soon observe what a great compass of real and useful knowledge this science includes; wherein, although nature, assisted by genius, may be very instrumental, yet a strong memory and constant application, together with example and precept, will be highly necessary.

POLITE CONVERSATION.
DIALOGUE I.

The Men.
Lord SPARKISH.
Lord SMART.
Sir JOHN LINGER.
Mr. NEVEROUT.
Colonel ATWIT.

The Ladies.
Lady SMART.
Miss NOTABLE.
Lady ANSWERALL.

Lord Sparkish and Colonel Atwit meet in the morning upon the Mall: Mr. Neverout joins them: they all go to breakfast at lady Smart's. Their conversation over their tea.

ST. JAMES'S PARK.

LORD SPARKISH *meeting* COL. ATWIT.

Col. WELL met, my lord.

Spark. Thank ye, colonel. A parson would have said, I hope we shall meet in heaven. When did you see Tom Neverout?

Col. He's just coming toward us. Talk of the devil—

NEVEROUT *comes up.*

Col. How do you do, Tom?

Never. Never the better for you.

Col. I hope you are never the worse.: but pray where's your manners? Don't you see my lord Sparkish?

Never. My lord, I beg your lordship's pardon.

Spark. Tom, how is it that you can't see the wood for trees? What wind blew you hither?

Never. Why, my lord, it is an ill wind blows nobody good; for it gives me the honour of seeing your lordship.

Col. Tom, you must go with us to lady Smart's to breakfast.

Never. Must! why, colonel, must's for the king.

[*Col. offering, in jest, to draw his sword.*

Col. Have you spoke with all your friends?

Never. Colonel, as you are stout be merciful.

Spark. Come, agree, agree; the law's costly.

[*Col. taking his hand from his hilt.*

Col. Well, Tom, you are never the worse man to be afraid of me. Come along.

Never. What! do you think I was born in a wood, to be afraid of an owl? I'll wait on you. I hope Miss Notable will be there; 'egad, she's very handsome, and has wit at will.

Col. Why, every one as they like, as the good woman said when she kiss'd her cow.

LORD SMART'S *House: they knock at the door; the Porter comes out.*

Spark. Pray are you the porter?

Porter. Yes, for want of a better.

Spark. Is your lady at home?

Porter. She was at home just now, but she's not gone out yet.

Never. I warrant this rogue's tongue is well hung.

LADY SMART'S *Ante-chamber.*

LADY SMART *and* LADY ANSWERALL *at the Tea-table.*

Lady S. My lord, your lordship's most humble servant.

Spark. Madam, you spoke too late; I was your ladyship's before.

Lady S. Oh! colonel, are you here?

Col. As sure as you're there, madam.

Lady S. O, Mr. Neverout! What, such a man alive!

Never. Ay, madam, alive, and alive like to be, at your ladyship's service.

Lady S. Well, I'll get a knife, and nick it down, that Mr. Neverout came to our house. And pray, what news, Mr. Neverout?

Never. Why, madam, queen Elizabeth's dead.

Lady S. Well, Mr. Neverout, I see you are no changeling.

MISS NOTABLE *comes in.*

Never. Miss, your slave: I hope your early rising will do you no harm. I find you are but just come out of the cloth market.

Miss. I always rise at eleven, whether it be day or not.

Col. Miss, I hope you are up for all day.

Miss. Yes, if I don't get a fall before night.

Col. Miss, I heard you were out of order; pray how are you now?

Miss. Pretty well, colonel, I thank you.

Col. Pretty and well, miss! that's two very good things.

Miss. I mean I am better than I was.

Never. Why then 'tis well you were sick.

Miss. What! Mr. Neverout, you take me up before I'm down.

Lady S. Come, let us leave off children's play, and go to push-pin.

Miss. [*To lady S.*] Pray, madam, give me some more sugar to my tea.

Col. O! miss, you must needs be very good humour'd, you love sweet things so well.

Never. Stir it up with the spoon, miss; for the deeper the sweeter.

Lady S. I assure you, miss, the colonel has made you a great compliment.

Miss. I am sorry for it; for I have heard say, complimenting is lying.

Lady S. [*To Lord Sparkish.*] My lord, methinks the sight of you is good for sore eyes; if we had known of your coming, we should have strewn rushes for you: how has your lordship done this long time?

Col. Faith, madam, he's better in health than in good conditions.

Spark. Well, I see there's no worse friend than one brings from home with one; and I am not the first man has carried a rod to whip himself.

Never. Here's poor miss has not a word to throw at a dog. Come, a penny for your thought.

Miss. It is not worth a farthing; for I was thinking of you.

COLONEL *rising up.*

Lady S. Colonel, where are you going so soon? I hope you did not come to fetch fire.

Col. Madam, I must needs go home for half an hour.

Miss. Why, colonel, they say the devil's at home.

Lady A. Well, but sit while you stay, 'tis as cheap sitting as standing.

Col. No, madam, while I'm standing, I'm going.

Miss. Nay, let him go; I promise him we won't tear his clothes to hold him.

Lady S. I suppose, colonel, we keep you from better company, I mean only as to myself.

Col. Madam, I am all obedience. [*Colonel sits down.*

Lady S. Lord, miss, how can you drink your tea so hot? sure your mouth's pav'd. How do you like this tea, colonel?

Col. Well enough, madam; but methinks it is a little more-ish.

Lady S. O! colonel, I understand you.—Betty, bring the cannister. I have but very little of this tea left; but I don't love to make two wants of one; want when I have it, and want when I have it not. He, he, he, he! [*Laughs.*

Lady A. [*To the maid.*] Why, sure, Betty, you are bewitched; the cream is burnt too.

Betty. Why, madam, the bishop has set his foot in it.

Lady S. Go, run, girl, and warm some fresh cream.

Betty. Indeed, madam, there's none left; for the cat has eaten it all.

Lady S. I doubt it was a cat with two legs.

Miss. Colonel, don't you love bread and butter with your tea?

Col. Yes, in a morning, miss; for they say, butter is gold in a morning, silver at noon, but it is lead at night.

Never. Miss, the weather is so hot that my butter melts on my bread.

Lady A. Why, butter, I've heard 'em say, is mad twice a-year.

Spark. [*To the maid.*] Mrs. Betty, how does your body politic?

Col. Fie, my lord, you'll make Mrs. Betty blush.

Lady S. Blush! ay, blush like a blue dog.

Never. Pray, Mrs. Betty, are you not Tom Johnson's daughter?

Betty. So my mother tells me, sir.

Spark. But, Mrs. Betty, I hear you are in love.

Betty. My lord, I thank God I hate nobody; I am in charity with all the world.

Lady S. Why, wench, I think thy tongue runs upon wheels this morning. How came you by that scratch upon your nose? Have you been fighting with the cats?

Col. [*To Miss.*] Miss, when will you be married?

Miss. One of these odd-come-shortly's, colonel.

Never. Yes; they say the match is half made; the spark is willing but miss is not.

Miss. I suppose the gentleman has got his own consent for it.

Lady A. Pray my lord, did you walk through the Park in the rain?

Spark. Yes, madam, we were neither sugar nor salt; we were not afraid the rain would melt us. He, he, he!   [*Laughs.*

Col. It rained, and the sun shone at the same time.

Never. Why, then the devil was beating his wife behind the door with a shoulder of mutton. [*Laughs.*

Col. A blind man would be glad to see that.

Lady S. Mr. Neverout, methinks you stand in your own light.

Never. Ah! madam, I have done so all my life.

Spark. I'm sure he sits in mine. Pr'ythee, Tom, sit a little farther; I believe your father was no glazier.

Lady S. Miss, dear girl, fill me out a dish of tea, for I'm very lazy.

Miss *fills a dish of tea, sweetens it, and then tastes it.*

Lady S. What, miss, will you be my taster?

Miss. No, madam; but they say 'tis an ill cook that can't lick her own fingers.

Never. Pray, miss, fill me another.

Miss. Will you have it now, or stay till you get it?

Lady A. But, colonel, they say you went to court last night very drunk; nay, I'm told for certain, you had been among the Philistines: no wonder the cat wink'd, when both her eyes were out.

Col. Indeed, madam, that's a lie.

Lady A. 'Tis better I should lie than you should lose your good manners: besides, I don't lie; I sit.

Never. O! faith, colonel, you must own you had a drop in your eye; when I left you, you were half seas over.

Spark. Well, I fear lady Answerall can't live long, she has so much wit.

Never. No; she can't live, that's certain; but she may linger thirty or forty years.

Miss. Live long! ay, longer than a cat or a dog, or a better thing.

Lady A. O! miss, you must give your vardi too!

Spark. Miss, shall I fill you another dish of tea?

Miss. Indeed, my lord, I have drank enough.

Spark. Come, it will do you more good than a month's fasting; here, take it.

Miss. No, I thank your lordship; enough's as good as a feast.

Spark. Well; but if you always say no, you'll never be married.

Lady A. Do, my lord, give her a dish; for they say maids will say no, and take it.

Spark. Well; and I dare say miss is a maid, in thought, word, and deed.

Never. I would not take my oath of that.

Miss. Pray, sir, speak for yourself.

Lady S. Fie, miss; they say maids should be seen and not heard.

Lady A. Good miss, stir the fire, that the tea-kettle may boil.—You have done it very well: now it burns purely. Well, miss, you'll have a cheerful husband.

Miss. Indeed, your ladyship could have stirred it much better.

Lady A. I know that very well, hussy; but I won't keep a dog and bark myself.

Never. What! you are stuck, miss.

Miss. Not at all; for her ladyship meant you.

Never. O! faith, miss, you are in Lob's pound; get out as you can.

Miss. I won't quarrel with my bread and butter for all that; I know when I'm well.

Lady A. Well; but, miss—

Never. Ah! dear madam, let the matter fall; take pity on poor miss; don't throw water on a drowned rat.

Miss. Indeed, Mr. Neverout, you should be cut for the simples this morning; say a word more and you had as good eat your nails.

Spark. Pray, miss, will you be so good as to favour us with a song?

Miss. Indeed, my lord, I can't; for I have a great cold.

Col. O! miss, they say all good singers have colds.

Spark. Pray, madam, does not miss sing very well?

Lady A. She sings, as one may say, my lord.

Miss. I hear Mr. Neverout has a very good voice.

Col. Yes, Tom sings well, but his luck's naught.

Never. Faith, colonel, you hit yourself a devilish box on the ear.

Col. Miss, will you take a pinch of snuff?

Miss. No, colonel, you must know that I never take snuff but when I am angry.

Lady A. Yes, yes, she can take snuff, but she has never a box to put it in.

Miss. Pray, colonel, let me see that box.

Col. Madam, there's never a C upon it.

Miss. Maybe there is, colonel.

Col. Ay, but May bees don't fly now, miss.

Never. Colonel, why so hard upon poor miss? Don't set your wit against a child. Miss, give me a blow, and I'll beat him.

Miss. So she prayed me to tell you.

Spark. Pray, my lady Smart, what kin are you to lord Pozz?

Lady S. Why, his grandmother and mine had four elbows.

Lady A. Well, methinks here's a silent meeting. Come, miss, hold up your head, girl; there's money bid for you. [*Miss starts.*

Miss. Lord, madam, you frighten me out of my seven senses!

Spark. Well, I must be going.

Lady A. I have seen hastier people than you stay all night.

Col. [*To lady Smart.*] Tom Neverout and I are to leap to-morrow for a guinea.

Miss. I believe, colonel, Mr. Neverout can leap at a crust better than you.

Never. Miss, your tongue runs before your wit: nothing can tame you but a husband.

Miss. Peace! I think I hear the church-clock.

Never. Why, you know, as the fool thinks—

Lady S. Mr. Neverout, your handkerchief's fallen.

Miss. Let him set his foot on it, that it mayn't fly in his face.

Never. Well, miss—

Miss. Ay, ay; many a one says well that thinks ill.

Never. Well, miss, I'll think on this.

Miss. That's rhyme, if you take it in time.

Never. What! I see you are a poet.

Miss. Yes, if I had but the wit to show it.

Never. Miss, will you be so kind as to fill me a dish of tea?

Miss. Pray let your betters be served before you; I'm just going to fill one for myself; and, you know, the parson always christens his own child first.

Never. But I saw you fill one just now for the colonel: well, I find kissing goes by favour.

Miss. But pray, Mr. Neverout, what lady was that you were talking with in the side-box last Tuesday?

Never. Miss, can you keep a secret?

Miss. Yes, I can.

Never. Well, miss, and so can I.

Col. Odd-so! I have cut my thumb with this cursed knife!

Lady A. Ay; that was your mother's fault, because she only warned you not to cut your fingers.

Lady S. No, no; 'tis only fools cut their fingers, but wise folks cut their thumbs.

Miss. I'm sorry for it, but I can't cry.

Col. Don't you think miss is grown?

Lady A. Ay, ill weeds grow apace.

A puff of smoke comes down the chimney.

Lady A. Lord, madam, does your ladyship's chimney smoke?

Col. No, madam; but they say smoke always pursues the fair, and your ladyship sat nearest.

Lady S. Madam, do you love bohea tea?

Lady A. Why, madam, I must confess I do love it, but it does not love me.

Miss. [*To lady Smart.*] Indeed, madam, your ladyship is very sparing of your tea; I protest, the last I took was no more than water bewitch'd.

Col. Pray, miss, if I may be so bold, what lover gave you that fine etui?

Miss. Don't you know?—then keep counsel.

Lady A. I'll tell you, colonel, who gave it her: it was the best lover she will ever have while she lives—her own dear papa.

Never. Methinks, miss, I don't much like the colour of that ribbon.

Miss. Why, then, Mr. Neverout, do you see, if you don't much like it, you may look off it.

Spark. I don't doubt, madam, but your ladyship has heard that sir John Brisk has got an employment at court.

Lady S. Yes, yes; and I warrant he thinks himself no small fool now.

Never. Yes, madam; I have heard some people take him for a wise man.

Lady S. Ay, ay; some are wise, and some are otherwise.

Lady A. Do you know him, Mr. Neverout?

Never. Know him! ay, as well as the beggar knows his dish.

Col. Well, I can only say that he has better luck than honester folks. But, pray, how came he to get his employment?

Spark. Why, by chance, as the man killed the devil.

Never. Why, miss, you are in a brown study: what's the matter? Methinks you look like Mumchance, that twas hanged for saying nothing.

Miss. I'd have you to know, I scorn your words.

Never. Well, but scornful dogs will eat dirty puddings.

Miss. Well, my comfort is, your tongue is no slander. What! you would not have one be always on the high grin?

Never. Cry mapsticks, madam; no offence, I hope.

NOTES

i

NOTES

THE text adopted for these selections is Scott's 2nd edition, as reprinted by Messrs. Bickers, 1883-4. It is the standard text, though by no means what a perfect text of Swift should be. The 1841 2-volume edition, which was apparently based upon an independent collation of the original editions, has, however, been compared; and, in cases of discrepancy, reference has been made to the first, or best, editions of the several works. The spelling and punctuation have been reduced to the modern system, except when (as in *phrensy* and a few other words) the present spelling is manifestly wrong. Objectionable words, phrases, and paragraphs, have invariably been expunged. When a whole paragraph or several sentences have been omitted, a statement to that effect is given in the notes, and the place of omission is generally indicated by dots . . . .; but when the omission consists only of a single word, or a short phrase, no indication is given that anything has been left out; it was felt that in such cases dots would only interrupt the reading and suggest the nature of the words expunged. Footnotes and marginal references to classical authors are also omitted, as immaterial and distracting the attention. Such principles would of course be inapplicable to a critical edition of the works of Swift: but, in a volume of selections, the main object is to avoid everything that interferes with the clear understanding of the writer's meaning, and that distracts the reader from the due appreciation of the style. For the notes, besides the usual sources, valuable suggestions have been made by Dr. Richard Garnett, Mr. John Ashton, Mr. J. Dykes Campbell, and by Mr. Sidney J. Low, who has contributed some of the notes on the political situation described in the *Examiners* and the *Conduct of the Allies*.

THE TALE OF A TUB.

The origin of the title has been frequently debated, but beyond the fact that it was a proverbial phrase, employed by Sir Thomas More and others to denote any rambling and incoherent story, much as "a cock and bull story" is used now, very little has been elicited as to its origin. The attempt to trace the expression to an incident in Apuleius reproduced by Boccaccio (7th Day) seems a trifle far-fetched. The meaning is tolerably clearly conveyed in the lines of Bale's *Comedye Concernynge Thre Lawes*, 1538 :—

> Ye saye thy folowe your lawe
> And varye not a strawe
> Whych is a tale of a tubbe.

Page 7. *A large Cloud.* Cp. *Antony and Cleopatra*, Act iv. Sc. 12 :—

> *Ant.* Sometime we see a cloud that's dragonish :
> A vapour, sometime, like a bear, or lion,
> A tower'd citadel, a pendent rock,
> A forked mountain, or blue promontory
> With trees upon 't, that nod unto the world,
> And mock our eyes with air : . . .
> That which is now a horse, even with a thought
> The rack dislimns, and makes it indistinct
> As water is in water.

Page 8. Durfey or "D'Urfey," says Scott, "who stood the force of so much wit, was a playwright and song-writer. He appears to have been an inoffensive, good-humoured, thoughtless character, and was endured and laughed at by Dryden, by Steele, . . . and at length by Pope, who, in a spirit between contempt and charity, wrote a prologue for his last play," which includes these lines :—

> He scorn'd to borrow from the wits of yore,
> But ever writ, as none e'er writ before . . .

Though plays for honour in old time he made,
'Tis now for better reasons,—to be paid.
Believe him, he has known the world too long,
And seen the death of much immortal song.

Dennis was a trenchant critic and an inferior poet of the day, whose attacks upon Pope and upon Addison's Cato induced the former to retaliate in a pamphlet called "The Narrative of Dr. Robert Norris concerning the strange and deplorable Frenzy of Mr. John Dennis;" and Dennis's tragedy of *Appius* is alluded to by the same poet in the *Essay on Criticism* :—

But Appius reddens at each word you speak,
And stares, tremendous, with a threatening eye,
Like some fierce tyrant in old tapestry.

Page 8. The *friend of your governor* is Sir William Temple, Swift's patron, with whom Bentley and Wotton were then contending in the debate as to the respective merits of ancient and modern writers.

Page 9. The *many volumes* referred to are the well-known classical editions prepared for the use of the Dauphin, *in usum Delphini*.

Page 12. By *ladders* are here meant gallows.

Page 13. Dunton was a broken-down bookseller who published his *Life and Errors*, wherein he described every bookseller, printer, and stationer in London, together with the characters of seventeen bookbinders. He did not, however, draw up the collection of gallows orations suggested in the text.

The *stage itinerant* is the mountebank's platform, which leads, according to Swift, either to the conventicle or the gallows.

Page 15. *Rotten wood: i.e.*, the fanatic preacher must possess inward light and a head full of maggots; and the *two fates* of his works are to be burnt or worm-eaten.

Hiatus in MS. A device of Swift to avoid a long disquisition, especially when it was a case of proving a paradox. So on p. 36 he puts *Hic multa desiderantur*, "here much is wanting;" on p. 55, *Hic pauca desunt*, "here a little is gone," etc. Carlyle's *Sartor Resartus* contains examples of a similar device.

Page 16. Gresham College was then the meeting place of

the Royal Society, and Will's coffee house in Covent Garden was the favourite rendezvous of the poets and wits of the day.

Page 17. "*A smaller affair*—viz., about moving the earth." (Swift's note.)

[*are*], inserted for grammar's sake. Swift was often careless in trifles like this, and several other examples occur in the present selection: *e.g.*, on pp. 34, 165.

Briguing: Fr. *briguer*; "to canvass, solicit."

Husks. A couple of lines are here omitted; and also the list of the masterpieces of Grub Street which concludes the *Introduction*, in which Dryden, L'Estrange, Wotton, and others, are held up to ridicule.

Page 19. *Exantlation*: *i.e.* extraction: Lat. *exantlare* or *exanclare*.

Page 20. *The Egyptian Cercopithecus*: this long-tailed monkey is, by the classical authors generally, associated with the worship of the ancient Egyptians. Everyone remembers Juvenal's lines, (xv. 4,)

> Effigies sacri nitet aurea cercopitheci
> Dimidio magicae resonant ubi Memnone chordae
> Atque vetus Thebe centum jacet obruta portis.

Martial is also familiar with the animal, (xiv. 302,)

> Si mihi cauda foret, cercopithecus eram.

and Pliny describes, among the monsters of Aethiopia (viii. 72, ed. Sillig), "cercopithecos, nigris capitibus, pilo asini, et dissimilis ceteris voce." Cuvier's note on this passage (in Didot's edition, 1827) is very remarkable: "non desunt in India simiae quibus longior cauda, pilus leucophaeus, facies nigra; quales *entellus* et *malbrouk* (simia faunus)." The name of "Malbrouk," or Marlborough, must have been given to this variety of ape during the great war of the Spanish succession, and Swift may have heard of it, as he did hear most things. Beyond the fact that Swift was a Whig and Marlborough a Tory at the time of the writing of the *Tale of a Tub*, there is indeed no reason for supposing that Swift entertained at that early date the strong antipathy he afterwards felt for the great general: but it is at least a curious and hitherto unnoticed coincidence that the lice-eating long-tailed monkey of the *Tub* should have been known by the name of Malbrouk.

Water-tabby: anything water-marked or wavy was so called, as watered silk, moiré antique, etc.; derived, through the Fr. *tabis* and the Ital. *tabi*, from the Persian '*ottâby*, a striped and watered cotton-silk, made at Baghdad.

Page 24. *I am first sculler.* The watermen of the Thames were divided into two classes; *oars*, *i.e.* pair-oars, and *scullers*, *i.e.* single rowers, and the latter were paid at half the rate of the former. The point of Swift's waterman's speech appears to be that the brothers could not expect a first-class boat, but must put up with a cheap sculler.

Page 25. The satire upon the schoolmen's methods of interpreting Scripture is rendered the more obvious by the use of their technical terms, such as *ex traduce*, "by original derivation," *totidem verbis*, "in so many words," &c., and by abbreviations such as Q. V. C., *i.e. quibusdam veteribus codicibus*, "in some ancient manuscripts."

Page 29. Between *arithmetic* and *What remains* an objectionable paragraph has been excised.

Page 32. After *fruitful*, more than two pages of Scott's edition have been omitted, in which Swift instances the evil effects of vapour in the wars of Henry IV. and Louis XIV. of France in a manner that will not bear citation.

Page 33. *clinamina*: inclinations or tendencies.

Page 34. *Cicero.* The quotation is from Ep. ad Divers, vii. 10, Trebatio; and the allusion as to the hackney coachmen refers to Trebatius' timid avoidance of the British war-chariots, in a subsequent letter (16).

Page 41. [*ecclesiastical*] was represented by asterisks in the early editions.

Ecce cornuta erat ejus facies: referring to the Vulgate version of Ex. xxxiv. 29, 35: "The skin of his face shone."

THE BATTLE OF THE BOOKS.

See note below, p. 272.

Page 51. The *large castle*, boast of *mathematics*, and the *palisadoes* and *modern way of fortification*, are allusions to some of the arguments used to prove the superiority of the moderns in the controversy which Swift satirizes.

Page 53. *Regent, i.e.* Richard Bentley, the Royal Librarian, and greatest scholar of the day, who had disputed the antiquity of the fables ascribed to Æsop, and had altogether refuted Temple's assumption of the antiquity of the spurious *Epistles of Phalaris*. He is consequently held up to special (and of course unmerited) ridicule, and is described as the Thersites of the army of the moderns in the battle, where he was useful "for his talent of railing."

Page 55. *The wounded aga.* Dr. Harvey, whose discovery of the circulation of the blood was questioned by Temple.

The asterisks are intended in mock-generosity to screen the names of the vanquished.

Page 56. *Gondibert*, a heroic poem by Sir W. Davenant. Sir John *Denham*, the author of *Cooper's Hill*, the inequality of whose poems is alluded to. *S. Wesley*, "a wretched scribbler," who did the life of Christ into verse. *Perrault* and *Fontenelle*, two of the French writers who began the futile discussion on the relative merits of old and modern books.

Page 57. *Called him father,* an allusion to Dryden's somewhat ambitious view of his own relationship to Virgil. Swift entertained an unreasonable dislike of "Glorious John," perhaps because Dryden had expressed an unflattering opinion of Swift's early Pindarics: "Cousin Swift, you will never be a poet."

Page 58. *Æsculapius turned off the point*, because Blackmore's skill as a physician made amends for his weakness as a poet. Swift was curiously indulgent to Blackmore, whose poetic vein was none of the purest. The following lines from *Verses to be placed under the Picture of England's Arch-Poet*, contained in the *Miscellanies* of Pope, Arbuthnot, and Gay, 1727, express the current opinion of Blackmore's productions:—

> See who ne'er was or will be half-read,
> Who first sung Arthur, then sung Alfred, . . .
> Maul'd *Human Wit* in one thick satire,
> Next in three books sunk *Human Nature;*
> Undid *Creation* at a jerk,
> And of *Redemption* made d——d work;
> Then took his muse at once and dipp'd her
> Full in the middle of the Scripture;
> What wonders there the man grown old did!
> Sternhold himself he out-Sternholded.

Creech, a clergyman, translated Lucretius and Horace.

Afra the Amazon: Mrs. Afra Behn.

Page 59. *Shield given him by Venus:* Cowley's poem "The Mistress," which Swift seems to have preferred to his Pindarics. It is noteworthy, as Scott has remarked, that Swift entirely ignores Milton among the moderns, and that no dramatists take part in the combat.

Neglected quarter, i.e. the little known, and spurious Epistles of Phalaris. The long-drawn similes here are admirable imitations of the Virgilian manner.

Page 64. *Mother, i.e.* the goddess Criticism, a "malignant deity," with claws like a cat and the ears and voice of an ass, who lay "extended upon the spoils of numberless volumes," surrounded by her parents and children, Ignorance and Pride, Noise and Impudence, Dulness and Vanity, Positiveness and Pedantry.

Page 65. *Boyle* entered the controversy out of respect for Temple, *clad in armour of the gods*, because supported by Aldrich, Atterbury, and the rest of the Christ Church scholars, in his edition of Phalaris *new polished and gilt*.

ARGUMENT AGAINST ABOLISHING CHRISTIANITY.

This treatise, as Mr. Garnett has discovered, was reprinted in 1765, without Swift's name, with many mutilations, and under the title of *A Modest Address to the Wicked Authors of the Present Age*, by H. F. (Peter Annet); but a footnote, in which he expresses his dissent from "the Dean," shows that this worthy field-preacher did not intend to appropriate the authorship himself.

Page 72. Between *profound judgment* and *upon a thorough examination*, appears in the original a redundant *who*.

Page 73. *Asgil, Toland, Tindal,* and *Coward*, were leaders of the deistical writers of the time. Swift devoted several treatises, notably the *Remarks* on Tindal's *Rights of the Christian Church*, and the *Abstract of Mr. Collins's Discourse*, to the refutation of a school that was peculiarly obnoxious to him as a sound churchman.

Page 74. *Empson and Dudley*: the well-known extortionate lawyers of Henry VII.'s reign.

Page 77. *Margaritians, Toftians, and Valentinians*: after the names of three famous opera singers of the day, Mrs. Tofts, first of prime donne, Francisca Margherita de l'Epine, who married the well-known musician Dr. Pepusch, and the alto Valentino Urbini. The Italian opera was then not long introduced to England. Among the performances was that of *Camilla*, in 1707, "to be sung after the Italian manner. The parts of Latinus by Mr. Turner, Prenesto by Signiora Margarita, part in Italian, Turnus by Signior Valentino, in Italian, Metius by Mr. Ramondon, Linco by Mr. Leveridge, Camilla by Mrs. Tofts, Lavinia by the Baroness, most in Italian, Tullia by Mrs. Lindsey."—*Daily Courant*, Dec. 6, 1707; Ashton's *Social Life in the Reign of Queen Anne*, ii. 29.

Swift himself had no taste for the Italian opera, or for music generally. "We have a music meeting in our town to-night," he writes to Stella. "I went to a rehearsal of it, and there was Margarita and her sister, with another drab, and a parcel of fiddlers; I was weary, and would not go to the meeting."

Page 81. *Daggled-tail*, and not draggled, is the correct orthography.

GULLIVER'S TRAVELS.

In Lilliput and Brobdingnag Swift satirizes the government of England of the day, with its "violent faction at home and the danger of invasion from abroad" (p. 108), and many of the allusions are to contemporary events and persons. In the present selection, however, passages consisting mainly of such temporary and particular allusions have been avoided as far as possible, and those which apply almost to any society or government at any time have been preferred. Such passages call for little explanation; the point of the humour is for the most part visible enough; but among the allusions that have a special application it may be well to remark that the *high* and *low heels* (p. 109) represent the high and low church parties, between which the *heir to the Crown*, George II., is seen to hobble; that the *Big-endians* and Little-endians (p. 110) stood originally for Papists and Protestants, though they would apply quite as well to any two sects that differed in points of detail; and that Blefuscu (p. 111) was intended for France.

In an interesting paper in Notes and Queries, 2nd series, vol. vi. p. 124, the eminent mathematician, Prof. A. de Morgan, notices the skill with which Swift has concealed the elementary nature of his calculations: the Lilliputian being to man as 1 to 12, and man to the Brobdingnagian as 1 to 12. Once this is perceived, all the dimensions in the two voyages are obvious. But Swift takes peculiar care that the proportion should not be so evident at first sight. He describes the miniature men as "not six inches high," which does not necessarily suggest that an average man is "not six feet high." So in Brobdingnag, the farmer's stride is measured at "about ten yards, as near as I could guess," when the proportion to the human stride of $1\frac{8}{9}$ yard, or 30 inches, is not immediately perceived. Yet the relative size is accurately maintained throughout. The hedges are 120 feet high, *i.e.* 10 feet; the corn 40 feet, *i.e.* 3 feet, 4 inches; the step of the stile 6 feet, *i.e.* 6 inches, etc. Even in cubic contents Swift keeps carefully to his scale. The largest Lilliputian hogshead holds only half-a-pint: $\frac{1}{2}$ pint × 12 × 12 × 12 = 1,728 half pints, or 108 gallons, which is the cubit contents of a butt of ale, which is probably what Swift meant by the "largest hogshead." Prof. de Morgan thinks that the only instance in which Swift has overshot the mark is when he makes Gulliver, up to his neck in water, drag by a rope fifty line-of-battle ships, which had held 30,000 men. This is equivalent to drawing $1\frac{60}{78}$ths of a line-of-battle ship of Swift's own time, which would be a somewhat heavy pull for a man up to his neck in water. This mathematical investigation of *Gulliver* is, of course, immaterial to the point of the satire: but it is interesting to see how carefully Swift worked out his theory. Prof. de Morgan believed that he must have been assisted by some mathematician, Arbuthnot for instance: but this view is hardly borne out by the blunders which Swift made in the voyage to Laputa, which was specially directed against the Royal Society and scientific men generally. Prof. de Morgan was, however, somewhat hypercritical in objecting to the tailor's taking Gulliver's altitude by a quadrant, on the ground that such an observation would obtain an angle and not a linear measure; and it is surely carrying criticism too far to denounce Swift for serving up mutton in two dimensions, and cutting bread into parallelograms, which are plain superficies, as well as into cubical figures, such as cones and cylinders.

Page 115. *Brobdingnag.* It is curious that, though this name, according to Swift's own preface, is a misprint for Brobdingrag, which is much more pronounceable, the correct spelling has never been restored. He would, however, be a bold critic who would attempt to change it now. The arrival in Brobdingnag is, in the original, prefaced by the famous description of the storm, of which Scott remarks that it is "a parody upon the account of storms and naval manœuvres, frequent in old voyages, and is merely an assemblage of sea-terms, put together at random, but in such accurate imitation of the technicalities of the art, that seamen have been known to work hard to attain the proper meaning of it." So far is this from being true, that the description in question is a perfectly accurate account of the ordinary seaman's practice of the time, and is taken (as Mr. Knowles first pointed out in N. and Q., iv. i. 223), word for word from a seaman's handbook, Sturmy's *Compleat Mariner,* as anyone may see by consulting the 3rd edition, published in 1684, in the British Museum. All that Swift has done is to turn the present tense into the narrative past, and to omit some immaterial words and sentences. The identity of the two descriptions is beyond dispute; and there is nothing blameworthy in Swift's adapting the phraseology of a current technical handbook. But as the storm can no longer be regarded as peculiarly illustrative of his powers of description, the passage in question, celebrated as it is, has been omitted in the present selection. This is one of the very few cases in which Swift has been proved to have directly copied another writer. That he was indebted for many of his ideas to previous authors, notably to Rabelais, is beyond question; and the plan of the *Battle of the Books* is undoubtedly identical with that of F. de Callière's *Histoire poétique de la guerre nouvellement declarée entre les anciens et modernes,* Paris, 1688, though, as Swift protested he had never heard of the book, the resemblance must be only a coincidence. So, too, the notion of giants and dwarfs was certainly no original idea; the fancy had been retouched so lately as 1675, though with little skill, in Joshua Barnes's *Gerania; or, a new discovery of a little sort of people, anciently discoursed of, called Pygmies;* while a still more probable source for the bare notion of big and little people may have been (as was lately pointed out in the *Athenæum*, 1884, 536, 567) Martello's puppet play, *Lo Starnuto d'Ercole*, which was published at Bologna in 1723, and written some six years earlier. But in these and other parallel instances, Swift may indeed have obtained a hint which he worked up in his masterpieces, but it was only a hint. The consistent elaboration of the idea, the wealth of illustration, the perfect apposition of the satire, are his alone. As Johnson said of him, " no writer can easily be found that has borrowed so little."

Page 134. The institution of *flappers* is of course meant to ridicule the proverbial absence of mind of philosophers, and was probably suggested by the current anecdotes, true or false, of Sir Isaac Newton's peculiarities. The Laputa voyage is, however, the least successful part of the satire, and Swift seems himself to have spent more pains in improving it than he devoted to the other voyages, if we may judge from his manuscript corrections and additions contained in a copy of the first edition of *Gulliver*, which he gave to his friend Charles Ford, who in turn communicated the corrections to the publisher. This copy is now in the Forster Library, in the South Kensington Museum, and a careful collation I have made shows that most of these corrections, which occur mainly in the Laputa voyage, were inserted in subsequent editions. A few unimportant alterations appear to have escaped notice, or more probably were rejected on a second revision, to which the appearance of several corrections not marked in Ford's copy bears testimony. The only addition of any length in Ford's copy that has not been inserted in any edition occurs just before the final short paragraph of Chapter III. of Laputa, at the end of the description of the Flying Island. As an unpublished addition to *Gulliver* the passage possesses some interest, and it is therefore printed below (with the original spelling and punctuation, but neglecting typographical peculiarities), though, on its merits, its final rejection is not perhaps inexcusable.

AN UNPUBLISHED ADDITION TO LAPUTA.

ABOUT three years before my arrival among them, while the king was in his progress over his dominions, there happened an extraordinary accident which had like to have put a period to the fate of that monarchy, at least as it is now instituted. Lindalino the second city in the kingdom was the first his majesty visited in his progress. Three days after his departure, the inhabitants who had often complained of great oppressions, shut the town gates, seized on the governor, and with incredible speed and labour erected four large towers, one at every corner of the city (which is an exact square), equal in heigth (*sic*) to a strong pointed rock that stands directly in the center of the city. Upon the top of each tower, as well as upon the rock, they fixed a great loadstone, and in case their design should fail, they had provided a vast quantity of the most combustible fewel, hoping to burst therewith the adamantine bottom of the island if the loadstone project should miscarry.

It was eight months before the king had perfect notice that the Lindalinians were in rebellion. He then commanded that the island should be wafted over the city. The people were unanimous, and had laid in store of provisions, and a great river runs through the middle of the town. The king hovered over them several days to deprive them of the sun and the rain. He ordered many packthreads to be let down, yet not a person offered to send up a petition, but instead thereof, very bold demands, the redress of all their greivances (*sic*), great immunitys, the choice of their own governor, and other the like exorbitances. Upon which his majesty commanded all the inhabitants of the island to cast great stones from the lower gallery into the town; but the citizens had provided against this mischief by conveying their persons and effects into the four towers, and other strong buildings, and vaults under ground.

The king being now determined to reduce this proud people, ordered that the island should descend gently within fourty yards of the top of the towers and rock. This was accordingly done; but the officers employed in that work found the descent much speedier than usual, and by turning the loadstone could not without great difficulty keep it in a firm position, but found the island inclining to fall. They sent the king immediate intelligence of this astonishing event, and begged his majesty's permission to raise the island higher; the king consented, a general council was called, and the officers of the loadstone ordered to attend. One of the oldest and expertest among them obtained leave to try an experiment. He took a strong line of an hundred yards, and the island being raised over the town above the attracting power they had felt, he fastened a piece of adamant to the end of his line, which had in it a mixture of iron mineral, of the same nature with that whereof the bottom or lower surface of the island is composed, and from the lower gallery let it down slowly towards the top of the towers. The adamant was not descended four yards, before the officer felt it drawn so strongly downwards, that he could hardly pull it back. He then threw down several small pieces of adamant, and observed that they were all violently attracted by the top of the tower. The same experiment was made on the other three towers and on the rock, with the same effect.

This incident broke entirely the king's measures and (to dwell no longer on other circumstances) he was forced to give the town their own conditions.

I was assured by a great minister, that if the island had descended so near the town as not to be able to raise it self, the citizens were determined to fix it for ever, to kill the king and all his servants, and entirely change the government.

ENGLISH POLITICAL TRACTS.

Page 163. *The Examiner, No.* 15. The numbering of the *Examiners* here adopted is that of the original single sheets. In all texts of Swift, however, No. 14 appears as 13, and all the subsequent numbers are shifted one back. The reason is that when the *Examiners* were republished in 1712 in 12mo., No. 13, the paper immediately preceding Swift's first contribution, containing a strenuous plea for non-resistance, was omitted. Swift's first *Examiner* was No. 14, and his last No. 46 : or, in the later numbering, 13-45. There seems no good reason for following a numbering which is not that of the original publication.—No. 15 is directed against the Earl of Wharton (*a certain great man*, p. 167), who was lord-lieutenant of Ireland from Oct. 1708 to Oct. 1710; to which post graceful allusion is made on p. 164, where the devil is described as having been *viceroy of a great western province*. Swift had personal reasons for disliking Wharton, but the flagrant profligacy and venality of the viceroy's character and government amply justified the undying contempt and hatred which inspired Swift's repeated onslaughts.

Page 166. *Wooden shoes*: alluding to the French sympathies of which the Tories, *your best friends*, were accused.

Page 168. *Such counsel*: alluding to the Whigs, monied men, dissenters, the war, and the national debt. The funded debt, which began in 1692 with £1,200,000 borrowed at ten per cent. by the Whig Montague had grown to fifty millions by the time of the treaty of Utrecht: and this indebtedness was a ground of serious alarm to Swift and the Tories.

Others who ... were only able to give reputation and success to the Revolution: i.e. noblemen, who, like Danby and Nottingham, without embracing Whig principles, made the Revolution possible by their aid.

Page 169. *This mighty change* refers to the case of Dr. Sacheverell, put on his trial by the Whigs in 1710, for preaching non-resistance, which produced a Tory reaction, and the fall of the Whigs in the same year.

Page 170. *Violences of either party*. Swift, though a party man, was no mere partisan. "Whoever," he wrote in the *Sentiments of a Church of England Man*, "has a true value for Church and State would be sure to avoid the extremes of Whig for the sake of the former, and the extremes of Tory on account of the latter."

Page 171. *The Examiner, No.* 16. The *Review* was Defoe's weekly paper, and the *Observator* was conducted by another Whig, John Tutchin, a former adherent of Monmouth, whom Jeffreys ordered to be flogged through some of the western towns. Pope alludes to his punishment in the well-known lines,

"Earless on high stood unabashed De Foe,
And Tutchin flagrant from the scourge below."

The *non-juror* was the Rev. Charles Lesley, an Irish non-juring clergyman, who promulgated Jacobite opinions in the *Rehearsal*. He also wrote numerous tracts against the Deists, whence Swift's *respect and esteem*.

The following account of the weekly papers of the year is taken from a pamphlet, ascribed by some to Gay, entitled, *The Present State of Wit*, and printed in 1711. Swift mentions it in the Journal to Stella, May 14, 1711, and says he thinks "Steele and Addison were privy to the printing of it."

"As to our weekly papers, the poor *Review* is quite exhausted, and grown so very contemptible, that though he has provoked all his brothers of the quill round, none of them will enter into controversy with him. This fellow, who had excellent natural parts, but wanted a small foundation of learning, is a lively instance of those wits, who, as an ingenious author says, 'will endure but one skimming.' The *Observator* was almost in the same condition ; but since our party struggles have run so high, he is much mended for the better; which is imputed to the charitable assistance of some outlying friends. These two authors might, however, have flourished some time longer, had not the controversy been taken up by much abler hands. The *Examiner* is a paper which all men, who speak without prejudice, allow to be well written. Though his subject will admit of no greater variety, he is continually placing it in so many different lights, and endeavouring to inculcate the same thing by so many beautiful changes of expression, that men who are concerned in no party may read him with pleasure. His way of assuming the question in debate is extremely artful ; and his letter to Crassus is, I think, a masterpiece. As these papers are supposed to have been written by several different hands, the critics will tell you that they can discern a difference in their styles and beauties, and pretend to observe, that the first *Examiners* abound chiefly in wit, the last in humour. Soon after their first appearance, came out a paper, from the other side, called the *Whig Examiner*, written with so much fire and in so excellent a style, as put the Tories in no small pain for their favourite hero. Every one cried Bickerstaff must be the author ; and people were the more confirmed in this opinion upon its being so soon laid down, which seemed to show that it was only written to bind the *Examiners* to their good behaviour, and was never designed to be a weekly paper. The *Examiners*, therefore, have no one to combat with at present, but their friend the *Medley* ; the author of which paper, though he seems to be a man of good sense, and expresses it luckily enough now and then, is, I think, for the most part, perfectly a stranger to fine writing. I presume I need not tell you, that the *Examiner* carries much the more sale, as it is supposed to be written by the direction and under the eye of some great persons who sit at the helm of affairs, and is consequently looked on as a sort of public notice which way they are steering us. The reputed author is Dr. Swift, with the assistance sometimes of Dr. Atterbury and Mr. Prior. . . . Before

I proceed further in the account of our weekly papers, it will be necessary to inform you that, at the beginning of the winter, to the infinite surprise of all men, Mr. Steele flung up his *Tatler*; and, instead of Isaac Bickerstaff, subscribed himself Richard Steele to the last of those papers, after a handsome compliment to the town for their kind acceptance of his endeavours to divert them. . . . The expiration of Bickerstaff's lucubrations was attended with much the same consequences as the death of Melibœus's ox in Virgil; as the latter engendered swarms of bees, the former immediately produced whole swarms of little satirical scribblers. . . . One cause for the laying down the *Tatler* was want of matter; and, indeed, this was the prevailing opinion in town, when we were surprised all at once by a paper called the *Spectator*, which was promised to be continued every day, and was written in so excellent a style, with so nice a judgment, and such a noble profession of wit and humour, that it was not difficult to determine it could come from no other hands than those that had penned the lucubrations. . . . The *Spectator*, whom we regard as our shelter from that cloud of false wit and impertinence which was breaking in upon us, is in every one's hand and a constant topic for our morning conversation at tea tables and coffee-houses. We had at first, indeed, no manner of notion how a diurnal paper could be continued in the spirit and style of our present *Spectators*; but, to our no small surprise, we find them still rising upon us, and can only wonder from whence so prodigious a run of wit and learning can proceed; since some of our best judges seem to think that they have hitherto in general outshone even the Squire's first *Tatlers*."

Page 173. *Two great men:* Marlborough and Godolphin came into office as Tories, and became Whigs on the war policy. Whigs and Tories professed to hold much the same views on the main questions of constitutional theory: except the extreme non-resistance Tories, whom Swift ignores.

Page 174. *Half-a-dozen others.* Swift probably means that, accepting the term Whig as it was used at the Revolution, when it meant a supporter of constitutionalism, the name might be applied to most of the Tories who came into office in 1710; for they accepted the Revolution, supported the Act of Settlement, and discountenanced the theory of kingship by divine right. Like the Whigs they (nominally at least) considered that Anne reigned by a parliamentary title. Among the ministers was the Duke of Shrewsbury, Lord High Treasurer, who had always been a prominent Whig.

Page 175. *The Pretender.* The Revolution of 1688 had been carried out with great unanimity. The bulk of the nation acquiesced in the step which got rid of a Roman Catholic sovereign, who was anxious to change the religion of the English people by French aid. But the Revolution brought over a foreign dynasty, and threw the administration into the hands of a faction which seemed to represent only one, and that not the most important, interest in the state. A reaction soon took place; a formidable Jacobite party numbering many of the High Churchmen was in existence throughout William III.'s reign. With the accession of Anne the Jacobite cause gained rather than lost. James II. was now dead, and his son, the Pretender, might claim exemption from the guilt of his father's sins. No one now thought of dethroning the reigning sovereign; comparatively few were ready to risk much to bring back the Stuarts; but at the same time very many people in England would have gladly acquiesced in the succession of James Edward on the death of Anne. This the Tory leaders knew, and some of them were engaged in constant intercourse with St. Germains, with the more or less definite object of proclaiming the Prince on the Queen's death. In fact the whole of the active Tory party was tainted with the suspicion of Jacobitism; and the suspicion was a strong card in the hands of their rivals. For the hatred to foreigners and Papists was as keen as ever among the country gentlemen and landed proprietors on whom the Tory leaders relied. This Swift knew, and he was extremely anxious to disclaim the imputation of favouring the Pretender. In his case the disclaimer was doubtless sincere. It is probable that to the end he was not made fully acquainted with the measures by which Bolingbroke was preparing for a restoration of the Stuarts.

Page 176. *Supposed father.* It was in many quarters believed that the Pretender, James Edward, who was born in June, 1688, was only a supposititious child of James II. and Mary of Modena.

Piece of secret history, &c. Referring probably to Marlborough's and Godolphin's trafficking with James II. after the Revolution, and in particular their betrayal of the intended expedition to Brest in 1694, to him. The affair was probably known to Harley.

Page 176, 28 seq. The title of Anne depended on the Bill of Rights (1 *Will. and Mary, s.* 2, *cap.* 2), which declares "that William and Mary, Prince and Princess of Orange, be, and be declared, King and Queen of England, France, and Ireland, and the dominions thereunto belonging . . . and after their deceases the said crown and royal dignity of the said kingdoms and dominions to be to the heirs of the body of the said Princess [Mary]; and for default of such issue to the Princess Anne of Denmark and the heirs of her body."

Page 177. *Supreme power.* A reminiscence of Hobbes, whose doctrine of the supremacy of the sovereign power in a state had no small influence upon the Tory theory of Government.

That settlement, &c. The reference is to the Bill of Rights, Art. VIII. "Thereunto the said Lords Spiritual and Temporal, and Commons, do, in the name of all the people aforesaid, most humbly and faithfully submit themselves, their heirs, and posterities, for ever." The words are repeated in the Act of Settlement, 1700 (12 *and* 13 *Will. iii.*).

Page 178. *The Conduct of the Allies.* The War of the Spanish Succession was ostensibly entered upon (May, 1702) by England, the Netherlands, the Emperor, and the German Princes, in order to set aside the will of Charles II. of Spain, by which the whole of the Spanish dominions had been left to Philip of Anjou, the grandson of Louis XIV. of France. It was rightly felt that if the resources of both the French and Spanish monarchies were at the disposal of the House of Bourbon, England, Holland, and the minor German princes would no longer be safe from the ambition of the French king. Hence it was that William III. and Marlborough strove to bring the Protestant states to support the counter-claim of the Austrian Archduke Charles on the Spanish crown. So far, though Swift would not allow it, the Whigs might urge that they were pursuing a policy necessary alike to Europe and to England. But the victories of Marlborough and Eugene in Flanders and Germany, and the financial exhaustion of his country, reduced Louis XIV. to the greatest distress. In 1706, and again in 1709, he made overtures of peace on terms which should have satisfied the legitimate desires of the allies. He would have consented to give the Dutch the "barrier" fortresses of the frontier, including even Lille and

Tournay, and to allow the claims of the Archduke to Spain and her colonial possessions, only reserving for his grandson the Italian dominions of the Spanish monarchy. But by this time the Whig interest in England had become identified with the war policy. To have made peace might have concentrated public attention or home politics, and especially on church matters, in which their rivals were the popular party. Louis' offers were rejected, contrary to the advice of Marlborough himself. In 1710 Louis was in such straits that he made even more favourable proposals. Besides giving up territory to the Dutch, the Empire, the Duke of Savoy, and to the English (in North America) he consented to surrender the *whole* Spanish monarchy to the Archduke Charles. But the English ministry, as if determined to drive him to desperation, imposed on him the intolerably humiliating condition that he should join with the allies in expelling his grandson Philip from Spain. To this Louis would not consent, and the conferences were broken off. After 1710 then, at any rate, Swift might fairly claim that every justification or excuse for the war was over. Further in the autumn of 1711 the Emperor Joseph II. died, and the Archduke Charles succeeded to the imperial dominions. This put an entirely different aspect on the matter. Had the allies succeeded in forcing Louis to submit, and driving Philip V. from Spain, the Spanish and Austrian territories would have been united under one ruler, and the monarchy of Charles V. would have been restored. Swift might well urge that it was useless to spend English blood and treasure to limit the growth of the House of Bourbon, when the only result would be to aggrandise enormously the House of Hapsburg.

Page 185. Swift was perfectly right in thinking that the Spanish Bourbons would speedily forget their French origin. Within ten years from the date of this pamphlet England and France are found in alliance against Spain.

PROPOSAL FOR CORRECTING THE ENGLISH TONGUE.

Page 193. Swift's ideas of ethnology and the history of language are not to be implicitly accepted.

Page 196. *Your lordship cite.* It is curious to find Swift, a clergyman, basing his appreciation of the style of the authorized version upon Harley's citations, rather than his own experience in the Offices of the Church.

TRACTS RELATING TO IRELAND.

The Swearer's Bank. Page 208. *Tradesmen.* . . . A short paragraph is here omitted.

The Drapier's Letters. Why Swift used the French form of the word Draper is not known. A list of bonds relating to the forfeited estates, dated Dublin, 1690, has the form "linnen-draper."

Page 210. *The Report* is the favourable report of the Committee of the Privy Council on Wood's coinage.

Page 211. The *two* Irish *Houses of Parliament*, the Corporation of Dublin, Grand Juries and guilds, had petitioned against the new coinage before Swift took the matter up. It is, therefore, inaccurate to describe him as stirring up the Irish by a factitious party cry: the people were already roused, and Swift only guided and strengthened their opposition.

Page 213. *Our ancestors.* Swift's limited view of the Irish is here evident: he is mainly concerned for the descendants of the Englishry, "the true English," (p. 226), and disclaims any connection with "the savage Irish whom our ancestors conquered" (p. 225). The disabilities of the English Irish here enumerated are more fully described on p. 238.

Page 221. *Primate:* Dr. Hugh Boulter, of Christ Church, Oxford, Archbishop of Armagh.

Page 223. *Molyneux*, a friend of Locke, published a tract against the oppressive trade laws against Ireland.

Page 225. *Side . . . But.* About three pages of Scott's edition are here omitted, in which Swift gives what he represents as Wood's and his friends' case according to the English tracts.

Page 227. *Kettle and furnace:* in allusion to Wood's business of ironmonger.

Swallowing the halfpence in fireballs: a fine example of Swift's method of logical *reductio ad absurdum.*

Page 228. *As remote from thunder:* " Procul à Jove, procul à fulmine."

Modest Proposal. Page 234. Psalmanazar's *Description of*

the Island of Formosa, 1705, was an audacious hoax, which the author eventually retracted.

Page 235. *Foreign fineries.* Swift was never tired of writing on this point : urging the people of Ireland to retaliate upon the atrocious English navigation laws by using only home manufactures. His *Proposal for the Universal Use of Irish Manufactures* appeared in 1720, and so alarmed the Government that they prosecuted the printer : but the Grand Jury brought him in Not Guilty, and persisted in their verdict until the Chief Justice had sent them back nine times and kept them eleven hours, when they gave in so far as to leave the verdict to the discretion of the judge ; and the Government found themselves compelled to drop so unpopular a case, and entered a *nolle prosequi*. The *Drapier's Letters* frequently refer to the restrictions on exportation, and advise a consistent adoption of home wear. In *Maxims Controlled*, and the *Short View of the State of Ireland*, both papers of the deepest interest, the same counsel is repeated : in the latter, Swift writes, " Ireland is the only kingdom I ever heard or read of, either in ancient or modern story, which was denied the liberty of exporting their native commodities and manufactures wherever they pleased, except to countries at war with their own prince or state ; yet this privilege, by the superiority of mere power, is refused us in the most momentous parts of commerce,—besides an Act of Navigation, to which we neve consented, pinned down upon us and rigorously executed." Similar passages occur in many of Swift's other papers on Ireland, an account of which is given in *Fraser's Magazine* for Sept., 1881.

Page 238. *Other expedients.* This is a list of Swift's remedies for the wretched condition of Ireland, which shows that he saw clearly enough into the difficult problem, and also proves that many of the burdens which still oppress the Irish people were much more grievous in Swift's time. His remedies are, it may be noticed, less legislative than moral. He would raise the spirit and rouse the energy of the Irish to counteract the oppression of England, rather than attempt to cure the evils they laboured under by new enactments.

POLITE CONVERSATION.

Page 244. *Age of six and thirty.* As some ingenuous reader of the *Polite Conversation* has been at the trouble of taking this and similar statements *au pied de la lettre*, it may be well to point out that Swift was not thirty-six in 1695, but only twenty-seven; and further, that the *conversation* was not written or thought of in 1695, but was composed in 1731. The same interpreter is inclined to accept the *hundred years* of p. 247 in an equally exact spirit; where the period is obviously ironical.

Page 252. *Push-pin:* probably "spelikans,"—essentially a children's play.

Page 256. *Vardi: par Dieu.—Lob's pound:* prison.

Page 259. *Etui:* the little case, generally of repoussé silver, attached to a lady's chatelaine, for holding needles and bodkins.

Page 261. *Cry mapsticks:* This expression has been much discussed. Some regard it as equivalent to a confession of humiliation, as though Neverout compared himself to a seller of mopsticks, or to one who deserves to be beaten with them. I believe myself that, like many oaths and exclamations of the time, *Mapsticks* is a corruption of some Latin or French phrase, and I incline to *Pax tecum* as its original. Neverout has been having a tiff with Miss Notable, and ends it (like a schoolboy's "*pax*") with "Cry Mapsticks, [I cry "*pax tecum*,"] madam! No offence, I hope."

www.ingramcontent.com/pod-product-compliance
Lightning Source LLC
Chambersburg PA
CBHW031904220426
43663CB00006B/758